Resolving Environmental Conflicts

Second Edition

Social-Environmental Sustainability Series

Series Editor

Chris Maser

Published Titles

Economics and Ecology: United for a Sustainable World,
Charles R. Beaton and Chris Maser

Resolving Environmental Conflicts, Second Edition,
Chris Maser and Carol A. Pollio

Social-Environmental Planning: The Design Interface Between Everyforest
and Everycity, **Chris Maser**

Sustainable Development: Principles, Frameworks, and Case Studies,
Okechukwu Ukaga, Chris Maser, and Michael Reichenbach

Resolving Environmental Conflicts

Second Edition

Chris Maser and Carol A. Pollio

CRC Press
Taylor & Francis Group
Boca Raton   London   New York

CRC Press is an imprint of the
Taylor & Francis Group, an **informa** business

CRC Press
Taylor & Francis Group
6000 Broken Sound Parkway NW, Suite 300
Boca Raton, FL 33487-2742

© 2012 by Taylor and Francis Group, LLC
CRC Press is an imprint of Taylor & Francis Group, an Informa business

No claim to original U.S. Government works

Printed in the United States of America on acid-free paper
10 9 8 7 6 5 4 3 2 1

International Standard Book Number: 978-1-4398-5608-6 (Hardback)

Library of Congress Cataloging-in-Publication Data

Maser, Chris.
    Resolving environmental conflicts / Chris Maser, Carol A. Pollio. -- 2nd ed.
      p. cm. -- (Social-environmental sustainability)
    Includes bibliographical references and index.
    ISBN 978-1-4398-5608-6
    1. Environmental policy. 2. Environmental protection. 3. Environmental mediation. I. Pollio, Carol A., 1957- II. Title.

GE170.M369 2012
333.7--dc22
                                                      2011004419

Visit the Taylor & Francis Web site at
http://www.taylorandfrancis.com

and the CRC Press Web site at
http://www.crcpress.com

To Zane, my wife and best friend for 30 years. What she has taught me about

the nobler, feminine aspects of life is an inner treasure beyond words.

Chris

This book is dedicated to the many mentors I have had along the

way, each of them guiding me and sharing their insights on resolving

conflict to benefit our natural resources and habitat. I decided to

collaborate on this project in the hope that sharing my experiences

would be helpful to those following in my footsteps—to pay forward

all the gifts that were given to me throughout the years.

Carol

Contents

Section II   The Legacy of Resolving Environmental Conflicts

Editor's Note

There are two primary emotions: love and fear. All other emotional expressions are merely aspects of these two. Kindness, compassion, and patience are the hallmark of love, whereas anger, violence, and impatience are the stamp of fear. Thus, where unconditional love dwells, there dwells peace and contentment also, and fear cannot abide. Where fear dwells, there dwells discord and discontent also, and peace cannot abide. Conflict is a choice born out of the fear of loss, be it for one's physical life, financial security, personal identity, or coveting the possession of another. Moreover, the dynamics of conflict are essentially the same, whether interpersonal, intertribal, international, or interreligious. Strife, after all, is dependent on the notion of inequality: I'm right; you're wrong. I'm superior; you're lesser. I belong; you don't. This is mine to do with as I wish; it's not yours.

Conflict resolution is based on the art of helping people with disparate points of view find enough common ground to sheath their weapons and listen to one another for their common good. As it turns out, people agree on 80 percent of virtually everything, unbeknownst to them, and disagree on 20 percent, which becomes the sole focus of their disagreement. If, therefore, combatants can be helped to see and move toward the 80 percent agreement, the 20 percent is more easily negotiated. Ultimately, however, it is necessary for the participants to formulate a shared vision toward which to strive, one that accommodates all viewpoints to everyone's long-term benefit. Only then can the barrier between combatants dissolve into mutual respect, acceptance, and potential friendship—only then is a conflict truly resolved.

Chris Maser, Series Editor

Editor's Note

There are two primary emotions: love and fear. All other emotional expressions are merely aspects of these two. Kindness, compassion, and patience are the hallmark of love, whereas anger, violence, and impatience are the stamp of fear. Thus, where unconditional love dwells, there dwells peace and contentment also, and fear cannot abide. Where fear dwells, there dwells discord and discontent also, and peace cannot abide. Conflict is a choice born out of the fear of loss, be it for one's physical life, financial security, personal identity, or coveting the possession of another. Moreover, the dynamics of conflict are essentially the same, whether interpersonal, intertribal, international, or interreligious. Strife, after all, is dependent on the notion of inequality: I'm right; you're wrong. I'm superior; you're lesser. I belong; you don't. This is mine to do with as I wish; it's not yours.

Conflict resolution is based on the art of helping people with disparate points of view find enough common ground to sheath their weapons and listen to one another for their common good. As it turns out, people agree on 80 percent of virtually everything, unbeknownst to them, and disagree on 20 percent, which becomes the sole focus of their disagreement. If, therefore, combatants can be helped to see and move toward the 80 percent agreement, the 20 percent is more easily negotiated. Ultimately, however, it is necessary for the participants to formulate a shared vision toward which to strive, one that accommodates all viewpoints to everyone's long-term benefit. Only then can the barrier between combatants dissolve into mutual respect, acceptance, and potential friendship—only then is a conflict truly resolved.

Chris Maser, Series Editor

Foreword

One far wiser than I has stated that, "(t)he brotherhood of the well-intentioned exists even though it is impossible to organize it anywhere." This book epitomizes the above statement. *Resolving Environmental Conflicts* contains new ideas about an important subject, and defines a new paradigm as to how we must begin to think about they we live, the way we use our resources, and the way we interact with our fellow humans and other life forms within our biosphere.

Over the last 60 years or so, our environmental consciousness has been raised considerably. Rachel Carson warned us in "Silent Spring" that our actions have dire consequences. Nevertheless, we have enjoyed the fruits of our industrial production with relative abandon, but at a cost of unsustainable consumption of resources and perhaps the irreversible poisoning of our environment. Despite our rampant consumerism, however, a worldwide environmental movement was born, our consciousness was raised, and we began to understand some of the unrealized costs of our miraculous "progress" as we lept boldly into a "brave new world" of plenty and prosperity.

Simply put, *Resolving Environmental Conflicts* is a working manual for those involved in mediation. It discusses techniques and methods of mediation, provides principles useful for understanding the milieu of environmental conflicts, and examines the varying responsibilities of the participant parties to the mediation process. It also lays the foundation for arriving at cooperative solutions to unresolved environmental dilemmas. The specialist reader will appreciate the readiness of the work in describing the difficulty of the process and the importance of the outcomes sought. Being considerably more than a "how to" directive, the book examines the "whys" of the mediation process and broadens the knowledge base by providing the philosophical underpinnings of "a new environmental responsibility." This broadening aspect makes the work of instant value not only to raising the consciousness of the responsible citizen in critical aspects of social-environmental sustainability but also by training the mediator in the art of bringing environmental conflicts to sustainable conclusions.

Since the Middle Ages, we have had exceptionally good weather, allowing improvements in agriculture, combined with advances in our sciences. Our human population bourgeoned in this abundance, and we have eradicated many common diseases that long plagued humankind. Advances in manufacturing, transportation, medicine, hygiene, and healthcare have all combined to bring our species to a position of preeminence on this planet. Moreover, we have even begun some small steps toward leaving our earthly confines and exploring the greater universe beyond our planetary home. This progress has been marvelous, nee breathtaking. Unfortunately, it actually does take our breath away because we have so polluted the air and water that we are suffering unprecedented rates of environmentally related ailments in addition to rendering numbers of sensitive species of both plants and animals nearly extinct within one human lifetime.

The authors provide an irrefutable truth for the potential mediator to consider: The children of today, tomorrow, and beyond are unheralded participants in *every* environmental mediation that takes place. They, who have no voice, are the ultimate recipients of our largess and our folly as well as our wisdom, and must be considered in the environmental bequest we pass forward. Our natural patrimony is neither unlimited nor indestructible. It must be accounted for in light of sustainment, efficient use, and careful nurturing. The commonwealth has need for a healthy biosphere into the indefinite future and our husbanding of resources, conservation of nature, and protection of our environment are priorities that must become part of the body politic, the common culture, and our economic order if this planet is to continue as our home. Our longevity as a species is directly related to our willingness to conserve our environment. To be successful, it must to be a collective task.

When nuclear weapons appeared during the last century, J. Robert Oppenheimer quoted the Hindu scripture as the first atomic bomb was being tested: "Behold, I have become death, the destroyer of worlds." Thousands of these weapons were stockpiled during the cold war, and now we have begun to realize the futility of a weapon too terrible to use. Our security is not enhanced, and our resulting instability is something that should frighten any sane individual. At least in this one regard there is almost universal agreement that nuclear weapons must be eliminated from the world's arsenals because their unmanageable destructive power has made them an anathema. The call to eliminate nuclear weapons was perhaps our first global step in prescribing our environmental priority and choosing to protect the natural environment in recognition of our bid for survival.

Over 95 percent of all the scientist who ever lived are alive today, and we are told by some that the polar ice caps are shrinking at an alarming rate, the great ocean currents responsible for our weather are diminished, and the oceans are undergoing substantial chemical changes. In addition, the ozone layer in the Southern hemisphere is being rapidly depleted with serious consequences, 9 of the past 15 years are the warmest in recorded history, the warming of the globe has spawned more frequent and severe tropical storms, and all of these things will have combined, detrimental effects on plant and animal life on the planet. Yet, all this scientific knowledge has not convinced us to recognize that the immutable laws of nature cannot be suspended or put in abeyance to protect the profits of the unconcerned, the interests of the uncaring, or even the health and welfare of the unaware.

Nearly all of the reputable graduate programs in public policy and law schools in this country offer courses in environmental policy and law, but these courses stress comprehensive regulations, balancing economic interests within communities. In addition, they allow limited degradation of the planetary resources to mitigate particularized losses to balance sheets and minimize balanced uses of scarce resources, which are sought within the confines of a competitive economy. But, none of these requisites recognize the inviolable biophysical principles of nature, prioritize the use of limited resources accordingly, or consider the deleterious effects of toxic wastes.

We must begin to understand a new paradigm, and this book is a seminal text to use in beginning to teach this paradigm to personnel at all levels of government. The increasing unwillingness to change personal values and lifestyles until forced to do so has been a hallmark of humankind since the inception of agriculture and civilization, but we have reached a point at which change is increasingly being forced upon us. This book points us in that direction by examining the parameters of that change and meets out some of the skills necessary to traverse the intensifying global imbroglio. I predict it will become a standard text for training public officials, environmental specialists, and mediators and will be the subject of informed conversations for some time to come.

J. Holmes Armstead, J.D., Ph.D., LL.D., D.Litt., D.H.L. (hc)
Professor, US Naval War College (ret.)
Monterey, California

Acknowledgments

The following people, listed in alphabetical order, were kind enough to review the manuscript of the first edition and help me improve it: John Baldwin (director, Institute for a Sustainable Environment, University of Oregon, Eugene); Joyce K. Berry (assistant professor, Human Dimensions and Policy in Natural Resources, Colorado State University, Fort Collins); Ron Clarke (professor emeritus, Religious Studies, Oregon State University, Corvallis, now deceased); David Hunt (mediation trainer, Salem, OR); James R. Karr (director, Institute for Environmental Studies, University of Washington, Seattle); Christine Kirk (community policing, Albany Police Department, Albany, OR); Deen Selwood (program coordinator, Turtle Island Earth Stewards Society, Vancouver, British Columbia, Canada); Bob Tarrant (retired director, U.S. Department of Agriculture Forest Service Pacific Northwest Research Station, Portland, OR, and professor emeritus, Forest Science, Oregon State University, Corvallis, now deceased); and Julia Wondelleck (assistant professor, Resource Policy and Behavior, University of Michigan, Ann Arbor).

I now thank Carol Pollio for agreeing to be my coauthor in writing this second edition; she added her valuable experiences, which broadened the scope of the message. And once again, my wife, Zane, graciously accepted being a "writer's widow" while I worked on this book. I am sincerely grateful for all the help.

I (Carol) appreciate the support, assistance, and high spirits of Chris as my editor, colleague, and friend in crafting this work, and the patience and understanding of my longtime friend, Ray, in helping this dream of mine come to fruition.

We are both grateful to Irma Shagla-Britton for taking the wonderful photograph on the cover of this book and for allowing us to use it.

Introduction

We are now beginning the second decade of the twenty-first century, a century in which once abundant natural resources have rapidly dwindled to scarcity while the human population of the world continues to grow at an exponential rate. We citizens of this planet must now address a moral question for the rest of this century and beyond: Do those living today owe anything to the future? If your answer is "No," *do not read further.*

If your answer is "Yes," however, then we must now determine what and how much we owe future generations lest our present collision course continue unabated until we eventually destroy the environmental options for all generations. Be forewarned, however, that meeting the obligation we say we have—whatever we determine it is—will require a renewed sense of personal and social justice, one that causes us as individuals and society to act now for the simultaneous environmental benefit of both the present and the future. But what direction must our renewed sense of personal and social commitments take? Personal growth is vital to the answer because the level of consciousness that causes a problem in the first place is not the level of consciousness that can fix it.

Our personal and social reticence to deal openly and honestly with this question calls to mind a salient paragraph from a speech Winston Churchill delivered to the British Parliament on May 2, 1935, as he saw with clear foreboding the onrushing threat of Nazi Germany to Europe and the British people:

> When the situation was manageable it was neglected, and now that it is thoroughly out of hand we apply too late the remedies which then might have effected a cure. There is nothing new in the story. . . . It falls into that long, dismal catalogue of the fruitlessness of experience and the confirmed unteachability of mankind. Want of foresight, unwillingness to act when action would be simple and effective, lack of clear thinking, confusion of counsel until the emergency comes, until self-preservation strikes its jarring gong—these are the features which constitute the endless repetition of history.[1]

Consider that civilizations have evolved by similar steps: growth of intelligence through discoveries and inventions; advancement through the ideas of government, family, and property—all based on a slow accumulation of experimental knowledge. As such, civilizations have much in common, and their evolutionary stages are connected with one another in a natural sequence of cultural development.

The arts of subsistence and the achievements of technology can be used to distinguish the periods of human progress. People lived by gathering fruits and nuts; learned to hunt, fish, and use fire; invented the spear and atlatl and then the bow and arrow. They developed the art of making pottery, learned to domesticate animals and cultivate plants, began using adobe and stone in building houses, and learned to smelt iron and use it in tools. Finally, what we call civilization began with the invention of a written language, culminating in all the wonders of the modern era.

Each civilization has also been marked by its birth, maturation, and demise, the last brought about by uncontrolled population growth that outstripped the source of available energy, be it loss of topsoil, deforestation, or the continued despoliation of its water source. But in olden times, the survivors could move on to less-populated, more fertile areas as their civilizations collapsed. Today, there is nowhere left on Earth to go.

Yet, having learned little or nothing from history, as Churchill pointed out, our society is currently destroying the very environment from which it sprang and on which it relies for continuance. Surely, society as we know it cannot be the final evolutionary stage for human existence. But what lies beyond our current notion of society? What is the next frontier for "civilized" people to conquer? Is it outer space, as so often stated? No, it is inner space, the conquest of oneself, which many assert is life's most arduous task. As the Buddha said, "Though he should conquer a thousand men in the battlefield a thousand times, yet he, indeed, who would conquer himself is the noblest victor."[2]

In the material world, self-conquest means bringing one's thoughts and behaviors in line with the immutable biophysical laws governing the world in which one lives, such as the law of cause and effect. In the spiritual realm, self-conquest means disciplining one's thoughts and behaviors in accord with the highest spiritual and social truths handed down throughout the ages, such as love your neighbor as yourself and treat others as you want them to treat you.

The outcome of self-conquest is social-environmental sustainability, which must be the next cultural stage toward which we struggle. This is the frontier beyond self-centeredness and its stepchild, conflict, which destroys human dignity, degrades the productive capacity of our global ecosystem, and forecloses options for all generations.

To fulfill our obligation as environmental trustees for the children we bring into the world requires fundamental changes in our social consciousness and cultural norms, changes that will demand choices different from those we have heretofore made, which means thinking and acting anew. But, "a great many people," as American psychologist William James observed, "think they are thinking when they are merely rearranging their prejudices."[3]

To change anything, we must, through the choices we make, reach beyond where we are, beyond where we feel safe. We must dare to move ahead, even if we do not fully understand where we are going or the price of getting there because perfect knowledge will always elude us. Furthermore, we must become students of processes and let go our advocacy of positions and embattlements over winning agreement with narrow points of view. This is important because our ever-increasing knowledge rapidly outstrips the ability of our current paradigm, based on old knowledge, to explain the new in terms of the old.

True progress toward an ecologically sound environment and a socially just culture will be initially expensive in both money and effort, but in the end not only will be mandated by shifting public values but also will be progressively less expensive over time. The longer we wait, however, the more disastrous becomes the environmental condition, the more disputes will arise as a result of our declining quality of life, and the more expensive and difficult become the necessary social changes.

No biological shortcuts, technological quick fixes, or political rhetoric can mend what is broken. Dramatic, fundamental change is necessary if we are really concerned with bettering the quality of life—even that of next year. It is not a question of whether we can or cannot change, but one of, Will we change or won't we? Change is a choice, a choice of individuals reflected in the collective of society and mirrored in the landscape throughout the generations.

Can environmental conflicts be resolved? Emphatically, yes! But, they must be ground on the personal growth of the disputants.

Therefore, to resolve environmental conflicts, the mediation process not only must have the greatest and longest-lasting personal and social effect possible but also must be as healing as possible because outcomes of such conflicts are, above all, intergenerational. This means it is the present generation's responsibility to serve the future, not the future generations' responsibility to serve the present. (*Facilitate*, in the sense it is used in this book, means to conduct a process of communication whereby people are assisted in freeing themselves from difficulties and obstacles in making decisions that either avoid or eliminate environmental conflict by forging commonly held values into a shared vision toward which to build collectively.)

Environmental conflicts are created by the choices people make and thus can be resolved by electing different choices with resolution so firmly in mind that it naturally leads to a shared vision of the future toward which to build. Because people are often consciously blind to the motives of their choices, however, some kind of process is needed to help resolve conflicts by overcoming blind spots, the first step toward a shared vision. We choose the term *mediation*, which comes from the Latin *medius* ("middle") as opposed the word *facilitate*, which comes from the Latin *facilis*, meaning "easy."

There are many reasons mediation is necessary to the resolution of a conflict, but we are going to interweave into this book only a few by helping people understand that

1. Nature—not humanity—is ultimately in control and sets inviolate, biophysical rules of engagement in the experiment of life, all of which are intergenerational.

2. Solar energy is the only "free" resource and true investment in planet Earth over geological time; Earth-based resources are ultimately finite reinvestments in our global ecosystem—a condition now exacerbated by a worldwide overpopulation of humans and an unjust distribution of available resources.

3. Science can do the job it was designed to do only when we have resolved our environmental conflicts and are willing to accept scientific data for what it is meant to be: tentative insight into universal relationships.

4. The environment and our children, their children, and their children's children are the silent parties in almost every conflict.

5. People are one another's learning partners, and conflict is one of life's classrooms.

6. Through conflict resolution, we can reframe our understanding of the issues and renegotiate our participation with one another and our environment and in so doing realize what costs we are committing our children and those of the future to pay for *our* decisions and behavior.

7. Environmental conflicts are squandering Earth's finite resources through the primacy of competition, which is a luxury society can no longer afford.

8. Conflict is a choice, and we always have the option of choosing to choose again.

9. Social-environmental sustainability is also a choice, but it requires a collective vision to see beyond the strictly self-serving ambitions that foster conflict to the cooperative principles of a shared vision that serves everyone's well-being as equally as possible.

This book covers some of the basic transformative concepts that over the years we have found vital in helping resolve environmental conflicts, bringing them to closure in a shared vision of the future, and then implementing that vision as sustainably as possible. Because one must learn the basic philosophy from which the art is born before procedural "dos" and "don'ts" make any sense, our book is meant as a synthesis of essential principles, not a strict "how to" book of mediation procedures.

Although some important procedural aspects of mediation per se are discussed, there is standard, well-documented literature on the procedures in general, which does not need to be repeated here. The discussion therefore is confined specifically to points concerning mediation as it applies to personal growth and thus resolution at the true causal level. But, if we were to write a book on the general procedures of mediation, it would sound like a combination of *As a Man Thinketh* by James Allen,[4] *The Tao of Leadership* by John Heider,[5] and *Leadership Is an Art* by Max DePree,[6] with a liberal dose of common sense, compassion, and humility.

For whom is this book written? It is written for people who are interested in creating or furthering social-environmental sustainability and furthering the course of peace at all levels of society. These people include, but are not restricted to, community leaders, such as city mayors, city councilors, and county commissioners; bioregional visionaries; aboriginal Americans and Canadians; Shinto priests; government agencies; and conservation groups in the United States and abroad. It is also written for professional mediators interested in helping people grow toward a higher level of consciousness of cause and effect and thus personal responsibility, as well as for those who are interested in becoming mediators. And, it is written for whoever is considering a mediation process as a means of resolving an environmental dispute but is unsure of which approach to select. (The different approaches are discussed in Chapter 1.)

Why is this book written? It is written to give people the necessary philosophical underpinnings for practicing the type of conflict resolution that not only settles a dispute but also heals the people. Although we always endeavor to leave behind a working knowledge of the process itself each time we mediate the resolution of a dispute, we cannot impart in so short a time that which has taken us much of our life to learn. It is therefore our hope that this book will encourage the many would-be mediators springing up around the world to consider a true healing approach to conflict resolution as the best way to achieve long-term social-environmental sustainability.

To become a mediator, one must learn to be a sifter, taking something from here and something from there, which is incorporated into one's own style. Sifting is essential to one's continual growth as a servant of the parties in any environmental conflict.

This book has two parts. Section I opens with a brief comparison of approaches to conflict resolution and a quick look at how we generally mediate disputes, which creates a context for what follows. The rest of Section I is an examination of what goes into the mediation process, beginning with the "givens" of any environmental conflict. The givens are those biophysical and social principles that must be understood, accepted, and acted on if a conflict is to be resolved. One of our main purposes is to help people understand the debt they are committing all generations of the future to pay through decisions they make during the resolution process—beginning with their children and their children's children.

It is imperative that people become aware of the long-term effects of their decisions. We say this because children are one of the two silent parties in all environmental conflicts; the land and its productive capacity is the other. All disputants must understand the social, environmental, and economic circumstances to which they are committing the future because, if the outcome of a conflict is a deficit in terms of the children's future options, the productive capacity of the ecosystem, or both, it is analogous to "taxation without representation," and that goes against everything democracy symbolizes.

We do not presume to cover all the possible givens for resolving environmental conflicts, only to provide those basic concepts that we find to be critical and recurring. Anything more is beyond the scope of this book.

The givens are grouped under eight subheadings: (1) conflict as a choice; (2) the inviolate biophysical principles; (3) the interactive social principles; (4) the human equation; (5) communication, the interpersonal element; (6) the process as the decision; (7) conflict as a learning partnership; and (8) practicing mediation as a gift of social-environmental healing. These are by no means discrete entities but rather interrelated and interactive areas of resolution in every conflict.

An environmental conflict is mediated toward its natural conclusion, a shared vision of a sustainable future toward which to build. Such a vision is the necessary culmination of every mediation process dealing with conflict resolution if society, as we know it, is to survive the twenty-first century. This is a critical idea because parts are often mistaken for wholes, and ideas are often viewed as complete when in fact they are not. Such is frequently the case with the resolution of an environmental conflict, when the goal is seen only as the solution of an immediate problem, which equates to *symptomatic thinking.*

Section II goes beyond shared vision to examine notions of development, sustainability, and community. The process plans for sustainable community development within the context of a sustainable landscape. This means that a community committed to sustainable development is not seeking some mythical "balance" between its economics and its environment. Rather, it seeks the synergism of ecology and culture, including economy, to promote a healthy, sustainable environment that enriches the lives of all its inhabitants—both human and nonhuman. Sustainable community development gives people a chance to employ such cardinal principles of culture as democracy, beauty, utility, durability, and sustainability in the planning process.

The sustainable community development of the future must begin in the elementary schools of today, and it must begin by children learning the art of mediating their differences before they become destructive conflicts. This does not mean that every child must necessarily become a skilled mediator. But, it does mean that every child would have available a basic understanding of how to use the principles of conflict resolution in deciding the best way to deal with stressful, personal issues and interpersonal differences, beginning at home while growing up.

We think it possible that learning skills of conflict resolution at a young age can begin to break the escalating dysfunctional cycle of family abuse by helping children understand that there are behavioral models other than those at home from which to choose. In addition, the constructive principles we employ in resolving conflicts can help a child learn how to retain or take back their personhood by revealing that empowerment is a viable alternative to the role of victim. Thus, every child from a dysfunctional family who chooses a peaceful model of resolving differences will carry forward into his or her family a greater degree of socially functional behavior.

If learning the skills of conflict resolution can help shift a child's focus from socially dysfunctional to socially functional behaviors, then environmental conflicts may decline in both frequency and intensity, which would go a long way toward protecting the options of all future generations. In this way, we could give children the peaceful tools of empowerment with which to begin helping themselves in the present for the future.

Bear in mind, however, that the future is always rooted in the present. It is therefore necessary to commence teaching and using the principles and skills of environmental conflict resolution now if present generations are to grow toward social-environmental sustainability while there is still time to approach it.

As we write this book, we introduce our personal experiences by saying: Chris found this . . . , or Carol did such and such, which resulted in . . . . These examples are to help you, the reader, understand that the resolution of every conflict is a unique journey of similar processes and novel outcomes.

Beyond how Carol and I conduct our respective mediation processes are eleven givens that must be understood if a conflict of any kind is to be resolved through personal growth toward a high level of consciousness: (1) approaches to conflict resolution; (2) conflict as a choice; (3) biophysical principles of sustainability; (4) social principles of sustainability; (5) the human equation; (6) communication, the interpersonal element; (7) the process as the decision; (8) conflict as a learning partnership; (9) practicing the mediation of conscience; (10) resolution: social-environmental conflict brought to a shared vision; and (11) modifying our belief systems regarding change.

References

1. Robert R. James, ed., *Winston S. Churchill: His Complete Speeches, 1897–1963*. Chelsea House, New York (1974) 6:5592.
2. *The Teaching of Buddha*. Bukkyo Dendo Kyokai, Tokyo, Japan (1966).
3. Richard Alan Krieger, *Civilization's Quotations: Life's Ideal*. Algora, New York (2002).
4. James Allen. *As a Man Thinketh*. Grosset & Dunlap, New York (1981).
5. John Heider. *The Tao of Leadership: Leadership Strategies for a New Age*. Bantam Books, New York (1986).
6. Max DePree. *Leadership Is an Art*. Dell Trade Paperback, New York (1989).

About the Authors

Chris Maser was trained in zoology and ecology and worked for 25 years as a research scientist in agricultural, coastal, desert, forest, valley grassland, shrub steppe, and subarctic settings in various parts of the world before realizing that science is not designed to answer the vast majority of questions society is asking it to address. Science deals with an understanding of biophysical relationships; society asks questions about human values.

Chris gave up active scientific research in 1987 and has since worked to unify scientific knowledge with social values in helping to create sustainable communities and landscapes, part of which entails his facilitating the resolution of social-environmental conflicts. He has over 286 publications, including 34 books, mostly dealing with some aspect of social-environmental sustainability. In addition, he is listed in *Who's Who in the West*, *American Men and Women of Science*, *Contemporary Authors*, and *International Authors and Writers Who's Who*.

As an author, international lecturer, and facilitator in resolving environmental disputes, creating vision statements, and assisting in sustainable community development, Chris is committed to telling it as he sees it to give people an honest, open appraisal, based on extensive experience, of innovative ways to resolve their conflicts and unite their community in a sustainable way in relationship to their surrounding landscape, the source of the natural wealth of the community. This is important because people can most easily deal with required changes when they feel safe and know someone is there to guide the process as gently as possible, all the while protecting their dignity and looking out for their well-being.

Although he has worked and lectured in Canada, Egypt, France, Germany, Japan, Malaysia, Mexico, Nepal, Slovakia, and Switzerland, he calls Corvallis, Oregon, home.

Carol A. Pollio began her career as a student trainee in the National Park Service in New Jersey in 1977. She soon learned that working collaboratively was what made her most successful in effecting conservation. As her career progressed, Carol gained recognition as an abandoned mine reclamation specialist, closing eleven abandoned mines in West Virginia and Virginia, and working with federal, state, and local agencies; non-governmental organizations; and communities to reclaim these environmentally degraded and unsafe sites. A field biologist for more than twenty-four years, Carol transitioned to the Washington Office of the U.S. Fish and Wildlife Service, a position she held for five years. She currently serves as the science advisor for the Ecological Services Program in the Northeast Regional Office.

Carol has served as a member of the U.S. Coast Guard Reserve for more than twenty-seven years and has attained the rank of Commander. She has been called to active duty twice in her career, once in support of Operation Noble Eagle/Iraqi Freedom and recently to serve as liaison officer on the *Deepwater Horizon*/Gulf of Mexico oil spill. She served for many years in deployable port security units, participating in foreign port exercises in Panama, Turkey, Portugal, and the United States.

Carol is also the Program Director for the American Public University and American Military University environmental studies program. In this role, she directs undergraduate and graduate programs in environmental science and public policy and teaches graduate-level courses in environmental impact assessment, wildlife management, watershed management, and conservation biology. In this role, she guides students through the adaptive management and structured decision-making processes and teaches them the importance of working collaboratively toward shared and sustainable solutions to complex environmental problems.

Carol's experience in on-the-ground restoration led her to develop strategies and skills in negotiation and conflict resolution. Her down-to-earth approach centers on respecting others, treating everyone as she would like to be treated, and finding common objectives toward which all can work to craft practical and sustainable solutions. Working with timber companies, coal miners, and the military, Carol has successfully balanced numerous competing needs and values to accomplish fish and wildlife habitat restoration.

After many career moves up and down the East Coast, Carol has chosen a small community on the Delaware Bay near Milford, Delaware, as her home.

Section I

Mediating Environmental Conflicts

1

Approaches to Mediation

Introduction

Mediation (facilitation, according to Bush and Folger) is generally understood as an informal process in which a neutral third party, one powerless to impose resolution, helps disputing parties seek a mutually acceptable settlement. As such, mediation has within itself the unique potential to raise the level of consciousness in the disputants, which engenders personal growth by helping them—in the very midst of conflict—to wrestle with difficult inner and outer circumstances, better understand cause and effect, assume greater ownership of personal responsibility, and thereby bridge human differences.[1]

Nevertheless, the unique potential of mediation to achieve a higher level of consciousness is receiving less and less emphasis in practice. This potential is therefore seldom realized, and when it is, it is generally serendipitous, rather than the result of the mediator's purposeful efforts. There is currently a crossroad facing mediation, one reflecting the two basic approaches: problem solving and personal growth, which raises the level of personal awareness.

Mediation at the Crossroads

The problem-solving approach to environmental conflicts—which is basically a business-oriented approach—emphasizes the capacity of mediation to find solutions that generate mutually acceptable settlements, almost always for the immediate benefit of adult humans, regardless of the effect of the settlement on children or the productive capacity of the environment. Mediators in this approach often endeavor to influence and

3

direct disputants toward settlement in general, even toward the specific terms of a settlement.

As mediation has evolved, the problem-solving approach has been increasingly emphasized, to the point at which this kind of directed, settlement-oriented outcome dominates the current movement. The premise of the problem-solving approach is that the most important goal is to maximize the greatest possible satisfaction for individuals engaged in a conflict. But as author Gail Sheehy points out, "Human institutions prepare people for continuity, not for change." To us, therefore, the limitations inherent in the problem-solving approach are precisely its narrowness in scope, rigid focus on quantifiable outcomes, and the increasing attempt to eliminate risk, all symptoms of its growing institutionalization.

Designer Milton Glaser captures well our concern with the uncritical institutionalizing of professionalism in mediating the resolution of disputes when he says, "Professionalism really means eliminating risk. Once you become good at something, everyone wants you to repeat it over and over again. But the more you eliminate risk, the closer you come to eliminating the act of creative intervention."

In contrast to the problem-solving approach, raising the combatants' level of consciousness emphasizes the capacity of mediation for personal growth, which is embodied in the ability to accept risk. Mediators therefore concentrate on helping parties empower themselves to define the issues and decide the settlement in their own terms and in their own time through a better understanding of one another's perspectives.

To accomplish this increased awareness, mediators avoid the directiveness associated with the problem-solving approach. Equally important, mediators help parties recognize and capitalize on the opportunities for personal growth inherently present in a conflict. This does not mean that satisfaction and fairness are unimportant; rather, it means that personal growth and more enlightened conduct are even more important.

The aim of mediation, as we practice it, is to help parties become better human beings by stimulating moral growth and transforming human character, which results in parties finding genuine solutions to their real problems. In addition, the private, nonjudgmental, noncoercive character of such mediation can provide disputants a safe haven in which to humanize themselves, despite the disputants having started out as fierce adversaries. This safety helps people feel and express varying degrees of understanding and concern for one another as they grow toward greater compassion, despite their disagreement.

The most important aspect of mediation is its ability to strengthen people's moral resolve and their ability to handle adverse circumstances beyond the immediate conflict. It therefore transforms society for the better by bringing out the intrinsic good in people.

A Brief Look at the Mediation Process as We Practice It

In mediation, it is not so much the procedural aspects that make the difference, but rather the nature and emphasis of the mediator's content within its context. Therefore, the only topic encompassed in this section is a brief look at the generalized procedure I follow while mediating the resolution of an environmental conflict.

As you read this chapter, remember that Carol and I are each a single person, and the ways we mediate the resolution of an environmental dispute, the framing of a vision statement, sustainable community development, or the entire process (from resolution of a conflict through sustainable community development) are but two ways. This does not make them the "right" ways or even the best ways.

The Mediation Process as Chris Practices It

I am deeply concerned with the philosophical foundation of the mediation I practice because I have lived under both a ruthless dictator and a Communist regime that were, at best, indifferent to human life. From these experiences, it is clear that coercion of any kind settles no differences and lays to rest no issues. It only degrades human beings, trashes their dignity, and thereby steals hope from their souls.

I did not set out to become a facilitator. In the beginning, I merely noticed that many of the environmental conflicts grew out of the incompatibility of human material desires with the sustainable capacity of the environment. This situation was compounded as the questions of value in society were increasingly subjected to "objective" scientific study, to derive "objective" scientific data, to provide "objective" scientific answers. Yet, despite millions of dollars and thousands of person hours devoted to such study, intrinsic cultural values and objective scientific data remain miles apart.

The original idea, therefore, was to help bridge this chasm by presenting participants with the ecological concepts (based on the best available data) and the social concepts (based on their expressed cultural values) within the context of systems thinking. My sole intent was to help them understand the information from an interactive, interconnected, interdependent ecological/social systems point of view, encompassing the past, present, and future. In this way, they could expand their common frame of reference in preparation for someone else to mediate the resolution of their dispute.

It was always emphasized that the data presented were the most up to date of which I was aware, but that *neither I nor anyone else knew what was "right" or had "the answer."* Over time, and much to my surprise, participants began asking me to stay with them and guide the entire mediation process. Having no idea what I was doing, I reluctantly agreed but limited myself to dealing with environmental conflicts.

All I had in my favor was an undying belief (1) in the inherent goodness of people; (2) that their blindness—their lack of conscious awareness—was born of ignorance, not malice; (3) that each person does the level best he or she knows how to do at all times; (4) that given a place in which to be safe, an empathetic ear with which to be heard, and the empowerment with which to overcome fear and ignorance, people could and would change their behavior for the better; (5) that there was no turning back once a person started down the path of personal growth, with its increasing sense of freedom through self-control and self-direction; and (6) that society as a whole is lifted up each time an individual grows and matures emotionally, spiritually, and intellectually.

My approach to mediation was intuitively transformative because it seems much more important to cure the cause and eliminate the symptom than merely to alleviate the symptom without touching its cause (the problem-solving approach). The approach I intuitively chose (1) assumes that human relationships take precedence over procedural outcomes; (2) opens people to a greater compassion for one another; (3) allows people to argue for and protect one another's dignity; (4) is a meticulous practice of the best principles democracy has to offer; (5) balances intellect with intuition; (6) improves society by allowing people to grow emotionally, spiritually, and intellectually; (7) focuses on the cause of a conflict; (8) helps participants understand the consequences of their choices within the context of Nature's impartial law of cause and effect; (9) allows the outcome of a conflict to be decided solely by the participants, despite the fact that resolution may not take place until some months after mediation is completed; and (10) inspires the possibility of social-environmental sustainability.

I go intentionally into mediation with little specific knowledge of the conflict or the participants. Although someone obviously contacts me about mediating the resolution of an environmental conflict, our conversation is kept to a minimum. Beyond that, I deal with as few participants as possible prior to the mediation process; if interaction is necessary, I avoid discussing the conflict. In this way, I am, as much as possible, unbiased during the process and detached from the outcome.

Further, I only agree to mediate a conflict when the disputants have exhausted every other avenue of settlement and have come up empty handed. Only when they have reached "their wit's end" are they ready to listen and to change, which makes true mediation possible. There are three basic parts to the way I mediate the resolution of a dispute: (1) the introduction, (2) the body, and (3) the conclusion.

Introduction

The introduction serves several purposes, which collectively set the stage for the mediation process. The first is to establish common ground among the participants and between the participants and the mediator. I usually use cards with the participants' names on them to arrange seating, so that participants sit next to someone not of their choosing and begin to mix. Next, we take some time to introduce ourselves and share a little about our respective backgrounds, often including interests and hobbies.

At other times, the participants may form into pairs with their neighbors, take a few moments to learn about each other, and then take turns introducing each other. In this way, preliminary communication is initiated, which simultaneously starts to bring each person "out of the closet" through mutual participation, which captures and holds their attention and has within it the seeds of trust.

The introduction serves to clarify why the participants are taking part in the process and what each hopes to gain from it. At this time, we discuss whether all necessary parties are in attendance; if not, why not; and what can be done to rectify the situation. Here, my task is to help the participants develop an inclusive attitude by helping them understand why all parties are necessary to the process and its outcome.

Next, I help them develop a receptive attitude toward the mediation process itself. This is done by helping them understand what it may hold that is beneficial to them personally, such as learning how to use the democratic process as a tool of self-government as well as community government.

The introduction also allows the disputants to learn what they can expect from me, what I expect from them, and what they can expect from one another. This is done in part by how I present myself as a person and in part by the collective establishment of the rules of conduct, such as waiting your turn to speak, being kind and polite at all times, and accepting one another's ideas without judgment.

Finally, the participants must understand that they will get as much or as little out of the mediation process as they are committed to putting into it. After all, it is theirs, not mine.

Body

The body is the main part of the mediation. When possible, I use a three-day process. The first day is spent discussing what an ecosystem is, how it functions, the reciprocal nature of how and why we treat a system as we do, and how and why it responds as it does. By using slide presentations, it is easier for the participants to begin shifting their thinking prior to their explaining to me what the dispute is about because they know that under this circumstance I am as unbiased as possible.

This format works well, as evidenced by a write-up in the U.S. Forest Service *Southwestern Region News*:

> Chris Maser ... spoke to a group of Forest Service employees, preser-vationists, conservationists, and industrialists in Albuquerque [NM] August 9 [1988]. ... Plans called for 30 to attend. There were 74 at the session with standing room only. ...
>
> ... [Maser], who neither "preached" nor "put down" views of old growth, stressed repeatedly the need for rethinking positions, prior education, and conclusions concerning forests and old growth. A theme that was woven constantly through a several-hour monologue was that of discussion, definition, and consensus. The meeting and discussion of forest issues by those involved ... is a necessity, he insisted. ...
>
> ... Maser, with patience, painted a picture of the cycles of the for-est, and the vital part of old growth. With meticulous care, he led the group through a labyrinth of long-term activity in the soils, which can, he insisted, produce a truly sustainable forest.
>
> A question and answer session followed the formal presentation. ... It was notable that there were few pointed or conflict-prone questions. Reaction ... from most participants was one of studied consideration of what had been presented, a reaction that we are convinced Maser was aiming for.[2]

The second day, with as much of a "systems" view as possible, we put the current conflict into a social-environmental context in the field, pref-erably in the area of contention. Going into the field is critical because it helps to make the abstract concepts of the first day into concrete experi-ences of immediate relevance. Here, the discussion begins by focusing on the teaching/learning of the first day, namely, on what an ecosystem is, how it functions, the reciprocal nature of how and why we treat a system as we do, and how and why it responds as it does.

During this time, each person in turn expresses his or her perception of the dispute from a personal understanding of how the ecosystem in question functions. The purpose is for each person to educate me about the dispute from a personal understanding of the whole and his or her perceived relation to the whole.

As each explanation unfolds, the person recounting it clarifies his or her understanding of personal perceptions, and the other parties hear for the first time the whole of someone else's story from that person's point of view. During this storytelling, I learn what the dispute is about because I hear it from various sides and am thus able to find common ground, differ-ences, negotiable areas, quagmires, and hidden potentials for resolution.

Because the ecological condition of the resources, which is the focal point of the conflict, has a historical perspective, it is necessary to help participants examine this perspective. From our examination of the concrete historical and current perspective, we progress to a more abstract, futuristic perspective. This perspective allows scrutiny of possible outcomes resulting from various kinds of decisions as each might affect the productive capacity of the environment, present and future. It is vital that combatants be able to move from the concrete to the abstract, based on their concept of current knowledge, if they are to craft a shared vision of the future as a resolution of their immediate conflict.

Toward this end, it is imperative to accept people where they are in terms of their understanding, which normally means using simple examples—often analogies—of how two or three components of a system might function together and then gradually expanding the examples to show how a more complex system might function as a whole. This includes helping participants to understand such concepts as change in terms of a continual, creative process; self-reinforcing feedback loops; isolated pieces versus interconnected, interactive functions; the dynamic disequilibrium of an ever-changing system; and so on.

By accepting people where they are in their understanding, it is possible to help them move from a known point of departure, with respect to their perceived knowledge, and from there toward new ideas and concepts while retaining their dignity intact. This process is greatly enhanced if one can lead people from more widely accepted ideas to those less widely held.

When I feel that I have an adequate understanding of the issues and the participants seem ready (usually by the third day), we discuss the concept of a vision, goals, and objectives. Once the participants have an understanding of these concepts, they begin to work out their vision and goals (it is not yet time for objectives), crafting them carefully on flip charts. Doing it this way, the vision and goals can usually be drafted and agreed to during the third day.

Occasionally, however, this does not work. If the participants just do not agree, they are sent off by themselves (sometimes for a day or a couple of weeks) with the instruction that each party in the dispute, which usually consists of a number of individuals, is to craft its own vision and goals. When they have completed the assignment, we reconvene, at which time each party shares its vision and goals with the others.

The purpose of one party presenting its vision and goals to the others is simply for the other people to help make sure—without judgment—that the stated vision and goals fit the agreed-on criteria. If they do not, the wording is corrected so that the criteria are in fact satisfied. Each party in turn presents its material, and each party in turn helps the others ensure that the criteria are met.

Once this process has been completed, all parties look for areas of overlap. I may help them out with questions, a powerful tool when used wisely, because questions open the door of possibility. For example, it was not possible to go to the moon until someone asked the question: Is it possible to go to the moon? At that moment, going to the moon became possible. To be effective, however, each question must (1) have a specific purpose, (2) contain a single idea, (3) be clear in meaning, (4) stimulate thought, (5) require a definite answer to bring closure to the human relationship induced by the question, and (6) relate to previous information.

For example, in a discussion about going to the moon, one might ask: Do you know what the moon is? The specific purpose is to find out if one knows what the moon is. Knowledge of the moon is the single idea contained in the question. The meaning of the question is clear: Do you or do you not know what the moon is? The question stimulates thought about what the moon is and may spark an idea of how one relates to it; if not, that can be addressed in a second question. The question, as asked, requires a definite answer, and the question relates to previous information.

Once the areas of agreement or willingness to compromise are found, they may constitute up to 80 percent or more of a common ground, and there may be little dispute left to negotiate. When this point has been reached, the parties are ready to conclude this phase of the mediation process.

Conclusion

In winding down the conclusion phase of the mediation process, the important elements of the dispute and its resolution are retraced, so the parties, having been consumed in the process, can now stand back and see in perspective how it works, which may give them a better understanding of the whole. This review both reinforces what they have learned and improves their retention of it for later reference. New ideas are not included at this time because they are likely to confuse the participants.

Finally, I must help them to determine what their next step is, usually another meeting to refine their initial draft of the vision and goals. They must decide how they want to do this and when. It is imperative, however, that they have their next meeting date set and committed to prior to adjourning.

Mediation in this way helps the parties create a shared vision and goals for a sustainable future in which they can all somehow benefit and in which they want to share. Only now do I consider the dispute largely, but not completely, resolved. Full resolution of an environmental conflict requires putting the shared vision into action.

Resolving an environmental conflict depends first on understanding the cause or causes of the conflict. Such understanding must uncover the chain of events set in motion by the participants' decisions, which in turn triggered cause-and-effect relationships within a range of alternative decisions and outcomes. My perception of a conflict must be as objective as possible and not based on judgment as dictated by my standard of right or wrong.

The Mediation Process as Carol Practices It

Most of my experience in mediation has been on the ground during commercial projects or reviews of federal permit applications for such projects, for which individuals have an immediate economic stake in the outcome and come to the table (or to visit a site) with a clear position. Participants in the meeting are ready for a fight and have usually decided that I am (meaning whom I represent) the enemy. It has taken many years to develop the necessary skills to defuse such a situation and bring a group like this to agreement—or at least a way forward.

There have been several times in my career when I worked with an individual who truly was the enemy—someone who used (or abused) their power to ensure that permits would be denied or projects halted in the name of the government or their organization. Animosity was the individual's idea of how to resolve environmental conflict—to win at any cost. In the individual's mind, a win was a "win for the environment," and that justified whatever means was necessary to accomplish that goal.

I always felt conflicted when I worked with those types of people. While I shared their concern for the environment, I also empathized with the farmer or miner who simply wanted to feed a family or keep making mortgage payments. I *did* want to make a difference for the environment—but not on those terms. I had no desire to create antagonistic relationships with people or find creative ways to thwart their progress. Yes, I wanted to conserve resources, but I also felt at my core that there must be a way to do so by working *with* people instead of against them.

In those early years, I frequently found myself apologizing for the behavior of supervisors and co-workers (as one wonderful mentor called it, "making nice") so that I could bring a group to agreement and move ahead with a project or plan. It was certainly uncomfortable to be put in that position, being sent to meetings after a supervisor or colleague had made a mess of things, but through that experience, I learned quite a few skills in mediation and facilitation.

Overcoming Animosity

Instead of developing an adversarial attitude, I chose to create an environment in which all participants were respected and felt safe to express their opinions and concerns. It sometimes meant being just as tough as the coal miner or voicing my opinion to the major general when it was not what they wanted to hear. But, I learned to do it in a way that was respectful and appropriate, not destructive and not in the form of a personal attack. This experience formed the basis of my mediation style—one of respect for every participant—and directs my actions in all that I do.

Engaging participants to work together positively can, at times, be a daunting task. In many instances, we bring a variety of barriers with us to the table. These barriers often come in the form of "bowling shirts," such things as uniforms, logo ball caps, company polo shirts, and so on. They are worn to meetings to state clearly: "This is who I am, and my position on this matter is clear." My first strategy as a mediator in these meetings is not to wear my bowling shirt. Instead of seeing me as "X from X agency," I want to be seen as a person, not a position. I also prefer to find neutral ground for the meeting, whether it be a neutral office or on site, somewhere that is not the battleground itself.

One of my most valuable tools is the social gathering. When I want a group to work together and see each other as people, not positions, I plan a gathering that has a social context to it, a barbeque, an open house with coffee and donuts, or a tour of a facility or field location with similar issues, followed by refreshments. By doing this, I have found that it not only sets the tone for the upcoming negotiations but also encourages participants to talk about themselves as people in a less formal, nonthreatening setting. I can tell you from personal experience that it is much harder to be angry with someone you shared your kids' baby photos with or joked with during a game of softball.

On-the-ground mediation is a lot less formal than Chris's mediation experiences. It is more the "down-and-dirty" variety, where you are face to face with an opponent who is directly involved and typically angry at you (or, as we discuss further, is expressing fear of the unknown as anger). So, how do you get started? I like to start with "the golden rule"—treat others as you would like to be treated.

Over the years, I have learned by talking with people during mediation that we have many similarities. Most people at the table will have many years of experience in their chosen field, including those in industry. They will be skilled at what they do, and many will have formal education similar to our own. For example, I was acting as a field office supervisor in Alabama a few years ago and had an interesting discussion with an employee ("John") I was sending to a meeting with the U.S. Army Corps of Engineers. We had done nothing but fight with the Corps and were truly at a stalemate on a number of projects.

I told John, "Remember that you're no different than that biologist at the Corps. You probably went to the same school, or even have the same degree. The only difference between you and him is where you got hired when you finished college."

He looked at me for a moment, and said, tentatively, "I never thought of it that way."

When I saw that I had him thinking, I said, "You both should be able to agree to do what's best for the resource, because that's the common ground you have as biologists. Try that approach and see how that works, because what we've been doing so far certainly hasn't worked."

I know I made an impact that day. I cannot say we solved all of our issues with that one meeting, but I can say that John changed the fundamental way he thought about "the enemy." To quote Walt Kelly, the Pogo cartoonist, "We have met the enemy ... and he is us."

Establishing Ground Rules

Establishing a foundation of respect is similar, whether in a small, more cohesive group, or in a larger, more contentious one. One helpful tool is the development of *ground rules* because they codify how members are to be treated and set the stage for all future meetings or negotiations. (We talk more about specific ground rules in Chapter 5.) The critical aspect of setting ground rules, the one that makes them "stick," is that the group both establishes them and agrees to abide by them. As the group mediator, I have walked numerous groups through this rule-making process. I typically begin with brainstorming a list of possible ground rules, then work with the participants to narrow it by grouping similar rules, followed by helping them simplify and clarify the rules, and finally by deciding exactly what each rule means to the participants.

As a caution, do not assume that you, as mediator, know what a rule means because it is common for it to mean something different to a participant based on their prior experience. Therefore, ask the participant who suggested it to explain its meaning. What is important about establishing ground rules is that every participant acknowledges, to the mediator, that they agree with the rules as written. This allows any participant to invoke the ground rules as a point of order in later negotiations.

Setting Objectives

Throughout the informal mediation process, bringing the group back to the ground rules and focusing them on the issues, versus their positions, are critical to a successful conclusion. However, once the process is moving, the question becomes one of keeping it going smoothly. This is where establishing specific objectives is important. If we do not craft SMART (specific, measurable, attainable, relevant, and time-bound) objectives, we may end up solving the wrong problem. Or worse yet, we waste endless time arguing about our positions instead of working toward a solution. Setting meaningful objectives can also be used to tease out the basic values of a group and identify their issues of concern. I use the setting of objectives as a means of doing just that in both formal and informal mediation.

As I work with the group through the objective-setting process, I am often able fairly quickly to find common ground between the parties involved. One example comes from the time I worked with the U.S. Marine Corps, as an adjacent landowner to my assigned national park.

Our missions were certainly at odds but not an unsurmountable barrier to working together. In one case, I met with staff from the Marine Corps base to review a timber sale near our mutual boundaries, which I felt could have an impact on the national park. I learned, through our discussion, that proceeds from timber sales were used to fund the salaries of the wildlife and habitat staff. Without this funding, there would be less habitat restoration work done. In fact, none would be done at all if we (the U.S. National Park Service) stopped timber sales altogether. We discovered that our mutual objective was to ensure that habitat restoration continued on both sides of the boundary. Agreement was quickly reached once everyone realized that finding a resolution, which allowed the military to continue small timber sales on base while adding a larger buffer to streams near or adjacent to the park, was in our mutual interest.

A group can easily find itself off track or, worse yet, spinning its wheels. I use similar tactics to those Chris mentioned to help the group find its "next step." Throughout the process, I compile a list of action items and commitments made by individuals or the group as a whole. These are reviewed prior to closing each meeting and at the beginning of each subsequent meeting. Each commitment or step is assigned a responsible party and a due date. This "to do" list is agreed to by all members and is a crucial tool to ensure that everyone is moving forward and operationalizing their commitments to the group. Although I use this list to track the progress of large, complex issues, it also serves to remind members of both their commitment and their accountability to the process. This sense of commitment and accountability is important because I find that group members are willing to enforce it as part of their contract with one another and to apply peer pressure when and where needed to keep the group moving forward.

It is also important to celebrate the accomplishments of the group as it moves through particularly long or complex projects or as a way to close negotiations on shorter-term projects or issues. Doing so reinforces the positive contributions group members have made and often sets the stage for future collaborative efforts. Celebrating can be as simple as ending with a social event, as formal as a well-planned media event, or some other form of public recognition. The method may vary, depending on the size, dynamic, and accomplishments of the group, but I have found that such celebrations, no matter how small, end the mediation process on a positive note—one that reinforces the accomplishment yet also encourages group members to continue to work together should the opportunity arise.

Structured Decision Making

In some cases, a more formal structure is useful for resolving environmental conflicts. An additional technique that is gaining popularity in environmental conflict resolution is *structured decision making*. Structured decision making was initially developed for use in the social sciences to assist in decisions related to child welfare. It is an organized approach that is best used in cases in which there are multiple stakeholders, complex issues, high levels of uncertainty, and the possible outcome has broad or significant economic, environmental, social, or political implications. Structured decision making is defined as

> An organized approach to **identifying and evaluating alternatives** that focuses on engaging stakeholders, experts, and decision makers in productive decision-oriented **analysis** and **dialogue** and that deals proactively with **complexity** and **judgment** in decision making. It provides a framework that becomes a decision-focused **roadmap** for integrating activities related to planning, analysis and consultation.[3] (boldface in original)

This tool is used in the Department of the Interior, primarily by the U.S. Fish and Wildlife Service, particularly in decisions concerning the Endangered Species Act. As early as 1995, the National Research Council recommended the use of a "structured problem-solving method" for dealing with scientific uncertainty in decisions concerning the Endangered Species Act.[4] The steps of structured decision making are

- *Problem definition*: What specific decision has to be made? What is the spatial and temporal scope of the decision? Will the decision be iterated over time?
- *Objectives*: What are the management objectives? Ideally, these are stated in quantitative terms, which relate to metrics that can be measured. Setting objectives falls in the realm of policy, and should be informed by legal and regulatory mandates, as well as stakeholder viewpoints. A number of methods for stakeholder elicitation and conflict resolution are appropriate for clarifying objectives.
- *Alternatives*: What are the different management actions to choose from? This element requires explicit articulation of the alternatives available to the decision maker. The range of permissible options is often constrained by legal or political considerations, but structured assessment may lead to creative new alternatives.
- *Consequences*: What are the consequences of different management actions? How much of the objectives would each alternative achieve? In structured decision making, we predict the consequences of the alternative actions with some type of model. Depending on the information available or the quantification desired for a structured decision process, consequences may be modeled with highly scientific computer applications or with

personal judgment elicited carefully and transparently. Ideally, models are quantitative, but they need not be; the important thing is that they link actions to consequences.

- *Trade-offs*: If there are multiple objectives, what are the trade-offs between and among one another? In most complex decisions, the best we can do is to choose intelligently among less-than-perfect alternatives. Numerous tools are available to help determine the relative importance or weights among conflicting objectives and to then compare alternatives across multiple attributes to find the "best" compromise solutions.

- *Uncertainty*: Because we rarely know precisely how management actions will affect natural systems, decisions are frequently made in the face of uncertainty. Uncertainty makes choosing among alternatives far more difficult. A good decision-making process will confront uncertainty explicitly and evaluate the likelihood of different outcomes and their possible consequences.

- *Risk Tolerance*: Identifying the uncertainty that impedes decision-making, then analyzing the risk that uncertainty presents to management is an important step in making a good decision. Understanding the level of risk a decision maker is willing to accept, or the risk response determined by law or policy, will make the decision-making process more objectives-driven, transparent, and defensible.

- *Linked decisions*: Many important decisions are linked over time. The key to dealing effectively with linked decisions is to isolate and resolve the near-term issues while sequencing the collection of information needed for future decisions.[5]

Chris and I use slightly different processes in our mediation efforts, but you can see that we share many similarities. There is no right or wrong way to move a group forward, only the way that works. The most important lesson here is to do what best suits your style and to be sincere in your desire to resolve the conflict at hand—understanding that conflict is a choice and thus resolution is also a choice.

References

1. Robert A. Baruch Bush and Joseph P. Folger. *The Promise of Mediation: Responding to Conflict through Empowerment and Recognition.* Jossey-Bass, San Francisco (1994).

2. USDA Forest Service. 1988. Maser: a man with a mission. *Southwest Regional News*, pp. 6, 16.
3. Structured Decision Making. http://www.structureddecisonmaking.org (accessed June 13, 2010).
4. National Research Council. *Science and the Endangered Species Act*. National Academies Press, Washington, DC (1995). http://www.nap.edu/openbook. php?record_id=4978&page=1 (accessed March 13, 2011).
5. Fish and Wildlife Service. Structured Decision Making Fact Sheet (October 2008). http://www.fws.gov/science/doc/structured_decision_making_fact sheet.pdf (accessed March 13, 2011).

2

Conflict Is a Choice

Introduction

Conflict is a choice of behavior. We resort to conflict in one way or another, at one level or another, because that is what we were taught to do as children. That is how we were taught to cope with change—those circumstances perceived as threatening to our survival. For example, we are waging a war against Nature, a war on cancer, a war on poverty, a war on obesity, a war on diseases of all kinds, a war on drugs, war of the sexes, and so on. We are we progressively making the world into an everyday combat zone with our thinking.

Looking around the world today, is it any wonder that various segments of the global society are blowing themselves to bits and in the process needlessly, recklessly squandering the natural resource base on which they and all future generations depend for survival? Children are being ushered into emotionally shattered lives, where their inner poverty will compound the outer poverty they face in the spiritual/cultural/economic chaos of disrupted lives; gutted cities; corrupt, power-hungry governments; and war-torn, fragmented landscapes. These generations may well grow up thinking that hatred and violent conflict are the norm, which continually fosters the unworkable paradigm of a black-and-white world, in which

- I'm right, and you're wrong.
- My religion is the only one that is right; thus, God is on my side, which makes you the infidel.
- You're either for me or against me.

Is such a future unavoidable? Must we increasingly become a world of victims in which there is no escape from an eternal dysfunctional cycle of abuse and combat? If abuse, and the combat it engenders, is indeed the lot of humanity, then time and history will grind wearily on to the only social outcome possible, the ultimate destruction of human society, taking much of life on Earth with it. Is this the lesson human history is to continue teaching as the activities of each day are recorded in the archives of eventide?

We think not. We see the world differently, and this difference is predicated largely on two things: (1) recognizing, accepting, and acting on the notion that conflict is a choice, which means we can choose peaceful ways of resolving differences; and (2) understanding that the peaceful way lies in the art of mediation that fosters personal growth, by which differences are resolved through inner shifts in consciousness. Such shifts alter the core perceptions from which conflict grows by increasing the social functionality of the participants and hence their tendencies toward peace.

Simply put, mediation can help combatants mirror their fears and sense of vulnerability to their opponents, thereby coaxing from deep within a sense of compassion that transcends each person's fear. As fear is transcended, perceived differences—the cradle of fear—become novel approaches to the commonalities of a shared vision. In fact, they often become the source of strength for a vision.

Finding no external fixes for internal fears, we must assume that the cause of conflict is internal to the combatants themselves, as it always is to us. For example, children are taught by adults' behavior that interpersonal conflict is simply a condition of life, a necessity of survival. Watching my parents, I did, as a child, the only thing a child knows how to do: I copied what I saw.[1]

We often assume that conflict is both open and visible because the term *conflict* brings to mind images of war and abuse, as well as homegrown, gang violence. For example, I (Carol) have no memory as a child of seeing my parents in conflict. Arguing, storming around the house, or raised voices were not considered acceptable ways to self-express. This lack of visible signs of conflict was a direct result of suppressing it, which sends the message that conflict was something neither done nor condoned in "public." As a result, I developed an avoidance of conflict—sitting through the debates of others without comment on an issue, even when I disagreed with someone in the group. This behavior took some effort to overcome—and sometimes still does.

As mediators, we must identify the hidden conflicts as well as the obvious ones. We see this often in conflict resolution, when meetings seemingly go well and agreement (or the appearance of it) brings us to a pleasant conclusion. Only at the next meeting, we come back to the issue again and discuss it further, and at the next meeting, and the next, and so on. If you have been in this situation, you have likely seen the avoidance of conflict in action. As with other types of responses to conflict, fear is often at the bottom of it. If I speak up, will others dislike me? Be angry with me? Ignore me? Ridicule or threaten me?

However, there are "no enemies out there," only frightened people who feel the need to defend themselves from potential loss of what they think they must have to survive—control of their own lives as they perceive them. Thus, as mediators, it is imperative that we understand why conflict is the chosen way of dealing with personal differences if we are to help the participants do anything more than temporarily alleviate the symptoms, which festered into open dispute. To do so, we must understand something of the underlying nature of conflict, beginning with the notion of each person's "right" of survival, however that is defined.

What Is a "Right"?

In medieval literature, brave knights came from across the land to be considered for membership at the Round Table. King Arthur designed its circular shape to arrange the knights democratically and give each an equal position. When a knight was granted membership at the Round Table, he was guaranteed equal stature with everyone else at the table and a right to be heard with equal voice.

Today, one understanding of a right is a legalistic, human construct based on some sense of moral privilege—of entitlement. Although a right in a democratic system of government is created by people and defined and guaranteed by law, access to a right may not be equally distributed across society. Conversely, a right does not apply to any person outside the select group unless that group purposely confers such a right on a specifically recognized individual, such as the disenfranchised.

In a true democracy, the whole protects all of its parts and the parts give obedience to the will of the whole. Ostensibly, therefore, a right in democracy gives everyone equality by sanctifying and impartially protecting certain socially acceptable behaviors while controlling unsanctioned ones. There is, however, a price exacted for having rights, even in a true democracy.

Rights have responsibilities attached to them. Thus, whenever a law is passed to protect the rights of the majority against the transgressions of the minority, everyone pays the same price—some loss of freedom of choice, of flexibility—because every law so passed is restrictive to everyone. Put succinctly, we give up personal freedoms to gain personal *rights*.

The problem is that rights, as granted by humans to one another in daily life, including in the United States, are based on access—not equality. Access is determined by some notion that one race, color, creed, sex, or age is superior to another, which means that differences and similarities are based on our subjective judgments about whatever those appearances are.

In American society, for example, men are still judged more capable than women in most kinds of work because society has placed more value on certain kinds of products (i.e., those demanding such masculine attributes as linear thinking and physical strength as opposed to those demanding such feminine attributes as relationship and physical gentleness).

With notable exceptions, the stereotype holds that perceived differences in outer (superficial) values become social judgments about the inherent (real) values of individual human beings. Superficial characteristics are thus translated into special rights or privileges simply because the individuals involved are different in some aspects and either perform certain actions differently or perform different actions. The greater the difference a person perceives between another person and themself (such as a millionaire versus a homeless street beggar), the more likely the person is to make black-and-white judgments about that other person's real value, as expressed through a personal notion of that person's rights.

Stated in a generic sense, such judgments are made against the standard I (in the generic sense) use to measure how everything around me fits into my comfort zone. I thus judge people as good or bad depending on how they conform to my standard of acceptability, a standard taught and reinforced by my parents and later by my peers and teachers. Such judgments are erroneous, however, because all I can ever judge is appearances. In addition, my standard is correct for me only; it is not validly imposed on anyone else. Nevertheless, I use socially constructed, hierarchical couplets of extrinsic differences (white male versus white female, white male versus black male, human versus Nature) as a basis for judging the equality of such things as one race versus another, men versus women, secular versus spiritual, right versus wrong, good versus evil, and so on.

The most extreme example of personal judgment is the use of superficial differences to justify a social end. One group of people thus declares itself superior to another group because it wants what the other group has. The "superior" group tells the "inferior" group that it has no rights and through this denial of rights justifies its abuse of fellow human beings.

When, for instance, the invading Spanish conquered the Pueblo Indians, they could not accept, let alone acknowledge, that they and the Pueblos were equally human. Had they acknowledged that truth, they could never have justified the wholesale murder of the Indians and theft of their land. In turn, when the invading Anglos conquered the Spanish, they could not accept, let alone acknowledge, that they and the Spanish were equally human. Had they acknowledged that truth, they could never have justified the wholesale murder of the Spanish and theft of their land. As modern conquests continue, so does the cycle.

The same principle holds for the indigenous peoples of the South American tropical forests. If the cattle barons ever admitted that the indigenous peoples living in the forests were their equals, they could not clear-cut and burn the forests to gain pasture for their beef herds. In creating the pastures, the cattle barons destroyed an ecosystem and stripped the indigenous peoples not only of their current livelihood but also of their future options and those of their children. If the cattle barons were to admit that the indigenous peoples are in every way their equals, then they would have to *treat* them as their equals. And that, in turn, means sharing control of their mutual social destiny.

It is not a question of who is better. Rather, it is a question of who is more afraid. It is a question of who has internalized all the assumed differences and therefore perceives another human being as an unknown entity. It is a question of who is so afraid of losing control of perceived rights that the person will do anything to keep control, regardless of social and environmental consequences. In the end, therefore, it becomes a question of the equality of differences.

The Equality of Differences

Notions of superiority and inferiority are based on personal, familial, and societal judgments about the intrinsic values of extrinsic differences. To illustrate, consider two questions about garbage collectors and medical doctors: Is collecting garbage as a social service of equal value to that of treating sick people? Is the social stature of a garbage collector equal to that of a medical doctor?

Most people, in Chris's experience, seem to think that the service performed by medical doctors is of greater social value than that performed by garbage collectors, and that doctors not only enjoy but also deserve a higher social status than garbage collectors. But, when judging garbage collectors versus medical doctors, most people focus on differences and fail to take similarities into account, one of which is that both occupations help maintain a healthy environment for people. Both occupations also rely on each other's services. In fact, doctors probably rely on garbage collectors more than garbage collectors rely on doctors.

How much more difficult would be the doctor's task if garbage collectors allowed human refuse to accumulate around houses and in streets? The outcome could be an epidemic of bubonic plague, a disease carried by rats that proliferate in human garbage and whose fleas transmit the disease. Once plague bacteria began spreading, doctors would have to marshal their numbers to treat the sick.

Garbage collectors serve society before the fact at a fundamental, collective level. Medical doctors tend to society after the fact, after someone is ill, one individual at a time. We therefore become personally acquainted with our doctors but not usually with our garbage collectors. Such a personal acquaintance greatly increases the value people tend to attribute to an individual's job because they have not only a more intimate sense of the person's intrinsic value but also a greater knowledge of how that person's profession contributes to society and their own welfare.

Nevertheless, garbage collectors are as vital to human health as medical doctors, only in a different way. Why, therefore, are they not afforded equal status in society? Perhaps the reason is that they do not need to attend school for seven to eight years to become sufficiently trained to collect garbage and therefore do not have a socially coveted title before their names. Perhaps it is because few people see them at work and therefore do not ponder the value of the service they perform. Perhaps it is because we do not go to garbage collectors to make us feel better when we are ill and thus do not form a personal relationship with them as we do with our doctors. (Have you, for instance, ever thanked your garbage collector for taking away your trash as you have thanked your doctor for making you feel better?) Perhaps it is because, compared to medical doctors, garbage collectors do not make nearly as much money, so we deem them less successful in a society where affluence is the measure of success and social status. Perhaps it is because they may be filthy and stink when they get off work instead of being clean and well groomed.

These things notwithstanding, garbage collectors and medical doctors are of equal value professionally, albeit different in how they serve the health needs of society. Further, their services are not only vital but also complementary in that they accomplish far more together than either could possibly accomplish alone.

There may be a number of judgmental reasons for these discrepancies in social stature, but none of them can be applied in the context of the real value of each person. An appropriate analogy might be the spokes of a wheel. Each spoke is slightly different and seemingly independent of the others, yet each is equal in its importance to the functioning of the wheel. Each spoke is connected at the center of the wheel and at the outer rim. Leave out one spoke and the strength and function of the wheel is to that extent diminished, although the effect might not become immediately apparent.

Each person has a gift to give, and each gift is unique to that person and critical to the social whole. All gifts are equal *and* different. What is true for individual human beings is true for cultures and societies because each is equal in its service to Earth. Each life, each culture, each society is equally important to the evolutionary success of our planet, whether we understand it or not. Each also has its own excellence and cannot be compared to any other. All differences among people, cultures, and societies are just that—differences. The hierarchies or judgmental levels of value are human constructs that have little or nothing to do with reality. Every life, culture, and society is a practice in evolution, and each is equal before the impartial law of cosmic unification and its subordinate but inviolate biophysical principles (discussed in Chapter 3).

We must therefore discard our view of Earth as a battlefield of subjective competition, where our "human superiority" reigns over that of Nature and where "my superiority" reigns over yours. We will all be better off if we instead consider Earth in terms of complementary efforts in which all gifts are equal and each in its own way is important to the health and well-being of the whole living system because life demands struggle and tenacity, which continually fit and refit each living thing to its function. Complementary efforts, such as those of garbage collectors and medical doctors, imply equality among people, and human equality brings us to the notion of the inalienable right of all people to environmental justice.

Environmental Justice Is Predicated on Human Equality

The concept of environmental justice, from the human point of view, asserts that we owe something to every person sharing the planet with us, both those present and those yet unborn. But, you may ask, what exactly do we have to give? The only things we have of value are the love, trust, respect, and wisdom gleaned from our life experiences, which are embodied in the ramifications of each and every option we pass forward. And, it is exactly because options encompass all we have to give those living today and all the children of tomorrow and beyond that environmental justice, as a concept, must of necessity be examined within the context of human equality.

A wonderful example of perceived inequality among humans took place some years ago in Chris's hometown of Corvallis, Oregon; it involved people living in the city versus those living in the country. A farmer had been arrested and fined for throwing garbage on somebody's lawn in town. But, as circumstances played out, it became apparent that, despite the Constitution of the United States, some people are a lot more equal than others. The episode went as follows:

> Joe City, who lived in Corvallis, took his garbage out to the country and dumped it on Bill Rural's property near Bill's house. Although Bill did not see Joe dump his garbage, he found an invoice in the garbage with Joe's name and address on it. So, Bill picked up all of Joe's garbage and drove into Corvallis, where he gave it back to Joe by dumping it on Joe's front lawn. Joe went to the police and complained.

Even though Bill said that the people of Corvallis were continually dumping their unwanted garbage on his land and that, in this case, he was sure it was Joe's garbage because of the invoice, Joe had legal standing and Bill did not. Bill was arrested and fined, but *nothing* happened to Joe—something that sent a clear message of inequality to Joe, to Bill, and to everyone else. The message: *It is okay for city folks to dump their garbage with legal impunity on the property of rural folks, but not vice versa.*

Let us look at this scenario another way. Rural people who value clean air and quality water have a right to enjoy these amenities, especially when they purposefully live "in the middle of nowhere." But, bureaucrats hundreds of miles away give cities and industries the right to pollute air and water because of economic and political pressures. They do this despite the fact that such pollution fouls the air and contaminates the water rural people have no choice but to use.

Human inequality has to do with fear and its companion, control. The person who harbors the most fear also harbors the greatest need to be in control of his or her external environment. This need to be in control is always fed by the need for the "inequality of others," who are often demonized in one way or another to steal with impunity their "personal rights" for self-interested gain.

Inequality, which translates into injustice, carries over into every institution in our land, but it is perhaps clearest in those agencies whose missions are to uphold and fulfill the legal mandates of protecting environmental quality for all citizens, present and future. It is seen everywhere: in the appalling lack of evenhandedness and in the bending of people within the agencies—including the Congress of the United States—to the political pressure of special interest groups at the expense of all generations. There have been times, however, when equality and justice counted for something, as Thucydides said of the Athenian code, "Praise is due to all who ... respect justice more than their position compels them to do." And in more recent times, the founding fathers of the United States did their level best, through the Declaration of Independence, the Constitution, and the Bill of Rights, to instill equality and justice in the new nation.

Nevertheless, agencies and individuals responsible for the welfare of the natural resources of our nation have functions prescribed by law, but not necessarily specified by law. Legislative bodies therefore permit a wide range of administrative discretion. Although this is as it should be, the system lacks a guiding precept for "public service," one that in fact means serving the whole of the public with the impartiality of justice for the common good of all generations.

These agencies and individuals are most often under great political pressure from special interest groups. This pressure, exerted through elected politicians, results in dedicated public servants being captives not only of the traditions of their organization but also of the fears and political weaknesses of their superiors. This means that true public servants are subjected to conflicting demands and receive no assurance or ethical governance, despite their dedication to such governance. As a result, our system of caring for the natural resources of the nation has neither an ethical standard, or ethos, nor a sense of social-environmental justice within society itself or toward the environment that nurtures and sustains society.

It is important to note, however, that this is unique to our culture in the United States. In other cultures, public servants have a position of trust and are held in the highest regard. According to Dr. Hans Bleiker of the Institute for Participatory Management and Planning, this distrust of public servants evolved during the formation of our democracy and continues to this day. We are a nation founded on distrust—what we proudly call our system of "checks and balances." Our forefathers established this system deliberately to ensure that no one person or branch of the government could move forward without the consent of the others. In contrast, Dr. Bleiker experienced the opposite in Sweden, where public officials are trusted, considered experts in their fields, and are treated with the utmost respect. Contrast that with the news stories and articles here in the United States, which consistently "bash" public service, and you will see what we mean. This negative behavior translates to a system in which it is up to the individual to maintain and uphold a set of ethics and standards, while being pressured by political and special interest groups, instead of a system in which the highest ethical standards are communicated, reinforced, and expected.[2]

Ethos, a Greek word meaning "character" or "tone," is best thought of as a set of guiding beliefs, which, as mentioned, is neither clearly articulated nor ubiquitous in most state and federal land management agencies. In phrasing this guiding direction, a distinction needs to be made between ethos and policy. Policy, written in explicit terms, can be in the form of an order—the letter of the law. Ethos, on the other hand, is implicit and includes a guiding set of human values—the heart of the law—that is understood but cannot easily be written. Yet ethos can be translated into policy should one wish to do so.

Instead of a clearly articulated ethos translated into a policy of environmental justice and human equality, however, our society is both arrogant and greedy. Arrogance arises from the ignorance that assumes present knowledge is both correct and unchanging. Greed, which fosters hoarding, is born out of the fear of loss, the fear of never having enough in the material sense. And both are justified—even hallowed—in the economic theory that underlies our capitalistic way of doing business, which is but a reflection of our social psyche, out of which arise competition and its attendant conflicts.

Perceived Resource Scarcity Accentuates Environmental Conflict

Nature affixes no human-derived values to either its components or the interactive whole. Its intrinsic value is sufficient unto itself. Humanity, on the other hand, puts its own values on some portions of the environment at the expense of others. People then compete for those items of Nature in which they find common value and waste those in which they do not.

That said, environmental conflict is born out of a perceived threat to a person's "right of survival," however that is defined. The perceived security of our right to survive is weighed against the number of choices we think are available to us as individuals and our ability to control our choices. Thus, as long as one party in a conflict thinks it can win agreement with its stance, which means to defend its perceived choices, that party will neither compromise nor change its position.

Perceived choices are ultimately affected by the real supply and demand for natural resources, the source of energy required by all life in one form or another. Perhaps with this in mind, former Soviet leader Mikhail Gorbachev asked: "If we're going to protect the planet's ecology, we're going to need to find alternatives to the consumerist dream that is attracting the world. Otherwise, how will we conserve our resources, and how will we avoid setting people against each other when resources are depleted?"[3]

The greater the supply of a particular resource, the greater the freedom of choice an individual has with respect to that resource. Conversely, the smaller the supply and the narrower the range of choices available often incites people to steal choices from one another to augment their own sense of insufficiency. And scarcity, real or perceived, is the breeding ground of environmental injustice, which rears its ugly head each time someone steals from another rather than taking responsibility for personal behavior and sharing equally. Here a paradox arises like the phoenix out of the ashes of conflict: The people who have the most often want the most and thus—perceiving a sense of scarcity—are usually the most competitive and combative in securing what they want.

An excellent example of environmental injustice occurred in 1991 when the people of Las Vegas and Clark County (in southern Nevada) attempted to take their neighbors' water against their neighbors' will. Las Vegas not only is built in a very fragile desert where no city should exist but also is made up of many people who squander more water than people anywhere Chris has ever been—and they can least afford it. Nevertheless, during the two years that he and his wife, Zane, lived in Las Vegas, the gutters of the streets ran almost every morning with great streams of water, some of which extended for a quarter of a mile or more.

The squandered water came from uncontrolled irrigation used solely to keep household and corporate lawns green. In addition, water was squandered on numerous artificial lakes and ponds and countless open swimming pools. Rather than conserving its limited supply, the city and county coveted the water of their northern neighbors and tried to figure out ways to get it, very much against the wishes and the will of those to whom it "belonged."

In short, rather than accepting the limitations of the desert in which they chose to live, the people of Las Vegas and Clark County were trying to usurp the choices of others. If they succeeded, then those who used water wisely and therefore had a greater number of options would be unjustly penalized for their thrift. The people of Las Vegas and Clark County, on the other hand, could continue squandering water with impunity by taking from others, thus avoiding personal restraint and accountability for their extravagant use of water.

The variety of available choices dictates the amount of control people feel they have. This consequently affects their sense of security about their survival. What would happen should you perceive your array of choices as fading or when they have suddenly been ripped away, as would happen if the people of Las Vegas and Clark County ever manage to steal their neighbors' water? Have you ever been told that you can no longer do something you have always done and therefore have taken doing it for granted? How did you feel?

How would you feel if you were suddenly plucked from whatever you are doing without warning and for no apparent reason, thrown into prison without explanation or recourse, and held indefinitely against your will? Are there such innocent people behind bars now? The answer is yes.

How would you feel if you were jerked out of the only life you know, smuggled into an alien country, and sold into the bonds of slavery, never again to see anyone or anything you knew or to enjoy the rights you once had as a citizen of the United States? This is not a far-fetched scenario; slavery is very much alive in the world today—even here, in the United States.

How would you feel, as an average citizen with no political desires, if civil war (such as that occurring in Iraq, Afghanistan, and parts of Africa) erupted suddenly all around you, and you had nowhere to go while your family, home, and town were being blown apart? I (Chris) had a small taste of this powerless feeling when held at gunpoint on at least one occasion in Egypt while the country was under Nasser's dictatorial fist.

We ask these questions, even though they are not specifically resource oriented, in the hope that you can imagine how you would feel deep within if you were suddenly to lose your sense of safety and well-being—your sense of choice. We ask because we are convinced that conflicts arise from a deep, albeit usually unconscious, sense of potential loss—a chronic or acute fear of the future based on a socialized disaster mentality.

For example, the functional premise of the global stock market is based on the fear of loss. That is why people buy stocks when the market is high and sell them when the market is low. They are afraid of missing an opportunity to make more money when the market is high—hoping it will continue to climb. When, however, the market value falls, as it is destined to do, they panic and sell in fear of losing what capital they have in whatever stocks are declining in value. They lose in both cases, however. On the other hand, they would gain at both ends if they sold when the market was high and bought when it was low, but first they would have to overcome their fear of loss.

Resource Overexploitation: A Matter of Perceived Loss

According to a song popular some years ago, "freedom's just another word for nothing left to lose,"[4] which in a peculiar way speaks of an apparent human truth. When I (in the generic sense) am unconscious of a material value, I am free of its psychological grip. However, the instant I perceive a material value and anticipate possible material gain, I also perceive the psychological pain of potential loss.

The larger and more immediate the prospects for material gain, the greater the political power used to ensure and expedite exploitation because not to exploit is perceived as losing an opportunity to someone else. And, it is this notion of loss that people fight so hard to avoid. In this sense, it is more appropriate to think of resources managing humans than of humans managing resources.[5]

A great example of this is the U.S. argument against signing the Kyoto Protocol. According to former President George W. Bush, "The Kyoto treaty would have wrecked our economy, if I can be blunt."[6] A primary reason for this belief was that China was seen as a "free rider"—a nonindustrial country that could pollute at will, while other, more industrialized countries made efforts to reduce emissions at some (possibly significant) economic cost. Yet, in this instance, it seems we failed to recognize that it was our own unbridled exploitation of natural resources in the United States that allowed us to gain our position as a global economic power. In this case, what is "good for the goose" apparently is not "good for the gander" because we want to deny the economic opportunity for China—the same opportunity that we have enjoyed. Many see the United States as hypocritical in this regard because we exercised tremendous political power to avoid becoming a signatory to Kyoto—all to protect our economic interests, to our detriment and that of all generations and the planet as a whole.

Historically, then, any newly identified resource is inevitably overexploited, often to the point of collapse or extinction. Its overexploitation is based, first, on the perceived rights or entitlement of the exploiter to get his or her share before someone else does and, second, on the exploiter's right or entitlement to protect personal economic investment. There is more to it than this, however, because the concept of a healthy capitalistic system is one that is ever growing, ever expanding, but such a system is not biologically sustainable.

With renewable natural resources, such nonsustainable exploitation is a "ratchet effect," for which to ratchet means to constantly, albeit unevenly, increase the rate of exploitation of a resource.[7]

The ratchet effect works as follows: During periods of relative economic stability, the rate of harvest of a given renewable resource, say timber or salmon, tends to stabilize at a level that economic theory predicts can be sustained through some scale of time. Such levels, however, are almost always excessive because economists take existing unknown and unpredictable ecological variables and convert them, in theory at least, into known and predictable economic constant values to better calculate the expected return on a given monetary investment from a sustained harvest.

Then comes a sequence of good years in the market, in the availability of the resource, or both, and additional capital investments are encouraged in harvesting and processing because competitive economic growth is the root of capitalism. When conditions return to normal or even below normal, however, the industry, having overinvested, appeals to the government for help because substantial economic capital, and often many jobs, are at stake. The government typically responds with direct or indirect subsidies, which only encourage continual overharvesting.

The ratchet effect is thus caused by unrestrained economic investment to increase short-term yields in good times and strong opposition to losing those yields in bad economic times. This opposition to losing yields means there is great resistance to using a resource in a biologically sustainable manner because there is no predictability in yields and no guarantee of yield increases in the foreseeable future. In addition, our linear economic models of ever-increasing yield are built on the assumption that we can in fact have an economically *sustained* yield. This contrived concept fails in the face of the biological *sustainability* of a yield.

Then, because there is no mechanism in our linear economic models of ever-increasing yield that allows for the uncertainties of ecological cycles and variability or for the inevitable decreases in yield during down times in the market, the long-term outcome is a heavily subsidized industry— say, agriculture. Such an industry continually overharvests the resource (soil productivity in the case of agriculture) on an artificially created, sustained-yield basis that is not biologically sustainable.

When the notion of sustainability arises in a conflict, the parties marshal all scientific data favorable to their respective sides as "good" science and discount all unfavorable data as "bad" science. Environmental conflict is thus the stage on which science is politicized, largely obfuscating its service to society.

Because the availability of choices dictates the amount of control we humans feel we have with respect to our sense of security, a potential loss of money is the breeding ground for environmental injustice. This is the kind of environmental injustice in which the present generation steals from all future generations by overexploiting a resource rather than facing the uncertainty of giving up potential income.

There are important lessons in all of this for anyone mediating environmental conflicts. First, history suggests that a biologically sustainable use of any resource has never been achieved without first overexploiting it, despite historical warnings and contemporary data. If history is correct, resource problems are not environmental problems but rather human ones that we have created many times, in many places, under a wide variety of social, political, and economic systems.

Second, the fundamental issues involving resources, the environment, and people are complex and process driven. The integrated knowledge of multiple disciplines is required to understand them. These underlying complexities of the physical and biological systems preclude a simplistic approach to both management and conflict resolution. In addition, the wide natural variability and the compounding, cumulative influence of continual human activity mask the results of overexploitation until they are severe, which progressively increases their irreversibility.

Third, as long as the uncertainty of continual change is considered a condition to be avoided, nothing will be resolved. However, once the uncertainty of change is accepted as an inevitable, open-ended, novel, creative life process, most decision making is simply common sense. For example, common sense dictates that one would favor actions having the greatest potential for some reversibility, as opposed to those with little or none. Such reversibility can be ascertained by monitoring results and modifying actions and policy accordingly. It must be understood, however, that nothing in the universe is reversible because the process of change is a biophysical constant and thus always novel in its outcomes, as discussed in the next chapter.

Fourth, the seed of all conflict is a perceived loss of choice over our individual ideas, desires, and personal destinies based on those ideas and desires, which we interpret as a threat to our personal survival. The sense of loss, which usually translates into a lifelong fear of loss in some degree, originates in childhood as lessons from the expressed concerns of our parents.

Conflict Is a Mistake

The result of many childhood lessons is the perceived need for control, and anything that threatens our control is an enemy onto whom we can project blame for our fears and thereby justify them. But, who or what is the enemy? An enemy is one seeking to injure, overthrow, or confound an opponent; something harmful or deadly. Of course, *I* (in the generic sense) am not "the enemy" because I am convinced that *my* position and *my* values are the *right* ones, and everyone knows that the enemy is wrong. That is what we are taught. That is the eternal verity around which conflict rallies.

The problem is that when all sides feel justified in their points of view, there is little understanding that an enemy is anyone or anything opposing that view. Opposition to that view is thus perceived as a threat to survival, however it is defined. Herein lies the great irony: Most environmental conflicts are the spawn of misunderstandings, miscommunication, and misperceptions in one way or another. Conflict is thus often a mistake, a misjudgment of appearances, or an assumption that is avoidable because it is only one choice of response to a given circumstance. Other responses are available, should a person examine them and choose to accept an alternative.

Consider war, the ultimate destructive conflict, both socially and environmentally. War, as is all human conflict, is based on the personalities of the people involved (in this case, the leaders) and their common feelings about fear and enemies.

Once one side or the other perceives a threat to its survival, the single most important precipitating factor in the outbreak of war is in fact misperception, which manifests itself in a leader's self-image and view of the adversary's character, of the adversary's intentions, capabilities, and military power. Once misperception is in play, miscommunication closes in and joins hands with misjudgment to foster a distorted view of the adversary's character, which helps to precipitate the conflict.

If a leader on the brink of war believes the adversary will attack, the chances of war are fairly high. If both leaders share this perception about each other's intent, war becomes a virtual certainty.

But, it is a leader's misperception of the adversary's power, and willingness to use it, that is perhaps the quintessential cause of war. It is vital to remember, however, that it is not the actual distribution of power that precipitates a war; what precipitates war is the way in which a leader *thinks* the power is distributed. Thus, on the eve of each war, at least one leader, through miscommunication, misperceives and thus misjudges the other's available power and willingness to use it. In this sense, the beginning of each war is a folly of misperception. The war itself then slowly and agonizingly teaches people the terribly high cost of destructive conflict.[8]

Conflict Is Usually Based on the Misjudgment of Appearances

The lesson war has to teach us is that conflict of any kind is a cycle of attack and defense based on the fear of uncertainties and unknowns, which usually results in the *misjudgment of appearances*. Appearance is an outward aspect of something that comes into view; judgment is the process of forming an opinion or evaluation by discerning and comparing something believed or asserted. Therefore, those whom we (in the generic sense) define as enemies are those onto whom we affix blame for our perceived sense of insecurity, a perceived threat to our own survival.

Our judgments are almost always incorrect, however, because things are seldom as they appear, since appearance is external. If, therefore, we could but understand the inner motive of our "enemy," we would likely find a mirror reflection of our fears for our own survival. In that reflection, we would also find that we were mistaken about our enemy's motives, that we had made an incorrect judgment of our enemy's character or ability based on inadequate knowledge.

Well, you might ask, if we are not one another's enemies, what is the enemy? Of what are we really afraid? We are largely afraid of change, loss of something we value through circumstances we perceive as a threat to our sense of survival because we cannot control them.

Yet almost every circumstance we encounter in some way evokes an unanticipated change in our participation with life. In turn, each change we are obliged to make is a compromise in our sense of control, a frightening condition of life to most people in an increasingly complex world.

Control, often used as a synonym for power, is an interesting phenomenon in life. We pay dearly for control, but regardless of the price, there are limitations. We cannot, for example, control the wind, but we can trim the sails on our boat. The wind is the circumstance beyond our control, but by trimming the sails we can choose how our boat—and thus we—respond to the wind. And in our response, we are in control of ourselves, which de facto controls the outcome of the circumstance.

Have you ever had a "bad" day, a day when nothing went right, you felt out of sorts, and every little thing that could go awry delighted in doing so, which unduly annoyed you, causing you to say, "I'm at my wit's end! If one more thing happens, I'm going to explode!" Because you felt out of sorts, or not at peace with yourself, you were therefore compelled to control the environment around you. Your inner sense of survival was shaky, and the only way you could ride out the inner storm was to have outer calm.

Now think of a "good" day, a day when everything went right. You felt in tune with the world, and you had a feeling of inner control and peace—a day when you said, "Everything I touch turns to gold!" On that day, the external things that still delighted in going awry did so, but they did not bother you.

Was it, in fact, that the day was *good* or *bad*? Or was it how you felt about yourself and your sense of survival on that given day? The difference between the two days was simply how you responded to the circumstances based on how you were feeling about yourself.

That no one can control circumstances is a given, although people continually try, which results in either inner or outer conflict of some magnitude. But, we can control how we react to circumstances, and therein lies both our problem and its potential resolution.

Our inability to control circumstances in any meaningful way translates into fear of change because every circumstance causes something to shift, and every alteration is novel. We, however, tend to focus on a potentially negative outcome—be it relatively minor (such as finding a tiny nick in the fender of our new car) or catastrophic (such as flood waters pouring through our home). We thus perceive change as a loss of control that threatens our survival in one way or another. We therefore want to control circumstances whenever we can, so that other people—our perceived enemies—will have to risk change, but not us.

There are no true enemies, only people frightened of the same kinds of things that frighten us. We thus mistakenly reject these people as enemies, a judgment we use to justify our side of a conflict in the war of survival, the war to control circumstances beyond our control.

When we focus our attention on human enemies, we are really focusing on the wrong thing. The other person is not the enemy. Rather, it is our fear of the unknown, of losing our sense of control based on the familiar, which dehumanizes our soul. Conflict is thus our attempt to place our problem onto someone or something else, to move away from our fear, away from something we do not want to happen.

References

1. See the books by Alice Miller: (a) *The Drama of the Gifted Child*. Basic Books, New York (1981); (b) *For Your Own Good*. Farrar, Straus, Giroux, New York (1981); (c) *Thou Shalt Not Be Aware*. Farrar, Straus, Giroux, New York (1984); (d) *Pictures of a Childhood*. Farrar, Straus, Giroux, New York (1986); (e) *The Untouched Key*. Anchor Books, New York (1990); (f) *Banished Knowledge*. Doubleday, New York (1990); and (g) *Breaking Down the Wall of Silence*. Dutton Books, New York (1991).

2. Dr. Hans Bleiker. Institute for Participatory Management and Planning. Personal communication with Carol. (See http://www.ipmp.com regarding the institute.)
3. Colin Greer. The well-being of the world is at stake. *Parade Magazine*, January 23 (1994):4–5.
4. Kris Kristofferson. Me and Bobby McGee. http://www.bluesforpeace.com/lyrics/bobby-mcgee.htm (accessed March 13, 2010).
5. Donald Ludwig, Ray Hilborn, and Carl Walters. Uncertainty, resource exploitation, and conservation: lessons from history. *Science*, 260 (1993):17–36.
6. Interview with British broadcaster Trevor McDonald during 2005 G8 Summit in Scotland.
7. (a) Ludwig et al., Uncertainty, Resource Exploitation; and (b) Chris Maser. *Global Imperative: Harmonizing Culture and Nature*. Stillpoint, Walpole, NH (1992).
8. The foregoing discussion of war is based on John G. Stoessinger. *Why Nations Go to War*. St. Martin's Press, New York (1974).

3

Biophysical Principles of Sustainability

Introduction

Change often occurs between need and fear. On the one hand, we know we need to do things differently; on the other hand, we are terrified of facing the unknown and unfamiliar. To change our direction for the future, however, we must suspend our conventional notion about change and our ability to learn because there are no problems to resolve other than those we perceive as manifestations of how we think and act. The problems we face are a matter of who we are consciously. And many people prefer to err repeatedly rather than let go of some cherished belief, pet notion, or deified assumption.

To resolve any dispute, the mediation process must go beyond human valuation of a resource to disclose and examine the fundamental issue of how use of the resource will affect the long-term biological sustainability of the ecosystem of which it is a component. One must also recognize the long-term issues that need to be dealt with to resolve the long-term potential for destructive conflict. This is necessary because the environment and the sustainability of its resources are silent parties present in any dispute, which de facto will determine the options passed forward to future generations.

To accommodate the sustainability of the favorable ecological integrity of the environment—the "silent third party"—each person must understand the environmental postulates given in this chapter as a condition for resolving a specific conflict. We (Carol and Chris) say this because these posits, to the best of our knowledge, are among the biophysical underpinnings through which Nature operates and the philosophical valuations through which we accept our participation with Nature. Understanding these posits does not connote acceptance of or agreement with them. It does, however, connote acknowledging their validity as a current data set. This means, whatever decisions are made in resolving a conflict are made consciously by those who can be held accountable for their outcome.

Social-environmental justice dictates that the participants of an environmental conflict be held accountable for the outcome of its resolution because the effects of their decisions become the consequences for all generations to come. This is particularly poignant in the face of an exploding human population and rapidly dwindling resources.

The Waterbed Principle

As long as the human population was but a small fraction of its current size, the resources of Earth were considered unlimited. But even then, "The history of almost every civilization," observed British historian Arnold Toynbee, "furnishes examples of geographical expansion coinciding with deterioration in [environmental and, therefore, resource] quality."[1] Think of this interconnectedness as the *waterbed principle*, which simply demonstrates that you cannot touch any part of a filled waterbed without affecting the whole of it.

Today, there is much talk about "renewable" resources, but no longer so much about unlimited resources. Ultimately all resources are finite. Not only can we literally run out of a resource by exhausting its earthly supply, such as the extinction of a species and its attendant ecological function, but also can we alter an existing resource to render it useless to us, such as poisoning our drinking water through radioactive pollution. And we are doing both.

As a burgeoning human population demands more and more material commodities from a rapidly dwindling supply of raw materials, the ratio of resources apportioned to each human must decline. Further, those resources currently deemed renewable are only renewable as long as the system that produces them remains healthy and is exploited only in a biologically sustainable manner.

Consider, for example, the following scenario: As you hike in a wilderness area or wander through a national park, no matter how far removed you seem to be from the center of civilization, you are still breathing pollution. It is everywhere and will continue to worsen as long as decisions to placate big industry continually trump a global pursuit of dramatically cleaning the world's air.

We dare not kid ourselves about the importance of air quality. Our earthly survival, and progressively that of our children and their children unto all generations, ultimately depends on clean air. Air is the interactive thread connecting soil, water, biodiversity, human population density, sunlight, and climate. (Biodiversity refers to the variety of living species and their biological functions and processes.) This interactive thread exemplifies the waterbed principle.

Yet, we as a society, with our myriad data bits and seemingly vast knowledge, listen to the economists of the world and *assume* they are correct when they take such ecological variables as air, soil, water, sunlight, biodiversity, genetic diversity, climate, and more and convert them, in theory at least, into economic constants whose values are unchanging—or discount them altogether as externalities. Ecological variables are therefore omitted from consideration in our economic and planning models, and even from our thinking. Biodiversity and genetic diversity, on the other hand, are simply discounted when their consideration interferes with monetary profits; they are euphemistically termed "externalities." On top of it all is the nagging problem of human population growth. We talk about it and worry about it, but in the end we give only lip service to the one solution that can control it—total, real gender equality.

That notwithstanding, relationships among things are in constant flux as complex systems arise from subatomic and atomic particles in the giant process of evolution on Earth. In each higher level of complexity and organization, there is an increase in the size of the system and a corresponding decrease in the energies holding it together. Put differently, the forces that keep evolving systems intact, from a molecule to a human society, weaken as the size of the systems increases, yet the larger the system is, the more energy it requires to function. Such functional dynamics are characterized by their diversity as well as by the constraints of the overarching laws and subordinate principles that govern them.

These principles can be said to *govern* the world and our place in it because they form the behavioral constraints without which nothing could function in an orderly manner. In this sense, the law of cosmic unification—the supreme law—is analogous to the Constitution of the United States, a central covenant that informs the subservient courts of each state about the acceptability of its governing laws. In turn, the Commons Usufruct Law (discussed in Chapter 4) represents the constitution of the state, which instructs the citizens of what acceptable behavior is within the state. In this way, Nature's rules of engagement inform society of the latitude by which it can interpret the biophysical principles and survive in a sustainable manner.

Understanding the Law of Cosmic Unification

The *law of cosmic unification* is functionally derived from the synergistic effect of three universal laws: the first law of thermodynamics, the second law of thermodynamics, and the law of maximum entropy production.

The *first law of thermodynamics* states that the total amount of energy in the universe is constant, although it can be transformed from one form to another. Therefore, the amount of energy remains entirely the same, even if you could go forward or backward in time. For this reason, the contemporary notion of either "energy production" or "energy consumption" is a non sequitur. The *second law of thermodynamics* states that the amount of energy in forms available to do useful work can only diminish over time. The loss of available energy to perform certain tasks thus represents a diminishing capacity to maintain order at a certain level of manifestation (say a tree) and so increases disorder or entropy. This "disorder" ultimately represents the continuum of change and novelty—the manifestation of a different, simpler configuration of order, such as the remaining ashes from the tree when is burned. In turn, the *law of maximum entropy production* says that a system will select the path out of available paths that maximizes entropy at the fastest rate, given the existing constraints.[2]

The essence of maximum entropy simply means that, when any kind of constraint is removed, the flow of energy from a complex form to a simpler form speeds up to the maximum allowed by the relaxed constraint.[3] As it turns out, the law of maximum entropy production freed early hominids from one of the basic constraints of Nature when they adapted the intense entropy of burning wood to their everyday use. (A hominid, *hom·i·nid*, is any of the modern or extinct primates that belong to the taxonomic family Hominidae, *Hom·in·idae*, of which we are members.) Control of fire gave hominids the ability to live in habitats that heretofore had been too cold or where the seasonal temperature variations had been too great. It also allowed them to cook food, making parts of many plants and animals palatable and digestible when they were baked, roasted, or boiled. The charred remains of flint from prehistoric firesides on the shore of an ancient lake near the river Jordan in Israel indicates that our ancient ancestors had learned how to create fire 790,000 years ago.[4] Moreover, the increased supply of protein embodied in cooked meat is thought to have facilitated evolution of increasing hominid brain capacity, ultimately leading to our mental abilities.[5]

We, in contemporary society, are all familiar with the basis of this law even if we do not understand it. For example, we all know that our body loses heat in cold weather, but our sense of heat loss increases exponentially when wind chill is factored into the equation because our clothing has ceased to be as effective a barrier to the cold—a constraint to the loss of heat—it was before the wind became an issue. Moreover, the stronger and colder the wind, the faster our body loses its heat—the maximum entropy of the energy of our body whereby we stay warm. If the loss of body heat to wind chill is not constrained, hypothermia and death ensue, along with the beginnings of bodily decomposition—reorganization from the complex structure and function toward a simpler structure and function.

In other words, systems are by nature dissipative structures that release energy by various means, but inevitably by the quickest means possible. To illustrate, as a young forest grows old, it converts energy from the sun into living tissue that ultimately dies and accumulates as organic debris on the forest floor. There, through decomposition, the organic debris releases the energy stored in its dead tissue. Of course, rates of decomposition vary. A leaf rots quickly and releases its stored energy rapidly. Wood, on the other hand, generally rots more slowly, often over centuries in moist environments. As wood accumulates, so does energy stored in its fibers. Before the suppression of fires, they burned frequently enough to generally control the amount of energy stored in accumulating dead wood by burning it. These low-intensity fires protected a forest for decades, even centuries, from a catastrophic, killing fire. In this sense, a forest equates to a dissipative system in that energy acquired from the sun is released through the fastest means possible, be it gradually through decomposition or rapidly through a high-intensity fire. The ultimate constraint to the rate of entropic maximization, however, is the immediate weather in the short term and the overall climate in the long term.

Now, let us examine the notion of maximum entropy in a more familiar way. I (Chris) have a wood-burning stove in my home with which I heat the 1,300 square feet of my living space. To keep my house at a certain temperature, I must control the amount of energy I extract from the wood I burn. I do this in nine ways.

My first consideration is the kind of wood I choose, be it Douglas fir, western red cedar, western hemlock, bigleaf maple, Pacific madrone, Oregon ash, Oregon white oak, red alder, or a combination. My choice is important because each kind of wood has a different density and thus burns with a corresponding intensity. On one hand, the three coniferous woods (Douglas fir, western red cedar, and western hemlock) are relatively soft, require less oxygen to burn than hardwoods, burn quickly, but produce only moderate heat. On the other hand, such hardwoods as bigleaf maple, Pacific madrone, Oregon ash, Oregon white oak, and red alder produce substantial heat—of which oak, madrone, and maple probably produce the most, followed by ash and alder. But these hardwoods also require more oxygen to burn than the softwoods, and they burn more slowly.

The second concern is the quality of wood that I burn. Sound, well-seasoned wood burns far more efficiently than either wet, unseasoned wood or wood that is partially rotten. In this case, the quality of the wood also determines the effectiveness by which it heats my house. Good quality wood is far more effective in the production of heat than is wood of poor quality.

The third determination is the size and shape of the wood. Small pieces produce a lot of heat but are quick to disappear. Large pieces take more time to begin burning, but last longer and may or may not burn as hot when they really get going, depending on the kind of wood. Split wood has more surface area per volume and burns more rapidly than do round pieces of wood of the same size, such as large branches, because the latter have more volume than surface area.

The fourth decision is how wide to open the damper and thereby control the amount of air fanning the flames, which either increases the intensity of burning (opening the damper) or decreases the rate of burn (closing the damper). In each case, the length of time the damper is in a given position is part of the equation. The wider the damper is opened, the less the constraint, the hotter and faster the wood will burn, and the more rapidly heat will escape—the law of maximum entropy production. This law also addresses the speed with which wood is disorganized as wood and reorganized as ashes.

The fifth choice is how warm I want my house to be in terms of how cold it is outside. The colder it is outside, the more wood I must burn to maintain a certain level of heat—how much depends on the kind of wood I am burning. Conversely, the warmer it is outside, the less wood I must burn to maintain the same level of warmth.

The sixth consideration is how well my house is insulated against the intrusion of cold air and thus the escape of my indoor heat—both of which determine the amount of wood I must burn to maintain the temperature I want. Another facet of how much wood I must burn depends in part on whether clouds are holding the heat close to Earth, thus acting as a constraint to the heat leaking out of my house, or whether clear skies allow heat to bleed from my home and escape into outer space.

The seventh option is how often I open the outside door to go in and out of my house and so let cold air flow in to replace the warm air rushing out. I could ameliorate this exchange by having an enclosed porch between the door opening into my house and the door opening directly to the outside. A well-insulated porch would act as a dead-air space and would be a functional constraint to the loss of heat from my house as I access the outside.

The eighth alternative is when to heat my house and for how long. I can, for instance, reduce the amount of heat I require at night when I am snuggled in bed. If I go to bed early and get up early, it is about the same as going to bed late and getting up late. But if I go to bed early and get up late, I do not need to heat the house for as long as I would if I spent more time out of bed as opposed to in bed. Moreover, if it is well below freezing outside, I might have to keep the house warmer than otherwise to protect the water pipes from freezing.

And the ninth course of action, one that is both influenced by the other eight and influences them in turn, is how warmly I choose to dress while indoors. Whatever I wear constitutes a constraint to heat loss of a greater or lesser degree. Clearly, the warmer I dress, the less wood I must burn to stay warm, and vice versa. It is the same with how many blankets I have on my bed during the winter.

These nine seemingly independent courses of action coalesce into a synergistic suite of relationships, wherein a change in one automatically influences the other eight facets of the speed that energy from the burning wood escapes from my house. This said, the first and second laws of thermodynamics and the law of maximum entropy production meld to form the overall unifying law of the universe—the Law of Cosmic Unification—wherein all subordinate principles, both biophysical and social, are encompassed. With respect to the functional melding of these three laws, Rod Swenson of the Center for the Ecological Study of Perception and Action, Department of Psychology, University of Connecticut, says these three laws of thermodynamics "are special laws that sit above the other laws of physics as laws about laws or laws on which the other laws depend."[6] Stated a little differently, these three laws of physics coalesce to form the *supreme* "Law of Cosmic Unification," to which all biophysical and social principles governing Nature and human behavior are subordinate—yet simultaneously *inviolate*. Inviolate means that we manipulate the effects of a principle through our actions on Earth, but we do not—and cannot—alter the principle itself.

The Inviolate Biophysical Principles

Although we have done our best to present the principles in a logical order, it is difficult to be definitive because each principle forms an ever-interactive strand in the multidimensional web of energy interchange that constitutes the universe and our world within it. Moreover, a different possible order can be found each time they are read, and each arrangement seems logical. Because each principle affects all principles (like a water bed), every arrangement is equally correct.

Principle 1: Everything Is a Relationship

The universe is constituted of an ever-expanding web of biophysical feedback loops, each of which is novel and self-reinforcing. Each feedback loop is a conduit by which energy is moved from one place, one dimension, and one scale to another. And all we humans do—ever—is practice relationships within this web because the existence of everything in the universe is an expression of its relationship to everything else within the web. Moreover, all relationships are forever dynamic and thus constantly changing, from the wear on your toothbrush from daily use to the rotting lettuce you forgot in your refrigerator. Herein lies one of the foremost paradoxes of life: The ongoing process of change is a universal constant over which we have no control, much to our dismay.

Think, for example, what the difference is between a motion picture and a snapshot. Although a motion picture is composed of individual frames (instantaneous snapshots of the present moment), each frame is entrained in the continuum of time and thus cannot be held constant, as Roman Emperor Marcus Aurelius observed: "Time is a river of passing events, and strong is its current. No sooner is a thing brought to sight than it is swept by and another takes its place, and this too will be swept away."[7]

Yet we, in our fear of uncertainty, are continually trying to hold the circumstances of our life in the arena of constancy as depicted in a snapshot—hence, the frequently used term *preservation* in regard to this or that ecosystem, this or that building. But, jams and jellies are correctly referred to as "preserves" because they are heated during their preparation to kill all living organisms and thereby prevent noticeable change in their consistency.

Insects in amber are an example of true preservation in Nature. Amberization, the process by which fresh resin is transformed into amber, is so gentle that it forms the most complete type of fossilization known for small, delicate, soft-bodied organisms, such as insects. In fact, a small piece of amber found along the southern coast of England in 2006 contained a 140-million-year-old spider web constructed in the same orb configuration as that of today's garden spiders. This is 30 million years older than a previous spider web found encased in Spanish amber. The web demonstrates that spiders have been ensnaring their prey since the time of the dinosaurs. And because amber is three dimensional in form, it preserves color patterns and minute details of the exoskeleton of the organism, so allowing the study of microevolution, biogeography, mimicry, behavior, reconstruction of the environmental characteristics, the chronology of extinctions, paleosymbiosis,[8] and molecular phylogeny.[9] But the same dynamic cannot be employed outside an airtight container, such as a drop of amber or canning jar. In other words, whether natural or artificial, all functional systems are open because they all require the input of a sustainable supply of energy to function; conversely, a totally closed, functional system is a physical impossibility.

Principle 2: All Relationships Are Productive

I (Chris) have often heard people say that a particular piece of land is "unproductive" and needs to be "brought under management." Here, it must be rendered clear that every relationship is productive of a cause that has an *effect*, and the effect, which is the cause of another effect, *is* the product. Therefore, the notion of an unproductive parcel of ground or an unproductive political meeting is an illustration of the narrowness of human valuation because such judgment is viewed strictly within the extrinsic realm of personal values, usually economics—not the intrinsic realm of the dynamics of Nature that not only transcend our human understanding but also defy the validity of our economic assessments.

We are not, after all, so powerful a natural force that we can destroy an ecosystem because it still obeys the biophysical principles that determine how it functions at any point in time. Nevertheless, we can so severely alter an ecosystem that it is incapable of providing—for all time—those goods and services we require for a sustainable life. Bear in mind that the total surface area of the United States covered in paved roads precludes the ability of the soil to capture and store water or that we are currently impairing the ability of the ocean to sequester carbon dioxide (one of the main greenhouse gases) because we have so dramatically disrupted the population dynamics of the marine fishes by systematically overexploiting too many of the top predators.[10] All of the relationships that we affect are productive of some kind of outcome—a product. Now, whether the product is beneficial for our use or even amenable to our existence is another issue.

Principle 3: The Only True Investment Is Energy from Sunlight

The only true investment in the global ecosystem is energy from solar radiation (materialized sunlight); everything else is merely the recycling of already existing energy. In a business sense, for example, one makes money (economic capital) and then takes a percentage of those earnings and *recycles* them, puts them back as a cost into the maintenance of buildings and equipment to continue making a profit by protecting the integrity of the initial outlay of capital over time. In a business, one recycles economic capital *after* the profits have been earned.

Biological capital, on the other hand, must be "recycled" *before* the profits are earned. This means forgoing some potential monetary gain by leaving enough of the ecosystem intact for it to function in a sustainable manner. In a forest, for instance, one leaves some proportion of the merchantable trees (both alive and dead) to rot and recycle into the soil and thereby replenish the fabric of the living system. In rangelands, one leaves the forage plants in a viable condition so they can seed and protect the soil from erosion as well as add organic material to the long-term, ecological integrity of the soil.

People speak incorrectly about fertilization as an *investment* in a forest or grassland, when in fact it is merely recycling chemical compounds that already exist on Earth. In reality, people are simply taking energy (in the form of chemical compounds) from one place and putting them in another for a specific purpose. The so-called investments in the stock market are a similar shuffling of energy.

When people *invest* money in the stock market, they are really recycling energy from products and services of Nature that were acquired through human labor. The value of the labor is transferred symbolically to a dollar amount, thereby representing a predetermined amount of labor. Let us say you work for ten dollars an hour; then a $100 bill would equal ten hours of labor. Where is the *investment*? There is not any, but there is a symbolic recycling of the energy put forth by the denomination of money we spend.

Here you might argue that people invested their labor in earning the money. And I (Chris) would counter that whatever energy they put forth was merely a recycling of the energy they took in through the food they ate. Nevertheless, the energy embodied in the food may actually have simultaneously been a true investment and a recycling of already existing energy.

It has long been understood that green plants use the chlorophyll molecule to absorb sunlight and use its energy to synthesize carbohydrates (in this case, sugars) from carbon dioxide and water. This process is known as photosynthesis, for which *photo* means "light," and *synthesis* means the "fusion of energy," and is the basis for sustaining the life processes of all plants. The energy is derived from the sun (an original input) and combined with carbon dioxide and water (existing chemical compounds) to create a renewable source of usable energy. This process is analogous to an array of organic solar panels—the green plant.

Think of it this way: the plant (an array of solar panels) uses the green chlorophyll molecule (a *photoreceptor*, meaning receiver of light) to collect light from the sun within chloroplasts (small, enclosed structures in the plant that are analogous to individual solar panels). Then, through the process of photosynthesis, the sunlight is used to convert carbon dioxide and water to carbohydrates for use by the plant, a process that is comparable to converting the sunlight in solar panels on the roof of a building into electricity for our use. These carbohydrates, in turn, are partly stored energy from the sun—a new input of energy into the global ecosystem—and partly the storage of existing energy from the amalgam of carbon dioxide and water.[11]

When, therefore, we eat green plants, the carbohydrates are converted through our bodily functions into different sorts of energy. By that is meant the energy embodied in green plants is altered through digestion into the various types of energy our bodies require for their physiological functions. The *excess* energy (that not required for physiological functions) is expended in the form of physical motion, such as energy to do work. On the other hand, it is different when eating meat because the animal has already used the contribution of the sun to the energy matrix in its own bodily functions and its own physical acts of living, so all we get from eating flesh is recycled energy.

Principle 4: All Systems Are Defined by Their Function

The behavior of a system—any system—depends on how its individual parts interact as functional components of the whole, not on what an isolated part is doing. The whole, in turn, can only be understood through the relationships, the interaction of its parts. The only way anything can exist is encompassed in its interdependent relationship to everything else, which means an isolated fragment or an independent variable can exist *only on paper* as a figment of the human imagination.

Put differently, the false assumption is that an independent variable of one's choosing can exist in a system of one's choice and that it will indeed act as an independent variable. In reality, all systems are interdependent and thus rely on their pieces to act in concert as a functioning whole. This being the case, no individual piece can stand on its own *and* simultaneously be part of an interactive system. Thus, *there neither is nor can there be an independent variable* in any system, be it biological, biophysical, or mechanical, because every system is interactive by its very definition as a system.

What is more, every relationship is constantly adjusting itself to fit precisely into other relationships, which in turn are consequently adjusting themselves to fit precisely into all relationships, a dynamic that *precludes* the existence of an independent variable, so *no given thing can be held at a constant value beyond the number one* (the universal common denominator) because to do so would necessitate the detachment of the thing in question from the system as an independent variable. Therefore, all relationships are constituted by multiples of *one* in all its myriad forms, from quarks, atoms, molecules, and proteins, which comprise the building blocks of life, to the living organisms themselves, which collectively form the species and communities. The only way the number one can exist, as the sole representative of any form on Earth, is to be the last living individual of a species—something intimated on the tribal level by James Fenimore Cooper's 1826 book, *The Last of the Mohicans*—because extinction is forever.

Therefore, to understand a system as a functional whole, we need to understand how it fits into the larger system of which it is a part and so gives us a view of systems supporting systems supporting systems supporting systems, ad infinitum.

Principle 5: All Relationships Result in a Transfer of Energy

Although technically a *conduit* is a hollow tube of some sort, we use the term here to connote any system employed specifically for the transfer of energy from one place to another. Every living thing, from a virus to a bacterium, fungus, plant, insect, fish, amphibian, reptile, bird, mammal, and every cell in our body is a conduit for the collection, transformation, absorption, storage, transfer, and expulsion of energy. In fact, the function of the entire biophysical system is tied up in the collection, transformation, absorption, storage, transfer, and expulsion of energy—one gigantic, energy-balancing act.

Principle 6: All Relationships Are Self-Reinforcing Feedback Loops

Everything in the universe is connected to everything else in a cosmic web of interactive feedback loops, all entrained in self-reinforcing relationships that continually create novel, never-ending stories of cause and effect, stories that began with the eternal mystery of the original story, the original cause. Everything, from a microbe to a galaxy, is defined by its ever-shifting relationship to every other component of the cosmos. Thus, "freedom" (perceived as the lack of constraints) is merely a continuum of fluid relativity. In contraposition, every relationship is the embodiment of interactive constraints to the flow of energy—the very dynamic that perpetuates the relativity of freedom and thus all relationships.

Hence, every change (no matter how minute or how grand) constitutes a systemic modification that produces novel outcomes. A feedback loop, in this sense, comprises a reciprocal relationship among countless bursts of energy moving through specific strands in the cosmic web that cause forever-new, compounding changes at either end of the strand, as well as every connecting strand.[12] And here we often face a dichotomy with respect to our human interests.

On the one hand, while all feedback loops are self-reinforcing, their effects in Nature are neutral because Nature is impartial with respect to consequences. We, on the other hand, have definite desires as far as outcomes are involved and thus assign a preconceived value to what we think of as the end result of the biophysical feedback loops of Nature. A simple example might be the response of North American elk in the Pacific Northwestern United States to the alteration of their habitat. In this case, the competing values were (and still are) elk as an economically important game animal versus timber as an economically important commodity.

In the 1940s and 1950s in western Oregon, the timber industry often used the adage: Good timber management is good wildlife management. At the time, that claim seemed plausible because elk populations were growing in response to forests being clear-cut. By the mid-to-late 1960s and throughout the 1970s, however, elk populations began to exhibit significant declines. Although predation was run out as the obvious reason, it did not hold up under scrutiny since the large predators, such as wolves and grizzly bears, had long been extirpated, and the mountain lion population had been decimated because of the bounties placed on the big cats.

As it turned out, the cause of the decline in elk numbers was subtler and far more complicated than originally thought. The drop in elk numbers was in direct response to habitat alteration by the timber industry. This is not surprising since elk, like all wildlife, have specific habitat requirements that consist of food, water, shelter, space, privacy, and the overall connectivity of the habitat that constitutes these features. When any one of these elements is in short supply, it acts as a limiting factor or constraint with respect to the viability of the population of a species as a whole.

By way of illustration, here is a simplified example: In the early days before extensive logging began, the land was well clothed in trees, making food the factor that limited the number of elk in an area. As logging cleared large areas of forest, grasses and forbs grew abundantly, elk, being primarily grazers, became increasingly numerous. This relationship continued for some years, until—for an instant in time—the perfect balance between the requirements of food and shelter was reached. The proximity to water did not play as important a role in this balance because of the relative abundance of forest streams and because elk can travel vast distances to find water. Thus, hunters and loggers initially perceived clear-cut logging as the proverbial win-win situation (a positive, self-reinforcing feedback loop).

But, as it turned out, the main interplay among the potential limiting factors for elk was between food and shelter. At first, food was the limiting factor because elk were constrained in finding their preferred forage by the vast acres of contiguous forest. In contraposition, continued logging started to shift the habitat configuration in a way that proved detrimental to the elk because, while the habitat for feeding continued to increase with clear-cutting, that for shelter declined disproportionately. Accordingly, the shelter once provided by the forest became the factor that increasingly reversed the growth in numbers of the elk. Here it must be understood that shelter for elk consists of two categories—one for hiding in the face of potential danger (simply called *hiding cover*) and one for regulating the body temperature of the animal (called *thermal cover*).

Thermal cover often consists of a combination of forest thickets or stands of old trees coupled with topographical features that block the flow of air. As such, thermal cover allows the elk to cool their bodies in dense shade in summer and get into areas of calm, out of the bitter winds in winter, which markedly reduces the wind-chill factor and thus conserves their body heat.[13] At length, the hunters began to see the systematic, widespread clear-cutting of the forest as a losing situation for huntable populations of elk (a negative, self-reinforcing feedback loop), although they did not equate the loss of thermal cover as the cause.

Biological feedback loops are ultimately controlled by the climate of Earth and so are greatly influenced by the levels of atmospheric carbon dioxide (CO_2) over time. Evidence from ice cores and marine sediments indicate that changes in CO_2 over timescales beyond the glacial cycles are finely balanced and act to stabilize global temperatures.[14] What is more, the long-term balance between the emissions of CO_2 into the atmosphere through such events as volcanic eruptions and the removal of CO_2 from the atmosphere through such processes as its burial in deep-sea sediments holds true despite glacial–interglacial variations on relatively short timescales. Today, on the other hand, that part of the feedback loop by which CO_2 is removed from the atmosphere by the chemical breakdown of silicate rock in mountains (termed *weathering*), as well as carbonate minerals (those containing CO_3) that are buried in deep-sea sediments, is being severely disrupted—even overwhelmed—by human activities that are raising the level of CO_2 emissions.[15]

Principle 7: All Relationships Have One or More Trade-Offs

All relationships have a trade-off that may be neither readily apparent nor immediately understood. To illustrate, for most of the past 900 years, the buildings in London were clean; many of these buildings had cream-colored limestone façades. But then things began to change as a result of the introduction of coal-burning stoves. That notwithstanding, the rate of change was so slow the cumulative effects were not readily apparent until a threshold of visibility had been crossed, and the protracted exposure to the sooty pollution of city air began to turn the buildings dark gray and black. So it is that smutty buildings dominated the cities of Europe and the United States for most of the nineteenth and twentieth centuries.[16] In fact, archival photographs show that the limestone Cathedral of Learning on the University of Pittsburgh campus in Pennsylvania, built during a period of heavy pollution in the 1930s, became soiled while still under construction.[17]

Reductions in the air pollution in Pittsburgh began in the late 1940s and 1950s.[18] Rain has slowly washed the soiled areas of the forty-two-story Cathedral of Learning since then, leaving a white, eroded surface. The patterns of whitened areas in archival photographs show the greatest rates of cleansing occurred on the corners of the high elevations on the building, predominantly where the impact of both rain and wind is most intense. It is also clear that the discoloration of buildings is a dynamic process: The deposition of pollution is a relatively consistent process but is simultaneously washed away to varying degrees and patterns over the surface of the building. Moreover, sooty pollutants soiled buildings, such as the Cathedral of Learning, much more rapidly in the past than they are being cleaned by wind and rain in the present.[19]

In this century, though, the buildings will gradually become more colorful as the city air is cleaned through the promulgation of pollution-control laws and wind-swept rain that will wash away the encrusted soot. The outcome of such cleaning may well be multicolored buildings as the natural reddish of some limestone is accentuated or a yellowing process occurs as a result of pollutants that are more organic in constitution. What is more, the switch from coal to other fuels has cast the Tower of London in hues that are slightly yellow and reddish-brown. As the atmosphere is cleaned and thus dominated more by organic pollutants, a process of yellowing on stone buildings due to the oxidation of organic compounds in the fumes of diesel and gasoline may become of concern.[20] The oxidation of this increased organic content from the exhaust of motor vehicles may have overall aesthetic consequences for the management of historic buildings—namely, recognizing a shift away from the simple gypsum crusts of the past to those richer in organic materials and thus warmer tones, particularly browns and yellows.[21]

And this says nothing about plant life growing on cleansed buildings, a phenomenon made possible because vehicular exhaust emits less of the sulfate that is present in the pollution from coal—pollution that suppresses the growth of algae, lichens, and mosses. Consequently, buildings may come to exhibit greens, yellows, and reddish-brown in different places and various patterns because, while lichens and algae prefer humid environs, such as cracks, they can grow on flat surfaces as well.[22]

The foregoing deals only with the dynamics of Nature in response to soiling of such limestone buildings as the Cathedral of Learning by different types of pollution and the long-term cleansing effects of wind and rain. Added to the trade-offs among these variables is the diversity of preferences espoused in 2003 by employees of the university.

Whereas some university officials were in favor of scrubbing the building with baking soda to remove the black, 70-year-old industrial grim, Cliff Davidson, the environmental engineer from Carnegie Mellon University who studied the building, prefers to let Nature do the work. Although the whiter spots have been scrubbed by wind-driven rain over decades, according to Davidson, the darker spots in nooks and crannies might well remain for centuries, if they could be cleaned at all. In contrast, Doris Dyen, director of cultural conservation for the Rivers of Steel National Heritage Area, expressed appreciation of how buildings in Pittsburgh were being spruced up. "At the same time," she said, "you can lose a little bit of a sense of what Pittsburgh was like for 100 years when all the buildings were showing the effects of the 24-hour-a-day operation of the steel mills in the area." G. Alec Stewart, dean of the University Honors College, took yet a different tack: "It would make a stunning addition to the night skyline of Pittsburgh if we were able to illuminate it [the Cathedral of

Learning] as significant monuments are in other major cities," comparing it to the Washington Monument.[23]

So, what are some of the significant trade-offs with respect to the Cathedral of Learning?

1. Clean the building artificially in the short term *or* let Nature do it over time.

2. Clean the building to blend into the cityscape and thus forgo the sense of familiarity *or* maintain the soot-derived appearance and thus avoid rapid change.

3. Trade the sooty, vegetation-free exterior for an exhaust-enriched, vegetation-covered exterior of the building and thereby give up a sense of the 100-year history of Pittsburgh.

4. Illuminate the Cathedral of Learning from the outside to create a monument-like effect, such as that of the Washington Monument in the District of Columbia *or* keep the status quo.

In the end, each of these trade-offs is couched in terms of whether to change or not based largely on some cultural value that blends naturally into an emotional criterion.

Other relationships have much more discernible trade-offs. Take the springtime ozone hole over Antarctic as illustrative; it is finally shrinking after years of growing. As the hole grew in size due to the human-induced, ozone-destroying chemicals in the stratosphere, the risk of skin cancer increased because more ultraviolet radiation reached Earth. Although today the good news is that the ozone hole is now shrinking and, through a complicated cascade of effects, could fully close within this century, what about tomorrow? Because the hole in the stratospheric ozone layer does not absorb much ultraviolet radiation, it keeps the temperature of Antarctica much cooler than normal. A completely recovered ozone layer, on the other hand, could significantly boost atmospheric warming over and around the icy continent and ostensibly augment its melting.[24] In this case, what is good for humans may not be good for Antarctica and vice versa.

Principle 8: Change Is a Process of Eternal Becoming

Change, as a universal constant, is a continual process of inexorable novelty. It is a condition along a continuum that may reach a momentary pinnacle of harmony within our senses. Then the very process that created the harmony takes it away and replaces it with something else—always with something else. Change requires constancy as its foil in order to exist as a dynamic process of eternal becoming. Without constancy, change could neither exist nor be recognized.

We all cause change of some kind every day. I (Chris) remember a rather dramatic one I inadvertently made along a small stream flowing across the beach on its way to the sea. The stream, having eroded its way into the sand, created a small undercut that could not be seen from the top. Something captured my attention in the middle of the stream, and I stepped on the overhang to get a better look, causing the bank to cave in and me to get a really close-up view of the water. As a consequence of my misstep, I had both altered the configuration of the bank and caused innumerable grains of sand to be washed back into the sea from whence they had come several years earlier riding the crest of a storm wave.

Whereas mine was a small, personally created change in an infinitesimal part of the world, others are of gigantic proportions in their effects. People of civilizations that collapsed centuries ago are a good example of such gargantuan effects because they were probably oblivious to the impact that could be wrought by long-term shifts in climate. Although not likely to end the debate regarding what caused the demise of the Roman and Byzantine empires, new data suggest that a shift in climate may have been partly responsible. The plausibility of this notion has been given a scientific boost of credibility through studying the stalactites of Soreq Cave in Israel.[25]

Stalactites are the most familiar, bumpy, relatively icicle-shaped structures found hanging from the ceilings of limestone caves. They are formed when water accumulates minerals as it percolates through soil before seeping into a cave. If the journey of the water takes it through limestone, it typically leaches calcium carbonate and carbon dioxide in its descent. The instant the water seeps from the ceiling of a cave, some of the dissolved carbon dioxide in the fluid escapes into the air in the cave. This gentle, soda-pop-like fizzing process causes the droplet to become more acidic and so results in some of the calcium carbonate crystallizing on the ceiling of the cave, thereby initiating a stalactite. As this process is performed repeatedly, the separation of calcium carbonate from within the thin film of fluid flowing down its surface allows the stalactite to grow. The procedure is so slow it typically takes a century to add four-tenths of an inch (one centimeter) to the growth of a stalactite.[26] Moreover, stalactites, like tree rings, can tell stories of paleoclimatic events, such as the severe drought that took place on the Colorado Plateau in the mid-1100s.[27]

By using an ion microprobe, it has become possible to read the chemical deposition rings of the Soreq Cave stalactites with such precision that even seasonal increments of growth can be teased out of a given annual ring. The results indicate that a prolonged drought, beginning in the Levant region as far back as 200 years BCE and continuing to AD 1100, coincides with the fall of both empires. (Levant is the former name of that region of the eastern Mediterranean that encompasses modern-day Lebanon, Israel, and parts of Syria and Turkey.) Although determining why civilizations collapse is always more complicated than one might imagine, an inhospitable shift in climate might well be part of the equation that either forces people to adapt by changing their behavior or eliminates them.[28] The latter seems to be the case in China.

The historical record of the activity of the Asian monsoon is archived in an 1,800-year-old stalagmite found in Wanxiang Cave in the Gansu Province of north-central China. Mineral-rich waters dripping from the ceiling of the cave onto its floor year after year formed the stalagmite (a mirror image of a stalactite) that grew continuously for 1,800 years, from AD 190 to 2003. Like trees and the stalactites in the Soreq Cave of Israel, stalagmites have annual growth rings that can provide clues about local environmental conditions for a particular year. Chapters in the Wanxiang Cave stalagmite, written over the centuries, tell of variations in climate that are similar to those of the Little Ice Age, Medieval Warm Period, and the Dark-Age Cold Period recorded in Europe. Warmer years were associated with stronger East Asian monsoons.

By measuring the amount of oxygen-18 (a rare form of "heavy" oxygen) in the growth rings of the stalagmite, the years of weak summer monsoons with less rain can be pinpointed due to the large amounts of oxygen-18 in the rings. The information secreted within the life of the stalagmite tells the story of strong and weak monsoons, which in turn chronicle the rise and fall of several Chinese dynasties. This is an important deliberation because monsoon winds have for centuries carried rain-laden clouds northward from the Indian Ocean every summer, thereby providing nearly 80 percent of the annual precipitation between May and September in some parts of China—precipitation critical to the irrigation of crops.

In periods when the monsoons were strong, dynasties, such as the Tang (618–907) and the Northern Song (960–1127), enjoyed increased yields of rice. In fact, the yield of rice during the first several decades of the Northern Song dynasty allowed the population to increase from 60 million to as many as 120 million. But periods of weak monsoons ultimately spelled the demise of dynasties.

The Tang dynasty, for example, was established in AD 618 and is still determined to be a pinnacle of Chinese civilization, a kind of golden age from its inception until the ninth century, when the dynasty began to lose its grip. The Tang was dealt a deathblow in AD 873, when a growing drought turned horrific, and widespread famine took a heavy toll on both people and livestock. Henceforth, until its demise in AD 907, the Tang dynasty was plagued by civil unrest.

Weak monsoon seasons, when rains from the Indian Ocean no longer reached much of central and northern China, coincided with droughts and the declines of the Tang, Yuan (1271–1368), and Ming (1368–1644) dynasties, the last two characterized by continual popular unrest. Weak monsoons with dramatically diminished rainfall may also have helped trigger one of the most tumultuous eras in Chinese history, called the Five

Dynasties and Ten Kingdoms period, during which time five dynasties rose and fell within a few decades, and China fractured into several independent nation-states.

Data from the stalagmite indicate that the strength of past Asian monsoons was driven by the variability of natural influences—such as changes in solar cycles and global temperatures—until 1960, when anthropogenic activity appears to have superseded natural phenomena as the major driver of the monsoon seasons from the late twentieth century onward. In short, the Asian monsoon cycle has been disrupted by human-caused climate change.[29] Here, an observation by the British biologist Charles Darwin is apropos: "It is not the strongest of the species that survive, nor the most intelligent, but the one most responsive to change."[30]

Principle 9: All Relationships Are Irreverisible

Because change is a constant process orchestrated along the interactive web of universal relationships, it produces infinite novelty that precludes anything in the cosmos from ever being reversible. Take my (Chris's) misstep on the aforementioned edge of the stream. One moment I was standing on the level beach and the next I was conversing with the water. At the same time, the sand I had knocked into the stream was being summarily carried off to the sea. What of this dynamic was reversible? Nothing was reversible because I could not go back in time and make a different decision of where to place my foot. And, because we cannot go back in time, nothing can be restored to its former condition. All we can ever do is repair something that is broken so it can continue to function, albeit differently from in its original form. If you want a detailed discussion of this principle, read *Earth in Our Care*.[31]

Principle 10: All Systems Are Based on Composition, Structure, and Function

We perceive objects by means of their obvious structures or functions. *Structure* is the configuration of elements, parts, or constituents of something, be it simple or complex. The structure can be thought of as the organization, arrangement, or makeup of a thing. *Function*, on the other hand, is what a particular structure either can do or allows to be done to it or with it.

Let us examine a common object, a chair. When did the notion of a chair begin to take form? This is the first time in the far memory that one of our human ancestors sat on a piece of wood, which can be thought of as a "one-legged stool." From then, our ancestors have been modifying that piece of wood, both intellectually and practically, until stools with three or four legs were derived to fit various purposes, such as the old, close-to-the-ground, one-legged milking stool and today's tall, four-legged bar stools. But a stool is not necessarily restful. Then, somewhere in time, an ancestor had the idea of adding a back to a stool, and lo, the "chair" was born.

A chair is a chair because its structure gives it a particular shape. A chair can be characterized as a piece of furniture consisting of a seat, four legs, and a back; it is an object designed to accommodate a sitting person. If we add two arms, we have an *armchair* where we can sit and rest our arms. Should we now decide to add two rockers to the bottom of the legs on the chair, we have a *rocking chair* in which we can sit, rest our arms, and rock back and forth while doing so. Nevertheless, it is the seat that allows us to sit in the chair, and it is the act of sitting, the functional component allowed by the structure, that makes a chair a chair.

Suppose we remove the seat so the structure that supports our sitting no longer exists. Now to sit, we must sit on the ground between the legs of the once-chair. By definition, when we remove the seat of a chair, we no longer have a chair because we have altered the structure and therefore also altered its function. Now, if we leave the seat but remove the back, the chair reverts to a stool. Thus, the structure of an object defines its function, and the function of an object defines its necessary structure. How might the interrelationship of structure and function work in Nature?

To maintain ecological functions means that one must maintain the characteristics of the ecosystem in such a way that its processes are sustainable. The characteristics one must be concerned with are (1) composition, (2) structure, (3) function, and (4) the disturbance regimes of Nature that periodically alter the composition, structure, and function of an ecosystem.

We can, for example, change the composition of an ecosystem, such as the kinds and arrangement of plants in a forest or grassland; this alteration means that composition is malleable to human desire and thus negotiable within the context of cause and effect. In this case, composition is the determiner of the structure and function in that composition is the cause, rather than the effect, of the structure and function.

Composition determines the structure, and structure determines the function. Thus, by negotiating the composition, we simultaneously negotiate both the structure and function. On the other hand, once the composition is in place, the structure and function are set—unless, of course, the composition is altered, at which time both the structure and function are altered accordingly.

Returning momentarily to the chair analogy, suppose you have an armchair in which you can sit comfortably. What would happen if you either gained a lot of weight or lost a lot of weight but the size of the chair remained the same? If, on the one hand, you gained a lot of weight, you might no longer fit into your chair. On the other hand, if you lost much weight, the chair might be uncomfortably large. In the first case, you could alter the composition by removing the arms and thus be able to sit on the chair. In the second case, you might dismantle the chair, replace the large seat with a smaller one, and reassemble the chair.

In a similar but more complex fashion, the composition or kinds of plants and their age classes within a plant community create a certain structure that is characteristic of the plant community at any given age. It is the structure of the plant community that in turn creates and maintains certain functions. In addition, it is the composition, structure, and function of a plant community that determine what kinds of animals can live there, how many, and for how long.

Hence, if one changes the composition of a forest, one changes the structure, hence the function, and thus affects the animals. The animals in general are not just a reflection of the composition but ultimately constrained by it.

If townspeople want a particular animal or group of animals within an urban growth boundary, let us say a rich diversity of summering birds and colorful butterflies to attract tourist dollars from bird-watchers and tourists in general, members of the community would have to work backward by determining what kind of function to create. To do so, they would have to know what kind of structure to create, which means knowing what type of composition is necessary to produce the required habitats for the animals the community wants. Thus, once the composition is ensconced, the structure and its attendant functions operate as an interactive unit in terms of the habitat required for the animals.

People and Nature are continually changing the structure and function of this ecosystem or that ecosystem by manipulating the composition of its plants, an act that subsequently changes the composition of the animals dependent on the structure and function of the resultant habitat. By altering the composition of plants within an ecosystem, people and Nature alter its structure and, in turn, affect how it functions, which in turn determines not only what kinds of individuals and how many can live there but also what uses humans can make out of the ecosystem.

Principle 11: All Systems Have Cumulative Effects, Lag Periods, and Thresholds

Nature, as previously stated, has intrinsic value only and so allows each component of an ecosystem to develop its prescribed structure, carry out its ecological function, and interact with other components through their evolved, interdependent processes and self-reinforcing feedback loops. No component is more or less important than another; each may differ from the other in form, but all are complementary in function.

Our intellectual challenge is recognizing that no given factor can be singled out as the sole cause of anything. All things operate synergistically as cumulative effects that exhibit a lag period before fully manifesting themselves. Cumulative effects, which encompass many little, inherent novelties, cannot be understood statistically because ecological relationships are far more complex and far less predictable than our statistical models lead us to believe—a circumstance Francis Bacon may have been eluding to when he said, "The subtlety of Nature is greater many times over than the subtlety of the senses and understanding."[32] In essence, Bacon's observation recognizes that we live in the invisible present and thus cannot recognize cumulative effects.

The invisible present is our inability to stand at a given point in time and see the small, seemingly innocuous effects of our actions as they accumulate over weeks, months, and years. Obviously, we can all sense change—day becoming night, night turning into day, a hot summer changing into a cold winter, and so on. But some people who live for a long time in one place can see longer-term events and remember the winter of the exceptionally deep snow or a summer of deadly heat.

Despite such a gift, it is a rare individual who can sense, with any degree of precision, the changes that occur over the decades of their lives. At this scale of time, we tend to think of the world as being in some sort of steady state (with the exception of technology), and we typically underestimate the degree to which change has occurred—such as global warming. We are unable to sense slow changes directly, and we are even more limited in our abilities to interpret the relationships of cause and effect in these changes. Hence, the subtle processes that act quietly and unobtrusively over decades reside cloaked in the invisible present, such as gradual declines in habitat quality.

At length, however, cumulative effects, gathering themselves below our level of conscious awareness, suddenly become visible. By then it is too late to retract our decisions and actions even if the outcome they cause is decidedly negative with respect to our intentions. So it is that cumulative effects from our activities multiply unnoticed until something in the environment shifts dramatically enough for us to see the outcome through casual observation. That shift is defined by a threshold of tolerance in the system, beyond which the system as we knew it suddenly, visibly, becomes something else. Within our world, this same dynamic takes place in a vast array of scales in all natural and artificial systems, from the infinitesimal to the gigantic.

At a personal level, everyone experiences cumulative effects, lag periods, and thresholds when they become ill, even if it is just a common cold. For instance, if you go to a social function, you may become infected with the cold virus, something you would not know. In fact, you would be unaware of the virus now multiplying in your body, a phenomenon that may continue unnoticed for some days (the cumulative effects within the lag period, or in the parlance of disease, the *incubation period*). At length, you begin to sense something is wrong; you just do not feel "up to snuff" (the threshold); shortly thereafter, you have the full-blown symptoms of the classic cold. In this case, the entire process encompasses a few days—from infection to expression.

A shorter-term example of cumulative effects, lag period, and threshold is the cutting down of a neighbor's dying walnut tree. Initially, a man from the tree service sawed off the small branches with intact twigs. The effect was barely discernible at first, even as the branches began to pile up on the ground. Each severed branch represented a cumulative effect that would have been all but unnoticeable had they not been accumulating under the tree.

After an hour or so (lag period) of removing the small limbs on one side of the tree, the cumulative effects gradually became visible as they crossed the threshold. Had the same volume of twigs been removed from throughout the tree and simultaneously gathered and removed from the ground, the cumulative effects would not have been as apparent. Nevertheless, the tree was gradually transformed into a stark skeleton of larger branches and the main trunk. Then the large branches were cut off a section at a time, with the same visual effect as when the small ones had been removed, until only the trunk remained. The piecemeal removal of the tree created a slowly changing vista of the neighbor's house, until an unobstructed view of it appeared for the first time as another stark threshold was crossed.

If we now increase the spatial magnitude that encompasses the formation of the delta of a river, the timescale involved for the cumulative effects to cross the threshold of visibility may well require centuries to millennia. When a river reaches the sea, it slows and drops its load of sediment. As the amount of sediment accrues on the seabed, it diverts the flow of the river, causing it to deposit additional sediment loads in other areas (cumulative effects). Thus, over many years (lag period), the accumulated sediment begins to show above the water (threshold) and increasingly affects the flow of the river as it forms a classic delta. The speed with which the delta grows has numerous variables, such as the amount of precipitation within the drainage basin of the river in any given year, as well as the amount of its annual sediment load. Many of today's extant river deltas began developing around 8,500 years ago, as the global level of the seas stabilized following the end of the last Ice Age.[33] And so the process of change and novelty continues unabated in all its myriad and astounding scales.

Principle 12: All Systems Are Cyclical, but None Is a Perfect Circle

While all things in Nature are cyclical, no cycle is a perfect circle, despite such depictions in the scientific literature and textbooks. They are, instead, a coming together in time and space at a specific point, where one "end" of a cycle approximates—*but only approximates*—its "beginning" in a particular time and place. Between its beginning and its ending, a cycle can have any configuration of cosmic happenstance. Biophysical cycles can thus be likened to a coiled spring insofar as every coil approximates the curvature of its neighbor but always on a different spatial level (temporal level in Nature), thus never touching.

The size and relative flexibility of a metal spring determine how closely one coil approaches another—the small, flexible, coiled spring in a ballpoint pen juxtaposed to the large, stiff, coiled spring on the front axle of an eighteen-wheel truck. The smaller and more flexible a spring, the closer are its coils, like the cycles of annual plants in a backyard garden or a mountain meadow. Conversely, the larger and more rigid a spring, the more distant are its coils from one another, like the millennial cycles of Great Basin bristlecone pines growing on rocky slopes in the mountains of Nevada, where they are largely protected from fire, or a Norway spruce growing on a rocky promontory in the Alps of Switzerland.

Regardless of its size or flexibility, the coils of a spring are forever reaching outward. With respect to the biophysical cycles of Nature, they are forever moving toward the next level of novelty in the creative process and so are perpetually embracing the uncertainty of future conditions— never to repeat the exact outcome of an event as it once happened. This phenomenon occurs even in times of relative climatic stability. Be that as it may, progressive global warming will only intensify the uncertainties.

In human terms, life is composed of rhythms or routines that follow the cycles of the universe, from the minute to the infinite. We humans most commonly experience the nature of cycles in our pilgrimage through the days, months, and years of our lives wherein certain events are repetitive—day and night, the waxing and waning of the moon, the march of the seasons, and the coming and going of birthdays, all marking the circular passage we perceive as time within the curvature of space. In addition to the visible manifestation of these repetitive cycles, the biophysical processes of Nature are cyclical in various scales of time and space, a phenomenon that means all relationships are simultaneously cyclical in how they work and forever novel in their outcomes.

Some cycles revolve frequently enough to be well known in a person's lifetime, like the winter solstice. Others are completed only in the collective lifetimes of several generations, like the life cycle of a 3,000-year-old giant sequoia in the Sequoia National Park in California—hence the notion of the invisible present. Still others are so vast that their motion can only be assumed. Yet even they are not completely aloof because we are kept in touch with them through our interrelatedness and interdependence. Regarding cycles, farmer and author Wendell Berry said, "It is only in the processes of the natural world, and in analogous and related processes of human culture, that the new may grow usefully old, and the old be made new."[34]

Principle 13: Systemic Change Is Based on Self-Organized Criticality

When dealing with scale (a small mountain lake as opposed to the drainage basin of a large river, such as the Mississippi in the United States or the Ganges in India), scientists have traditionally analyzed large, interactive systems in the same way that they have studied small, orderly systems, mainly because their methods of study have proven so successful. The prevailing wisdom has been that the behavior of a large, complicated system could be predicted by studying its elements separately and by analyzing its microscopic mechanisms individually—the reductionist-mechanical thinking predominant in Western society that tends to view the world and all it contains through a lens of intellectual isolation. During the last few decades, however, it has become increasingly clear that many complicated systems, like forests, oceans, and even cities, do not yield to such traditional analysis.

Instead, large, complicated, interactive systems seem to evolve naturally to a critical state in which even a minor event starts a chain reaction that can affect any number of elements in the system and can lead to a dramatic alteration in the system. Although such systems produce more minor events than catastrophic ones, chain reactions of all sizes are an integral part of system dynamics. According to the theory called *self-organized criticality*, the mechanism that leads to minor events (analogous to the drop of a pin) is the same mechanism that leads to major events (analogous to an earthquake).[35] Not understanding this, analysts have typically blamed some rare set of circumstances (some exception to the rule) or some powerful combination of mechanisms when catastrophe strikes.

Nevertheless, ecosystems move inevitably toward a critical state, one that alters the ecosystem in some dramatic way. This dynamic makes ecosystems dissipative structures in that energy is built up through time only to be released in a disturbance of some kind, such as a fire, flood, or landslide, in some scale, ranging from a freshet in a stream to the eruption of a volcano, after which energy begins building again toward the next release of pent-up energy somewhere in time.

Such disturbances, as ecologists think of these events, can be long term and chronic, such as large movements of soil that take place over hundreds of years (termed an *earth flow*), or acute, such as the crescendo of a volcanic eruption that sends a pyroclastic flow sweeping down its side at amazing speed. (A *pyroclastic flow* is a turbulent mixture of hot gas and fragments of rock, such as pumice, that is violently ejected from a fissure and moves with great speed down the side of a volcano. *Pyroclastic* is Greek for "fire-broken.")

Here you might interject that neither a movement of soil nor a volcano is a living system in the classical sense. Although that is true, all disturbance regimes are part and parcel of the living systems they affect. Thus, interactive systems, from the habitat of a gnat to a tropical rain forest, perpetually organize themselves to a critical state wherein a minor event can start a chain reaction that leads to a catastrophic event—as far as living things are concerned—after which the system begins organizing itself toward the next critical state. Furthermore, such systems never reach a state of equilibrium but rather evolve from one semistable state to another. This dynamic is precisely why sustainability is a moving target—not a fixed end point or a steady state.

Principle 14: Dynamic Disequilibrium Rules All Systems

If change is a universal constant in which nothing is static, what is a natural state? In answering this question, it becomes apparent that the *balance of Nature* in the classical sense (disturb Nature and Nature will return to its former state after the disturbance is removed) does not hold. In fact, the so-called balance of Nature is a romanticized figment of the human imagination, something we conjured to fit our snapshot image of the world in which we live. In reality, Nature exists in a continual state of ever-shifting disequilibrium, wherein ecosystems are entrained in the irreversible process of change and novelty, thereby altering their composition, interactive feedback loops, and thus the use of available resources—irrespective of human influence. Perhaps the most outstanding evidence that an ecosystem is subject to constant change and disruption rather than remaining in a static balance comes from studies of naturally occurring external factors that dislocate ecosystems, and climate appears to be foremost among these factors.

After a fire, earthquake, volcanic eruption, flood, hurricane, or landslide, for example, a biological system may eventually be able to approximate what it was through resilience—the ability of the system to retain the integrity of its basic relationships. But, regardless of how closely an ecosystem might approximate its former state following a disturbance, the existence of every ecosystem is a tenuous balancing act because every system is in a continual state of reorganization that occurs over various scales of time, from the cycle of an old forest to a geological phenomenon, such as Mauna Loa, the active volcanic mountain in Hawaii.

Bear in mind, an old forest that is burned, blown over in a hurricane, or smashed in a tsunami could be replaced by another, albeit different, old forest on the same acreage. In this way, despite a repetitive disturbance regime, a forest ecosystem can remain a forest ecosystem. Thus, ancient forests around the world have been evolving from one critical, biophysical state to the next, from one natural catastrophe to the next. Whereas people can to some extent manipulate a forest, Mauna Loa is entrained in an eternal flux of physical novelty over which no human has a smidgen of control.

Finally, we, the human component of the world, must understand and accept that the foregoing laws and biophysical principles are an interactive thread in the tapestry of the natural/cultural world, which must be accounted for if society is to become a sustainable partner with its environment. As such, they are an essential and unavoidable part of the "commons."

References

1. Arnold J. Toynbee. *A Study of History*, Volumes I–VI (abridgement by D.C. Somervell). Oxford University Press, New York (1987).
2. (a) Rod Swenson. Emergent evolution and the global attractor: the evolutionary epistemology of entropy production maximization. *Proceedings of the 33rd Annual Meeting of the International Society for the Systems Sciences*, P. Leddington (ed.), 33(3), 46–53, 1989; and (b) Rod Swenson. Order, evolution, and natural law: fundamental relations in complex system theory. In: *Cybernetics and Applied Systems*, C. Negoita (ed.), 125–148. New York: Marcel Dekker, 1991.
3. Rod Swenson and Michael T. Turvey. Thermodynamic reasons for perception-action cycles. *Ecological Psychology*, 3 (1991):317–348.
4. (a) Wolfgang Haber. Energy, food, and land—the ecological traps of humankind. *Environmental Science and Pollution Research*, 14 (2007):359–365; and (b) David Robson. Proto-humans mastered fire 790,000 years ago. ABC News, October 28, 2008. http://abcnews.go.com/search?searchtext=David%20Robson.%20Proto-humans%20mastered%20fire%20790%2C000%20years%20ago (accessed February 27, 2009).
5. Ann Gibbons. Food for thought. *Science*, 316 (2007):1558–1560.
6. Rod Swenson. Spontaneous order, autocatakinetic closure, and the development of space-time. *Annals of the New York Academy of Sciences*, 901 (2000): 311–319.
7. Marcus Aurelius. BrainyQuote. http://www.brainyquote.com/quotes/authors/m/marcus_aurelius.html (accessed December 30, 2008).
8. G.O. Poinar, A.E. Treat, and R.V. Southeott. Mite parasitism of moths: examples of paleosymbiosis in Dominican amber. *Experientia*, 47 (1991):210–212.
9. The general discussion of amberization is based on: (a) George O. Poinar, Jr. Insects in amber. *Annual Review of Entomology*, 46 (1993):145–159; (b) Scientist: earth's oldest spider web discovered. London. *Corvallis Gazette-Times* (December 16, 2008); and (c) Enrique Peñalver, David. A. Grimaldi, and Xavier Delclòs. Early Cretaceous spider web with its prey. *Science*, 312 (2006):1761.
10. Chris Maser. *Earth in Our Care: Ecology, Economy, and Sustainability*. Rutgers University Press, Piscataway, NJ (2009).
11. (a) Yuan-Chug Cheng and Graham R. Fleming. Dynamics of light harvesting in photosynthesis. *Annual Review of Physical Chemistry*, 60 (2009):241–262; (b) Paul May. Chlorophyll. http://www.chm.bris.ac.uk/3motm/chlorophyll/chlorophyll_h.htm (accessed on January 5, 2009).

12. Maser. *Earth in Our Care.*
13. The discussion of elk is based in part on Jack Ward Thomas, Hugh Black, Jr., Richard J. Scherzinger, and Richard J. Pederson. Deer and elk. In: *Wildlife Habitats in Managed Forests: The Blue Mountains of Oregon and Washington*, 104–127. Jack Ward Thomas (technical editor). U.S. Department of Agriculture, Forest Service, Pacific Northwest Range and Experiment Station, Portland, OR, 1979. Agricultural Handbook No. 553.
14. David Archer. Carbon cycle: checking the thermostat. *Nature Geoscience*, 1 (2008):289–290.
15. Richard E. Zeebe and Ken Caldeira. Close mass balance of long-term carbon fluxes from ice-core CO_2 and ocean chemistry records. *Nature Geoscience*, 1 (2008):312–315.
16. The discussion of color changes in buildings is based on (a) Carlotta M. Grossi, Peter Brimblecombe, Rosa M. Esbert, and Francisco Javier Alonso. Color changes in architectural limestone from pollution and cleaning. *Color Research and Application*, 32 (2007):320–331; and (b) Catherine Brahic. Cleaner air to turn iconic buildings green: with atmospheric changes, limestone buildings will turn yellow, reddish-brown and green. *New Scientist*, http://www.newscientist.com/article/dn16198-cleaner-air-to-turn-iconic-buildings-green.html (accessed December 8, 2008).
17. C.I. Davidson, W. Tang, S. Finger, V. Etyemezian, M.F. Striegel, and S.I. Sherwood. Soiling patterns on a tall limestone building: changes over sixty years. *Environmental Science and Technology*, 34 (2000):560–565.
18. Cliff I. Davidson. Air pollution in Pittsburgh: a historical perspective. *Journal of the Air Pollution Control Association*, 29 (1979):1035–1041.
19. (a) V. Etyemezian, C.I. Davidson, M. Zufall, W. Dai, S. Finger, and M. Striegel. Impingement of rain drops on a tall building. *Atmospheric Environment*, 34 (2000):2399–2412; and (b) Vicken Etymezian, Cliff I. Davidson, Susan Finger, and others. Vertical gradients of pollutant concentrations and deposition fluxes at the Cathedral of Learning. *Journal of the American Institute for Conservation*, 37 (1998):187–210.
20. (a) Carlotta M. Grossi, Peter Brimblecombe, Rosa M. Esbert, and Francisco Javier Alonso. Color changes in architectural limestone from pollution and cleaning. *Color Research and Application*, 32 (2007):320–331; and (b) Alessandra Bonazza, Peter Brimblecombe, Carlota M. Grossi, and Cristina Sabbioni. Carbon in black crusts from the Tower of London. *Environmental Science and Technology*, 41 (2007):4199–4204.
21. Grossi et al., Color changes.
22. (a) Grossi et al., Color changes; and (b) Bonazza et al., Carbon in black crusts.
23. Bill Zlatos. Foes, lack of funds may scrub Cathedral of Learning cleaning. *Pittsburgh Tribune-Review* (July 6, 2003).
24. (a) Sid Perkins. As ozone hole heals, Antarctic could heat up. *Science News*, 174 (2008):10; (b) S.-W. Son, L.M. Polvani, D.W. Waugh, and others. The impact of stratospheric ozone recovery on the Southern Hemisphere westerly jet. *Science*, 320 (2008):1486–1489; and (c) J. Perlwitz, S. Pawson, R.L. Fogt, and others. Impact of stratospheric ozone hole recovery on Antarctic climate. *Geophysical Research Letters*, 35 (2008): L08714, doi:10.1029/2008GL033317. (accessed December 17, 2008.)

25. Lee Dye. Did Climate Change Kill the Roman Empire? http://abcnews. go.com/Technology/JustOneThing/story?id=6428550&page=1 (accessed December 10, 2008).

26. (a) Sid Perkins. Buried treasures. *Science News*, 169 (2006):266–268; (b) Martin B. Short, James C. Baygents, and Raymond E. Goldstein. Stalactite growth as a free-boundary problem. *Physics of Fluids*, 17 (2005):083101, 12 pp. (accessed December 17, 2008); and (c) M.B. Short, J.C. Baygents, J.W. Beck, and others. Stalactite growth as a free-boundary problem: a geometric law and its platonic ideal. *Physical Review Letters*, 94 (2005):018510, 4 pp. (accessed December 17, 2008).

27. D. Meko, C. A. Woodhouse, C. A. Baisan, and others. Medieval drought in the upper Colorado River Basin. *Geophysical Research Letters*, 34 (2007):L10705, doi:10.1029/2007GL029988 (accessed December 17, 2008).

28. (a) Ian J. Orland, Miryam Bar-Matthews, Noriko T. Kita, and others. Climate deterioration in the eastern Mediterranean as revealed by ion microprobe analysis of a speleothem that grew from 2.2 to 0.9 Ka in Soreq Cave, Israel. *Quaternary Research*, 71 (2009):27–35; (b) A. Kaufman, G.J. Wasserburg, D. Porcelli, and others. U-Th isotope systematics from the Soreq Cave, Israel and climatic correlations. *Earth and Planetary Science Letters*, 156 (1998):141–155; and (c) Avner Ayalon, Miryam Bar-Matthews, and Eytan Sass. Rainfall-recharge relationships within a karstic terrain in the eastern Mediterranean semi-arid region, Israel: $\delta^{18}O$ and δD characteristics. *Journal of Hydrology*, 207 (1998):18–31.

29. (a) Pingzhong Zhang, Hai Cheng, R. Lawrence Edwards, and others. A test of climate, sun, and culture relationships from an 1810-year Chinese cave record. *Science*, 322 (2008):940–942; (b) Kallie Szczepanski. When the Rains Stop, the Emperors Fall. http://asianhistory.about. com/od/asianenvironmentalhistory/a/ChinaMonsoon.htm (accessed January 5, 2009); (c) Ker Than. Chinese kingdoms rose, fell with monsoons? *National Geographic News*. http://news.nationalgeographic.com/news/2008/11/081106-monsoons-china.html (accessed January 10, 2009); and (d) Yongjin Wang, Hai Cheng, R. Lawrence Edwards, and others. Millennial- and orbital-scale changes in the East Asian monsoon over the past 224,000 years. *Nature*, 451 (2008):1090–1093.

30. Charles Darwin. *On the Origin of Species*. Modern Library, a Division of Random House Publishers, New York (1998).

31. Maser. *Earth in Our Care*.

32. Francis Bacon. http://Science.prodos.ORG (accessed January 2, 2009).

33. (a) Sid Perkins. O river deltas, where art thou? *Science News*, 172 (2007):118; and (b) Pippa L. Whitehouse, Mark B. Allen, and Glenn A. Milne. Glacial isostatic adjustment as a control on coastal processes: an example from the Siberian Arctic. *Geology*, 35 (2007):747–750.

34. Wendell Berry. The road and the wheel. *Earth Ethics*, 1 (1990):8–9.

35. Per Bak and Kan Chen. Self-organizing criticality. *Scientific American*, January (1991):46–53.

4

Social Principles of Sustainability

Introduction

Simply stated, a *commons* is something owned by everyone and so by no one. Moreover, the global commons is the "birthright" of every living thing—not just humans. From a human perspective, however, it is the vast realm of our shared heritage, which we typically enjoy and use free of toll or price. Air, water, and soil; sunlight and warmth; wind and stars; mountains and oceans; languages and cultures; knowledge and wisdom; peace and quiet; sharing and community; and the genetic building blocks of life—these are all aspects of the commons.

The commons has an intrinsic quality of just being there, without formal rules of conduct. People are free to breathe the air, drink the water, and share life's experiences without a contract, without paying a royalty, without needing to ask permission. The commons is simply waiting to be discovered and used.

For example, as a youth in the 1950s, and even as a young man in the earliest years of the 1960s, I (Chris) could stand on the shoulder of a mountain in the High Cascades of Oregon or Washington and gaze on a land clothed in ancient forest as far as I could see into the blue haze of the distance in any direction. My sojourns along the trails of deer and elk were accompanied by the wind as it sang in the trees and by the joy-filled sound of water bouncing along rocky channels. At others times, the water gave voice to its deafening roar as it suddenly poured itself into space from dizzying heights, only to once again gather itself at the bottom of the precipice and continue its appointed journey to the mother of all waters, the ocean.

Throughout those many springs and summers, the songs of wind and water were punctuated with the melodies of forest birds. Wilson's warblers sang in the tops of ancient firs, while the plaintive trill of the varied thrush drifted down the mountainside, and the liquid notes of winter wrens came ever so gently from among the fallen monarchs as they lay decomposing through the centuries on the forest floor. From somewhere high above the canopy of trees came the scream of a golden eagle, and from deep within the forest emanated the rapid, staccato drumming of a pileated woodpecker.

These were the sounds of my youth. This was the music that complemented the abiding silence of the forest—a silence that archived the history of centuries and millennia as the forest grew and changed, like an unfinished mural painted with the infinite novelty of perpetual creation.

And so it is that every aspect of the commons engages people in the wholeness of themselves. It fosters the most genuine of human emotions and stimulates interpersonal relationships to share the experience, which enhances its enjoyment and archives its memory.

The Paradox of Life

Herein lies a paradox: While we are compelled to share our life's experiences with one another to know we exist and have value, we are forever well and truly alone with each and every thought, each and every experience, and the emotion it evokes in our personal journey from birth through death. A baby comes into the world outside its mother's womb with its own experience of life within the womb and the birth process, something the baby can never share, even with his or her mother. In turn, the mother has her own experience of nurturing her child before birth, as well as the process of giving birth, which she can never share—not even with her child, albeit they coexisted for nine months of their respective lives in the most intimate connection two human beings can have.

When we die, we pass out of life as we know it, but without being able to share the experience, even when surrounded by family and friends. Therefore, we are born and we die *alone*—the only person in the world who will ever truly experience the essence of who we are in our life.

Even if we could verbally share an experience with someone who had been through a similar situation, we would still be alone with our own rendition of it because all we can share are metaphors of our feelings and emotions through a chosen combination of words available in the language we are speaking. In this sense, words can be likened to incandescent lightbulbs because each bulb can have a different shape, clarity, color, hue, brightness of color, intensity of the light based on wattage and can be energized by a 110- or 220-volt current, depending on the nation one is in (different shades of meaning based on the way individuals interpret such things as color and hue); yet all these various lightbulbs share the commonality of electrical impulse—the energy (feelings and emotions) that fuel them. Besides, our ability to share the exact meaning of the metaphors we choose depends on how conversant the person with whom we are visiting is with the language and the degree to which our experiential similarities coincide. We cannot, however, share the feelings, emotions, or thoughts themselves because they cannot be expressed directly through language, only through the metaphorical shadows they cast. Even two people in the midst of a deeply intimate, sexual union have vastly different, private experiences, which neither can accurately portray to the other.

If the notion of being alone is expanded into the arena of life, it soon becomes apparent that we are alone with each thought we have, each question we ask, each decision we make, each rainbow or flower we observe, each bird's song we hear or symphony we listen to, and each emotion we feel. We are alone—totally alone—within a psychological world of our own making, regardless of how extroverted or introverted we are. Be it a world of exceeding beauty or terrific horror, we are the sole creator of the life we experience, and we live it alone—both as creator of our thoughts and as prisoner of our thinking.

Our *aloneness*, in all its forms, is the essence of spiritual union with the Eternal Mystery, which transcends all words and their contrived meaning, because our solitude pares life down to only what is self-created and nothing more. Thus, solitude itself transcends all material understanding and in so doing is touched by the unifying paradox of the cosmos, namely, all things are interrelated and alone—alone and interrelated.

Nevertheless, whether we realize it or not, whether we admit it or not, we need one another because we must, to the best of our ability, share our *feelings* with at least one other person to find value in life. Nevertheless, the *reality of life is beyond words* because we cannot communicate our feelings through language and because all that is real for us is how we feel. And, it is precisely because the reality of life is silent that we need to care for something in which the language of the intellect is unnecessary, but the language of the heart, conveyed through touch, is vital, such as cohabiting with another person, raising a child, nurturing a pet, planting and tending a garden, or engaging in caring for the commons.[1]

Astronomer and author Carl Sagan points correctly to cosmic unity when he says, "In order to make an apple pie from scratch, you must first create the universe,"[2] which includes such gifts of Nature as clean air, pure water, fertile soil, a rainbow, northern lights, a beautiful sunset, or a 5,000-year-old bristlecone pine growing in a national park. Nature's commons, says author Jonathan Rowe, is the "hidden economy, everywhere present but rarely noticed."[3] Nevertheless, the biophysical services of Nature provide the basic ecological and social support systems of all life and well-being, such as air, soil, water, biodiversity, and sunlight, among others.

Air: The Breath of Life—And of Death

It is late afternoon on a clear, warm, sunny September day. A tiny spider climbs a tall stalk of grass in a subalpine meadow and raises its body into the air, almost standing on its head. From spinnerets on the tip of its abdomen, it ejects a mass of silken threads into the breeze. Suddenly, without visible warning, the spider is jerked off its stalk and borne skyward to join its relatives riding the warm afternoon air flowing up the mountainside, all casting their fortunes to the wind. Like their ancestors in centuries past, they float on air currents from the far corners of Earth, and some become the first inhabitants of newly formed South Seas islands.

Spiders are not the only things borne aloft on air currents. On August 26–27, 1883, Krakatoa (a small Indonesian island between Java and Sumatra) was virtually obliterated by explosive eruptions that sent volcanic ash high enough above Earth to ride the airways of the world for more than a year. This affected the climate by reducing the amount of sunlight reaching Earth, which in turn cooled the climate and affected all life.[4] Like the volcanic ash of Krakatoa, air also carries the reproductive spores of fungi and the pollen of various trees and grasses, as well as dust and microscopic organisms. And it carries life-giving oxygen and water and death-dealing pollution—the legacy of human society.

Air can therefore be likened to the key in a Chinese proverb: To every human is given the key to the gates of heaven, and the same key opens the gates of hell. In this case, air is the key that carries both life-giving oxygen and death-dealing pollution, and as pollution increases, the quality and utility of the air are decreased.

Soil: The Great Placenta

Soil is like an exchange membrane between the living (plant and animal) and nonliving components of the landscape. Derived from rock and organic matter, soil is built up by plants that live and die in it. It is also enriched by animals that feed on plants, void their bodily wastes, and eventually die, decay, and return to the soil as organic matter. Soil is by far the most alive and biologically diverse part of any terrestrial ecosystem. In addition, soil organisms are the regulators of most processes that translate into soil productivity.

Many cultures have emphasized in their religion and philosophy that humans must be trustees of the soil. Confucius saw in the thin mantle of

Earth the sustenance of all life and the minerals treasured by human society. A century later, Aristotle viewed the soil as the central mixing pot of air, fire, and water, which formed all things.

Most people cannot grasp these intangible, long-held beliefs. Thus, we pay scant attention to the soil because it is as common as air and, like air, is taken for granted. But if we pause and think about it, we see that human society is tied to the soil for reasons beyond measurable materialistic wealth.

Yet, in the name of short-term profits, people rob the soil of the very organic material necessary for its sustainable fertility. They also use artificial chemicals that poison the soil, alter the way its many hidden processes function, and pollute the water moving through it into the water system of the world.

Soil is the stage on which the entire human drama is enacted. If we continue to destroy the stage on which we depend for life, we will play a progressively ebbing role in a terminal tragedy of human society.

Water: A Captive of Gravity

Water and oxygen are the most important products produced from the forests of the world. Most of our usable water comes from snows high on forested mountain slopes. When snow melts, the water percolates through the soil. It is purified when flowing through healthy soil; it is poisoned when flowing through soil stripped of the processes of Nature and polluted with artificial chemicals. In addition, water bearing tons of toxic effluents flows directly into streams, rivers, estuaries, and the open ocean. Because water is a captive of gravity, all the pollutants it accumulates on its downhill journey eventually end up in the oceans, where they accumulate in ever-increasing concentrations.

Biodiversity: The Variety of Life

Because every ecosystem adapts in some way to changes in its environment, biodiversity acts as an ecological insurance policy for the flexibility of future human options. In turn, the degree of adaptability of a system depends on the richness of its biodiversity, which creates backups—duplication or repetition of the elements of a system. Backups provide alternative, functional channels in case of a failure and so retain the ability of a system to respond to continual change.

Each ecosystem contains redundancies that provide resilience to absorb change or to bounce back after disturbance. Biological redundancy strengthens the ability of an ecosystem to retain its integrity. This means that the loss of one or two species is not likely to result in such severe functional disruption as to cause ecosystem collapse because other species can make up for the functional loss.

At some point, however, the loss of one or more species will tip the balance and cause an irreversible change that can lower the quality and productivity of the system. This point of irreversibility is an unknown biological threshold; we do not know which species' extinction will trigger its effects, which is why it pays to save every species possible. Hence, the precautionary principle: Err on the side of prudence.

Species variety is important because each species has a shape and structure that allows certain functions to take place. These functions interact with those of other species to create a viable system. All biodiversity is ultimately governed by the genetic code that builds some redundancy into each ecosystem by replicating the character traits of a species.

A stable ecosystem may respond positively to disturbances to which it is adapted, but it also may be vulnerable to the introduction of foreign disturbances to which it is not adapted. Plant and animal diversity therefore buffers an ecosystem against disturbances from which it cannot recover. When we lose species, we lose not only their combination of structural and functional diversity but also their genetic diversity, which eventually results in complex ecosystems becoming simplified and unable to sustain either them or us.

A forest, for example, is a living entity that often completes a cycle of interdependent processes over several centuries, spanning many human generations. Yet with grossly incomplete, shortsighted knowledge and unquestioning faith in that knowledge, we predict the sustained-yield capability of economically designed tree plantations far into a problematic and unforeseeable future.

Based on these erroneous predictions, clear-cutting the old-growth forest and converting it to a biologically simplified plantation is traditionally justified economically, completely ignoring biodiversity—especially that which sustains the infrastructure of the forest soil. Destroy the soil, and the forest ceases to be. Destroy the forest, and the soil becomes further impoverished and erodes, which degrades water quality and diminishes the oxygen content of the air.

Sunlight: The Source of Global Energy

The sun has been worshipped for millennia, and the quality of its light has often been taken for granted. Sunlight powers most of the processes on Earth; we harvest the energy of the sun through the fruits and vegetables we eat. But what happens when air pollution—smog—reduces the intensity of sunlight before it reaches plants? What happens when the ozone shield disappears, allowing deadly ultraviolet rays to bombard Earth? What happens when both of these events occur simultaneously, as is now happening?

Impacts from our burgeoning human population, such as air pollution, now directly affect the quality of sunlight and energy reaching us. Like everything else, the quality of sunlight is an ecological variable that must be taken into account.

Human Population: A Matter of Gender Equality

We have been warned for decades that the human species is overpopulating Earth. Yet our population explodes, and the usable portion of Earth per individual shrinks, as does the allotted proportion of its resources, all of which become more quickly limiting when abused. We have tried many things to remedy this situation: education, birth control, feeding the hungry, shipping industrial technology to poor nations, and so on. In our opinion, however, we have not addressed the primary cause of overpopulation: the inequality between men and women.

Men have long dominated women. Through such domination, women are physically forced to produce most of the food in the world yet are allowed to own but an infinitesimal part of the land. And women have had only one way to be uniquely valued by men—by having babies, particularly *boys*.

Regardless of where I (Chris) have traveled, I have found that women who have a good education have fewer children and have them later in life. Education affords increased options and a variety of ways to be valued. If, therefore, we humans are serious about controlling our population, women must have an equal voice in all decisions and unequivocal access to opportunities for self- and social valuation. On the surface, this means such things as equal opportunity for education and jobs and equal pay for equal work. At its root, this means changing the male attitude of superiority toward women—a difficult task, but a vitally necessary one because we humans directly affect such foundation stones of social survival as air, soil, water, biodiversity, and population density—as well as sunlight indirectly.

If, for example, we choose to clean the air in our world, we will automatically clean the soil and water to some extent because airborne pollutants will no longer poison them, and the sunlight that reaches Earth will be unimpeded. If we then choose to treat the soil in such a way that we can grow what we desire without the use of artificial chemicals and if we stop using the soil as a dumping ground for toxic wastes and avoid overintensive agriculture, the soil can again filter and purify water. If we stop dumping waste effluents into the water, streams, rivers, estuaries, and oceans could—with time—become cleaner and healthier.

With clean and healthy air, soil, and water, we can also have clear, safe sunlight with which to power Earth and, with the eventual repair of the ozone shield, a more benign—and perhaps predictable—climate in which to live. In addition, effective population control can tailor human society to fit within the carrying capacity of the world.

A population in balance with its habitat will reduce demands on the resources of Earth. With reduced competition for resources can come the cooperation and coordination that will allow our landscapes to provide the maximum possible biodiversity. Protecting biodiversity translates into the gift of choice, which in turn translates into hope and dignity for future generations.

For the sake of discussion, let us add to this scenario the end of wars and their weapons. Such a world, a wonderful place in which to live and raise families, is possible, but this possibility ultimately hinges on clean air.

If we do everything outlined here—except clean the air, we will still pollute the entire Earth, from the blue arc of its heavens to the bottom of its deepest sea, in every corner of the globe. Clean air is the absolute "bottom line" for human survival. Without clean air, there eventually will be no difference in the way we destroy ourselves, either by nuclear war or air pollution, because our biosphere is composed of interdependent, interactive components, where one affects the whole, and the whole affects the one.

The paradox is that the thing of intangible value (such as scenic beauty) is the very thing that usually gives the most enjoyment to the greatest number of people over the longest time but turns no immediate profit. Commercial value, as opposed to intrinsic value, holds our mechanistic society captive; herein lies the conflict over the commons. Yet we humans have jointly inherited the commons, which is more basic to our lives and well-being than either the market or the state, as observed by British economist and philosopher Edmund Burke: "One of the first and most leading principles on which the commonwealth and the laws are consecrated is

[that] the temporary possessors and life-renters in it [should be mindful] of what is due to their posterity ... [and] should not think it among their rights to cut off the entail or commit waste on the inheritance by destroying at their pleasure the whole original fabric of society, hazarding to leave to those who come after them a ruin instead of a habitation."[5]

Burke's notion calls to mind a unifying construct of the commons, which can be thought of as the *Commons Usufruct Law*. *Usufruct* is a noun from ancient Roman law (and now a part of many civil law systems) that means one has the personal *right* to enjoy all the advantages derivable from the use of something that belongs to another, provided the substance of the thing being used is not injured in any way.[6] In Canada, for example, the indigenous First Nations people have a usufructuary right to hunt and fish without restriction on Crown lands. In a more industrialized setting, a farmer might rent an unused field to a neighbor, thus enabling that neighbor to sow and reap the harvest of that land or, perhaps, to use it as pasture for livestock.[7] On public rangelands in the western United States, this same arrangement between the federal government and a local rancher is known as a *grazing allotment*.

The legal definition of *usufruct* in the United States is as follows:

> Usufruct is a right in a property owned by another, normally for a limited time or until death. It is the right to use the property, to enjoy the fruits and income of the property, to rent the property out and to collect the rents, all to the exclusion of the underlying owner. The usufructuary has the full right to use the property but cannot dispose of the property nor can it be destroyed.
>
> The extent of usufruct is defined by agreement and may be for a stated term, covering only certain stated properties, it could be set to terminate if certain conditions are met, such as marriage of a child or remarriage of a spouse, it can be granted to several people to share jointly, and it can be given to one person for a period of time and to another after some stated event occurs.[8]

How the Commons Usufruct Law Arose

Until AD 1500, hunter-gatherers occupied fully one-third of the world, including all of Australia, most of North America, and large tracts of land in South America, Africa, and northeast Asia, where they lived in small groups without the overarching, disciplinary umbrella of a state or other centralized authority. They lived without standing armies or bureaucratic systems, and they exchanged goods and services without recourse to economic markets or taxation.[9]

With relatively simple technology (such as wood, bone, stone, fibers, and fire), they were able to meet their material needs with a modest expenditure of energy and have the time to enjoy what they had materially, socially, and spiritually. Although their material wants may have been few and finite and their technical skills relatively simple and unchanging, their technology was, on the whole, adequate to fulfill their requirements, a circumstance that says the hunting-gathering peoples were the original affluent societies.

Evidence indicates that these peoples lived surprisingly well together, despite the lack of a rigid social structure, solving their problems among themselves, largely without courts and without a particular propensity for violence. They also demonstrated a remarkable ability to thrive for long periods, sometimes thousands of years, in harmony with their environment. They were environmentally and socially harmonious and thus sustainable because they were egalitarian, and they were egalitarian because they were socially and environmentally harmonious. They intuitively understood the reciprocal, indissoluble connection between their social life and the sustainability of their inseparable environment.

The basic social unit of most hunting-gathering peoples, based on studies of contemporary hunter-gatherer societies, was the band, a small-scale nomadic group of fifteen to fifty people who were related through kinship. These bands were relatively egalitarian in that leadership was rather informal and subject to the constraints of popular opinion. Leadership tended to be by example instead of arbitrary order or decree because a leader could persuade, but not command. This form of leadership allowed for a degree of freedom unknown in more hierarchical societies, but at the same time put hunter-gatherers at a distinct disadvantage when they finally encountered centrally organized colonial authorities.[10]

Hunter-gatherers were by nature and necessity nomadic—a traditional form of wandering as a way of life by which people moved their encampment several times a year as they either searched for food or followed the known seasonal order of their food supply. "Home" *was* the journey in that belonging, dwelling, and livelihood were all components of it. Home, in this sense, was "en route."

The nomadic way of life was essentially a response to prevailing circumstances, as opposed to a matter of conviction. Nevertheless, a nomadic journey is in many ways a more flexible and adaptive response to life than is living in a settlement.

This element of mobility was also an important component of their politics because they "voted with their feet" by moving away from an unpopular leader rather than submitting to that person's rule. Further, such mobility was a means of settling conflicts, something that proved increasingly difficult as people became more sedentary.

Nomads were in many ways more in harmony with the environment than a sedentary culture because the rigors and uncertainties of a wandering lifestyle controlled, in part, the size of the overall human population while allowing little technological development. In this sense, wandering groups of people tended to be small, versatile, and mobile.

Although a nomadic people may in some cases have altered a spring of water for their use, dug a well, or hid an ostrich egg filled with water for emergencies, they were largely controlled by when and where they found water. Put differently, water brought nomads to it. On the other hand, the human wastes were simply left to recycle into the environment as a reinvestment of biological capital each time the people moved.

In addition, nomads, who carried their possessions with them as they moved about, introduced little technology of lasting consequence into the landscape, other than fire and the eventual extinction of some species of prey. Even though they may, in the short term, have depleted populations of local game animals or seasonal plants, they gave the land a chance to heal and replenish itself between seasons of use. Finally, the sense of place for a nomadic people was likely associated with a familiar circuit dictated by the whereabouts of seasonal foods and later pastures for their herds.

Another characteristic associated with mobility was the habit of hunter-gatherers to concentrate and disperse, which appears to represent the interplay of ecological necessity and social possibility. Rather than live in uniform-size assemblages throughout the year, they tended to disperse into small groups, the aforementioned 15 to 50 people, who spent part of the year foraging, only to gather again into much larger aggregates of 100 to 200 people at other times of the year, where the supply of food, say an abundance of fish, made such a gathering possible.[11]

Although hunter-gatherers had the right of personal ownership, it applied only to mobile property, that which they could carry with them, such as their hunting knives or gathering baskets. Such fixed property as land, on the other hand, was to be shared equally through rights of use but could not be personally controlled to the exclusion of others or the detriment of future generations.

Almost all hunter-gatherers, including nomadic herders and many village-based societies as well, shared a land tenure system based on the rights of common usage that, until recently, were far more common than regimes based on the rights of private property. In traditional systems of common property, the land is held in a kinship-based collective, while individuals own movable property. Rules of reciprocal accesses made it possible for an individual to satisfy the necessities of life by drawing on the resources of several territories, such as the shared rights among the indigenous Cherokee peoples of eastern North America.

In the traditional Cherokee economic system, both the land and its abundance would be shared among clans. One clan could gather, another could camp, and yet a third could hunt on the same land. There was a fluid right of common usage rather than a rigid individual right to private property. The value was thus placed on sharing and reciprocity, on the widest distribution of wealth, and on limiting the inequalities within the economic system.[12]

Sharing was the core value of social interaction among hunter-gatherers, with a strong emphasis on the importance of generalized reciprocity—the unconditional giving of something without any expectation of immediate return. The combination of generalized reciprocity and an absence of private ownership of land has led many anthropologists to consider the hunter-gatherer way of life as a "primitive communism," in the true sense of "communism."

Hunter-gatherer peoples lived with few material possessions for hundreds of thousands of years and enjoyed lives that were in many ways richer, freer, and more fulfilling than ours. These peoples so structured their lives that they wanted little, needed little, and found what they required at their disposal in their immediate surroundings. They were comfortable precisely because they achieved a balance between necessity and want, by being satisfied with little. There are, after all, two ways to wealth—working harder or wanting less.

The !Kung Bushmen of southern Africa, for example, spent only 12 to 19 hours a week getting food because their work was social and cooperative, which means they obtained their particular food items with the least possible expenditure of energy. Thus, they had abundant time for eating, drinking, playing, and general socializing. In addition, young people were not expected to work until well into their twenties, and no one was expected to work after age forty or so.

Hunter-gatherers also had much personal freedom. There were, among the !Kung Bushmen and the Hadza of Tanzania, either no leaders or only temporary leaders with severely limited authority. These societies had personal equality in that *everyone* belonged to the same social class *and* had gender equality. Their technologies and social systems, including their economies of having enough or a sense of "enoughness," allowed them to live sustainably for tens of thousands of years. One of the reasons they were sustainable is that they made no connection between what an individual produced and their economic security, so acquisition of things to ensure personal survival and material comfort was not an issue.[13]

The Precursor of the Environmental Conflicts of Today

With the advent of herding, agriculture, and progressive settlement, however, humanity created the concept of "wilderness," and so the distinctions between *tame* (meaning "controlled") and *wild* (meaning "uncontrolled") plants and animals began to emerge in the human psyche. Along with the notion of tame and wild plants and animals came the perceived need not only to "control" space but also to "own" it through boundaries in the form of landscape markers, pastures, fields, and villages. In this way, the uncontrolled land or wilderness of the hunter-gatherers came to be viewed in the minds of settled folk either as "free" for the taking or as a threat to their existence.

"One of the most important developments in the existence of human society was the successful shift from a subsistence economy based on foraging to one primarily based on food production derived from cultivated plants and domesticated animals."[14] Being able to grow one's own food was a substantial hedge against hunger and thus proved to be the impetus for settlement, which in turn became the foundation of civilization. Farming gave rise to social planning as once-nomadic tribes settled down and joined cooperative forces. Irrigation arose in response to the need of supporting growing populations—and so the discipline of agriculture was born. Around 5,000 BCE, the first cities were constructed in the southern part of the long valley, near the Persian Gulf, by an intelligent, resourceful, and energetic people who became known as the Sumerians. The Sumerians gradually extended their civilization northward over the decades to become the first great empire—Mesopotamia, the name given to this geographical area by the ancient Greeks, meaning "land between two rivers."[15]

Evidence indicates this early irrigation farming was accomplished through communally organized labor to construct and maintain the canals, which necessitated the scheduling of daily activities beyond individual households. Nevertheless, to support the inevitable increase in the local population required an economy in which farming was combined with hunting and gathering. The commitment to agriculture was more than simply the transition to a sedentary life structured around sustainable, small-scale production of food; it was also the commitment to a set of decisions and responses that resulted in fundamental organizational changes in society, increased risks and uncertainties, and shifts in social roles as a result of the dependence on irrigation technology.[16]

As indicated by the necessity of scheduling daily activities beyond individual households, agriculture brought with it both a sedentary way of life and a permanent change in the flow of living. Whereas the daily life of a hunter-gatherer was a seamless whole, a farmer's life became divided into *home* (rest) and *field* (work). While a hunter-gatherer had intrinsic value as a human being with respect to the community, a farmer's sense of self-worth became extrinsic, both personally and with respect to the community as symbolized by, and permanently attached to, "productivity"—a measure based primarily on how hard the farmer worked and thus the quantity of goods or services produced. In addition, the sedentary life of a farmer changed the notion of "property."

So, the dawn of agriculture, which ultimately gave birth to civilizations, created another powerful, albeit unconscious, bias in the human psyche. For the first time, humans saw themselves as clearly distinct—in their reasoning at least—from and superior to the rest of Nature. They therefore began to consider themselves as masters of, rather than members of, Nature's community of life. It seems that farmers had a mindset that was antibiodiversity from the beginning—an attitude that still prevails among the world's farmers of today. In fact, wild Nature, humankind's millennial life support system, suddenly came to be seen as a fierce competitor—a perpetual enemy to be vanquished when possible and subjugated when not.[17]

Until fairly recently, historically speaking, property in Britannia, as early England was known, was a matter of possessing the right to use land and its resources, and most areas had some kind of shared rights. Today the land itself is considered to be property, and the words for the British shared rights of old have all but disappeared: *estovers* (the "right to collect firewood"), *pannage* (the "right to put one's pigs in the woods"), *turbary* (the "right to cut turf"), and *pescary* (the "commoner's right to catch fish") are no longer in the British vocabulary. Now, while the landowner's rights are almost absolute, the common people no longer have the right of access to most lands in England.[18]

Although a few cultures (such as Bedouin clans in the Middle Eastern deserts and the Lapland reindeer herders) still live lightly on the land, most of humanity leaves a heavy footprint, consuming nearly a quarter of the biophysical productivity of Earth. In fact, land use continually transforms the terrestrial surface of Earth, thereby resulting in changes within biogeochemical cycles and thus the ability of ecosystems to deliver services critical to human well-being.[19]

Thus, while the hunter-gatherers created the Commons Usufruct Law spontaneously in their living, it is today being progressively eroded by people, especially in the industrialized countries. To arrest this erosion, we must understand and accept that the quality of our individual lives depends on the collective outcome of our personal motives, decisions, and actions as they coalesce in the environment over time, particularly with respect to our common inheritance.

It is today increasingly critical for us in the technological society we are creating globally both to understand and to accept that the Commons Usufruct Law and its governing principles are subordinate to the biophysical principles of the cosmic law of unification. And, just as the biophysical principles are inviolate in their governance of Nature, so the social principles of the Commons Usufruct Law are inviolate in their governance of a functional society in which long-term, social-environmental sustainability is the requisite outcome.

Social Principles of Engagement in a Sustainable Society

So what, at this juncture, can we, as a society, *relearn* from the hunter-gath-erers? We can relearn to live by the principles of social behavior embod-ied in the Commons Usufruct Law—principles that grew as unplanned, individual behaviors that simply emerged from a life epitomized by the continual novelty of reciprocal relationships between humans and Nature over the millennia. We say relearn because, as writer Carlo Levi once said, "the future has an ancient heart."[20]

Principle 1: Sharing Life's Experiences Connects Us to One Another

We are compelled to share our life experiences with one another as best we can to know we exist and have value, despite the fact that we are for-ever well and truly alone with each and every thought, each and every experience, and the emotion it evokes in our personal journey from birth through death.[21] And the best way to share experiences is by working together and taking care of one another along the way, which, inciden-tally, is the price of social-environmental sustainability.

Principle 2: Cooperation and Coordination Are the Bedrock of Sustaining the Social-Environmental Commons

When we couple cooperation and coordination with sharing and caring, it precludes the perceived need to compete for survival and social status, except in play—and perhaps storytelling. Linking individual well-being strictly to individual production is the road to competition, which in turn leads inevitably to social inequality, poverty, and environmental degrada-tion. Self-centeredness and acquisitiveness are not inherent traits of our species but rather acquired traits based on a sense of fear and insecu-rity within our social setting, which fosters the perceived need of our ego to impress others with our personal prowess, which means that more is always better and *enough* does not exist.

The separation of work from the rest of life, which began centuries ago with the inception of agriculture, is today fully manifested. Jobs are so fundamental to people's sense of identity and class distinction within the social hierarchy that many become severely depressed when they lose their jobs. Moreover, the competitive marketplace of today, in which people are "bought" and "sold" at the economic convenience of busi-nesses and corporations, is a breeding ground for stress-related illnesses due to the uncertainty and unpredictability of everyday life over which people feel increasingly out of control. Long-term stress not only wears down the body but also initiates the potential for high blood pressure, heart disease, mood disorders, and chronic pain brought on by relentless muscle tension.[22]

Principle 3: The Art of Living Lies in How We Practice Relationships

The art of living lies in how we practice relationships—beginning with ourselves—because practicing relationships is all we ever do in life. Wisdom dictates, therefore, that we live leisurely, which means to afford the necessary amount of time to engage fully each thought we have, each decision we make, each task we perform, and each person with whom we converse to fulfill the total capacity of a relationship for a quality experience. We learn to live fully in the measure in which we learn to live leisurely, a sentiment echoed by Henry David Thoreau: "The really efficient laborer will be found not to crowd his day with work, but will saunter to his task surrounded by a wide halo of ease and leisure."[23] If one lives leisurely, all aspects of life blend into a seamless whole in which contentment and joy can be found. In this sense, everyone can be a lifelong artist if he or she so chooses.

Principle 4: Success or Failure Lies in the Interpretation of an Event

On the one hand, all relationships are self-reinforcing feedback loops that in Nature are neutral in valuation because Nature has only intrinsic value. On the other hand, these same self-reinforcing feedback loops carry either a positive or a negative accent in human valuation because we want specific, predetermined outcomes to give us the illusion of being in control of circumstances. This human dynamic is the same as that driving the notion of success or failure, with each the interpretation of an event—but not the event itself.

I (Chris) was asked by a community in northern California to mediate their conflict over how to "restore" their river to its previous condition. During the process, some of the long-time, older residents began lamenting how "newcomers" into "their" valley had destroyed "their" river through years of overuse and abuse. Finally, a youth in his late teens, who had been in juvenile detention, spoke up and said, in effect: "I don't know what you are talking about. I've been working for three years with a crew to improve the river's condition. The river is so much better than when I started. What's your problem?"

Although the only thing the old-timers could see was the loss of what, to them, had been a "pristine condition," the boy perceived a vast improvement in a short period of time. The success or failure of the efforts to heal the river was perceived differently, depending on the individual's life experiences. In this case, the old-timers constantly reinforced their collective grief over the *negative* changes for which they blamed others, whereas the

boy was encouraged by his ability to nudge change in a *positive* direction—
to which the old-timers were blind but for which he took responsibility.

Principle 5: There Is More Beauty and Peace than Ugliness and Cruelty

There is more beauty and peace in the world than ugliness and cruelty.
In the end, it is a matter of what we choose to focus on—the beauty and
kindness that surround us if only we look for it *or* the large spoonful of
fear fed to us daily by the media. As Francis Bacon put it, "The best part
of beauty is that which no picture can express."[24] Even in the midst of
war, beauty exists in a smile, a hug, caring for a child, and the ever-fresh
face of a flower. In essence, ordinary people are motivated primarily by
their inner harmony and balance, which is expressed through their sense
of aesthetics.

Principle 6: People Must Be Equally Informed If They Are to Function as a Truly Democratic Society

For a group of people to be socially functional, they must be equally
informed about what is going on that affects them; in other words, there
must be no secrets that are actually or potentially detrimental to any
member. Inequality of any kind based on gender or social class is merely
fear of inadequacy disguised as privilege.

Principle 7: We Must Consciously Limit Our "Wants"

By consciously limiting our "wants," we can have enough to fulfill our
necessities as well as some of our most ardent desires comfortably —and
leave more for other people to do the same. In essence, there are two
ways to wealth: want less or work more. Unfortunately, the capitalistic
system of economics is based on dissatisfaction and a continual stimulus
to purchase superfluous items at the risk of personal debt, the long-term
expense of the environment, and thus growing impoverishment for all
future generations.

Principle 8: Every Decision Is the Author of a Never-Ending Story of Cause and Effect

With every act we consummate, we become the authors of a never-ending story, a mystery novel of everlasting change in the world. This is so
because every cause has an effect, and every effect is the cause of yet
another effect, ad infinitum.

Principle 9: Simplicity Is the Key to Contentment, Adaptability, and Survival

Any fool can complicate life, but it requires genius to keep things simple. Simplicity in living and dying depends on and seeks things small, sublime, and sustainable. What is more, simplicity is the key to contentment, adaptability, and survival as a culture; beyond some point, complexity becomes a decided disadvantage with respect to cultural longevity, just as it is to the evolutionary longevity of a species. As artist Hans Hoffman puts it, "The ability to simplify means to eliminate the unnecessary so that the necessary may speak."[25]

Principle 10: Marvel at the Abundance and Resilience of Earth

The notion of scarcity is largely an economic construct to foster consumerism and increase profits but is not necessarily an inherent part of human nature. We need to overcome our fear of economically contrived scarcity and marvel instead at the incredible abundance and resilience of Earth and our sacred duty to protect it for all generations.

Principle 11: Only Mobile Property Can Be Owned Outright

Mobile property can be owned, whereas such fixed property as land, which can be borrowed long term, is to be shared equally through rights of generational use. In other words, a person can borrow land as a trustee but cannot personally own land to the detriment of any generation. After all, no human being on Earth can create land. Thus, no human has the right to degrade or destroy that which they cannot create and all coming generations must use.

Principle 12: Nature, Spirituality, and Human Well-Being Are Paramount

Placing material wealth, as symbolized by the money chase, above Nature, spirituality, and human well-being is the road to social impoverishment, environmental degradation, and the collapse of societies and their life support systems.

Principle 13: Every Legal Citizen Deserves the Right to Vote

Every legal citizen of every country deserves the right to an equal vote of their conscience on how their country is to be governed because they and their children and their children's children must live with the consequences of the collective choices and actions.

Principle 14: We Must Choose—In That, We Have No Choice

Here, the abiding paradox of life is that we have a choice in everything we think and almost everything we do—except practicing relationships, experiencing ourselves as we experience relationships, choosing, changing the world, living without killing, and dying. In those we have *no* choice of what we do, but we *do* have a choice of how we do it—and we *must* choose because not to choose *is still a choice*. In addition, we make a new choice (even if it is doing nothing) each time a circumstance in our life changes, which, of course, is an ongoing process, be it the outworking of biophysical principles that govern life or how we view the life changes as we mature in years.

The constancy of change dictates the omnipresence of choice. Life can therefore be viewed as an eternal plethora of decisions, each of which is a fork in the path we follow. Each time a decision is made, others are forgone. Nevertheless, each decision creates a kaleidoscope of additional choices. In turn, choice is the author of both wisdom and folly, which manifest as the consequences of our decisions and actions. This last statement is particularly relevant, as Israeli statesman Abba Eban observes: "History teaches us that men and nations behave wisely once they have exhausted all other alternatives."[26]

Choices always have effects in the form of trade-offs and consequences that become the causes of still other effects, and so on. Some of the consequences of our choices we may not like, but we must choose just the same because not to choose is still a choice. In this sense, everything we think and do has a trade-off of positive *and* negative consequences at the time a thought is formed, a decision is made, and a choice of action is taken. Hence, each choice is a trade-off of hoped-for outcomes amid the unknowns and uncertainties of life. So it is day in and day out.

Principle 15: We Change the World Simply Because We Exist

As an inseparable part of Nature, we have no choice but to change the world in our living simply because we exist and use the energy of the world to survive. We do, however, have a choice in selecting the level of consciousness with which we treat our environment in the reciprocal relationships of life and living.

Principle 16: We Must Kill To Live

We must eat to live. To eat means we must kill or cause to be killed—whether plant or animal. If we choose not to eat in order not to kill, we kill ourselves through starvation. Therefore, we have no choice but to kill. Nevertheless, we do have a choice in the level of conscious awareness with which we kill and the suffering we create in the process.

Principle 17: This Present Moment, the Here and Now, Is All We Ever Have

The present moment is all we ever have in which to act. The past is a memory, and the future never comes. *Now* is the eternal moment.

These social principles of engagement are enshrined in everyday life, whether we recognize them or not. Moreover, they form the basis of how Carol and I practice the mediation of conflicts.

References

1. The foregoing discussion of being alone is from Chris Maser. *Of Paradoxes and Metaphors: Understanding Some of Life's Lessons*. Woven Strings Publishing, Amarillo, TX (2008). E-Book 254KB.
2. Carl Sagan. Quotation. http://www.firstscience.com/home/poems-and-quotes/quotes/carl-sagan-quote_2284.html (accessed January 2, 2009).
3. Jonathan Rowe. The hidden commons. *Yes! A Journal of Positive Futures*, Summer (2001):12–17.
4. Krakatoa. http://en.wikipedia.org/wiki/Krakatoa (accessed March 13, 2010).
5. Constitutional Law Foundation. Intergenerational Justice in the United States Constitution, the Stewardship Doctrine. http://www.conlaw.org/Intergenerational-II-2.htm (accessed March 13, 2010).
6. Random House. *Webster's Unabridged Dictionary*. Random House, New York (1999).
7. Mike Fritz. Pastureland survey shows lease rates still climbing. *Beef Magazine*. http://beefmagazine.com/cowcalfweekly/pastureland-survey-lease-rates/ (accessed January 8, 2009).
8. U.S. Legal. Definitions. http://definitions.uslegal.com/u/usufruct/ (accessed January 1, 2009).
9. The foregoing discussion is based on Richard B. Lee. Forward. In: *Limited Wants, Unlimited Means*, John Gowdy (ed.), pp. ix–xii. Island Press, Washington, DC, 1998.
10. The foregoing discussion is based on (a) Lee, Forward; and (b) John Gowdy. Introduction. In: *Limited Wants, Unlimited Means*, John Gowdy (ed.), pp. xv–xxix. Island Press, Washington, DC, 1998.
11. (a) Gowdy, Introduction; and (b) Marshall Sahlins. *The Original Affluent Society*. In: *Limited Wants, Unlimited Means*, John Gowdy (ed.), pp. 5–41. Island Press, Washington, DC, 1998.
12. The foregoing two paragraphs are based on Rebecca Adamson. People who are Indigenous to the Earth. *YES! A Journal of Positive Futures*, Winter (1997):26–27.
13. Gowdy, Introduction.

14. Tom D. Dillehay, Herbert H. Eling, Jr., and Jack Rossen. Preceramic irrigation canals in the Peruvian Andes. *Proceedings of the National Academy of Sciences of the United States of America,* 102 (2005):17241–17244.
15. The preceding two paragraphs are based on (a) Stacey Y. Abrams. The land between two rivers: the astronomy of ancient Mesopotamia. *The Electronic Journal of the Astronomical Society of the Atlantic,* 3(no. 2) (1991); and (2) The Fertile Crescent. http://visav.phys.uvic.ca/~babul/AstroCourses/P303/mesopotamia.html (accessed January 7, 2009).
16. The preceding two paragraphs are based on Dillehay et al., Preceramic irrigation canals.
17. Wolfgang Haber. Energy, food, and land—the ecological traps of humankind. *Environmental Science and Pollution Research,* 14 (2007):359–365.
18. George Monbiot. Land reform in Britain. *Resurgence,* 181 (1997):4–8.
19. Helmut Haberl, K. Heinz Erb, Fridolin Krausmann, and others. Quantifying and mapping the human appropriation of net primary production in earth's terrestrial ecosystems. *Proceedings of the National Academy of Sciences of the United States of America,* 104 (2007):12942–12947.
20. Leonard W. Moss. Observations on "The Day of the Dead" in Catania, Sicily. *The Journal of American Folklore,* 76 (1963):134–135.
21. Maser. *Of Paradoxes and Metaphors.*
22. Radha Chitale. Job Loss Can Make You Sick. http://abcnews.go.com/Business/WellnessNews/story?id=7530730&page=1 (accessed June 1, 2009).
23. Odell Shepard. *The Heart of Thoreau's Journals.* Courier Dover, New York (1961).
24. Francis Bacon. http://Science.prodos.org (accessed January 2, 2009).
25. Quotes by Hans Hoffman. http://quotationsbook.com/author/3495/ (accessed January 7, 2009).
26. Abba Eban. Quotation. http://www.quotationspage.com/quote/298.html (accessed January 10, 2009).

5

The Human Equation

Introduction

In any mediation process, people must be thought of and treated as though they are equal and deserving of love, trust, respect, and social-environmental justice, which asserts that we owe something to every other person sharing the planet with us, both those present and those yet unborn. But, you may ask, what exactly do we have to give? The only things we have of value are the love, trust, respect, and wisdom gleaned from our experiences embodied in each choice we pass forward. And it is exactly because options embody all we have to give those living today and the children of tomorrow and beyond that social-environmental justice as a concept must fit within the context of human equality.

It must therefore be understood that the resolution of any environmental dispute will in some way affect the next generation—for good or ill. In this sense, a decision in the present always represents a circumstance in the future, and if it bodes ill, it is analogous to taxation without representation. Each party must therefore be aware of how its decision will affect future generations.

If you wonder whether we even need to be concerned about the future, remember that adults are responsible for bringing children into the world. We are thus also responsible for being their voice and for protecting their options until the time when they can speak and act responsibly for themselves.

It has been our experience, however, that many people seem not to be overly concerned about what social-environmental circumstances future generations will inherit. Chris has heard it asked, for example, "Why can't these changes wait until I've retired? Then someone else can worry about them."

Whether people are concerned about future generations depends on the way they grew up and the family values they learned. How we learned to cope with circumstances as children influences how we treat one another as adults. Society is thus as peaceful or combative as we are as individuals.

The more a person is drawn toward peace and an optimistic view of the future, the more functional (psychologically healthy) he or she is. The more a person is drawn toward debilitating, destructive conflict, cynicism, and pessimism about the future, the more dysfunctional (psychologically unhealthy) that individual is.

To change anything in society, therefore, we must first look inward to confront, understand, and change ourselves, especially if we are going to act as a mediator in helping others to confront their fears and resolve their destructive conflicts. This process of self-evaluation and change puts the battle where it really belongs—within our own heart. As such, our inner struggles are the greatest learning experiences we will ever have. In addition, the greater our understanding of our own behavioral dynamics, of our own unresolved fears and pain, the easier it is for us to understand these dynamics in others and thus introduce compassion into the mediation of a conflict and wisdom into a vision created for the future.

Facilitating the resolution of a conflict requires a basic understanding of those family dynamics that shape us as individuals. We therefore discuss familial dysfunction as openly and honestly as we can, which means that we must at times tap into our own familial dysfunction while growing up. This is important, because to be a good mediator, we must risk being an imperfect human. We must be open, honest, and vulnerable, and we must have the courage to work continuously and seriously on healing our own dysfunctions.

Our experience has been that we probably never really leave our families; we take them with us wherever we go throughout the rest of our lives. We take not only our families, both emotionally and intellectually, but also our familial heritage.

However, Carol encountered a vivid example of the myth many people have of a common experience among families. During a particularly tense conflict, a colleague said, "I'm sure you were raised to say 'sir' and 'ma'am' to your parents, just like I was." Although Carol did not respond immediately, the comment stuck with her because she was not raised saying sir and ma'am. In fact, she risked punishment if she referred to her mother as ma'am. Because such titles are reserved for the elderly in her family, her mother considered such a formality to be an insult and often said, "I'm not your grandmother!"

We sometimes make the assumption that our family experience is a common one, in that other families are just like ours. It is sometimes difficult to imagine since we only know our own experiences, our own perceptual "truths," just how different our individual truths can be. After all, *our perception is our truth*, which means everyone—*everyone*—is right from his or her point of view.

That said, however, we must always remember that, while we all take our families with us, it does not mean we have had a common or shared experience because each of us was raised differently, within a different culture, and with unique experiences—even within the same family. If we want to be successful at implementing environmental projects and

policies, we must put aside our assumptions and learn to deal with *every-one* as equally as humanly possible.

Thus molded in the family template in an unknown and unknowable Universe, the most consistently pressing existential questions since the dawn of humanity have probably been: "Who am I?" and "What value do I have in the immensity of the ever-changing Unknown and Unknowable?" These are the fundamental questions we indirectly help the combatants to address whenever we mediate the resolution of a conflict.

First, however, we must have some understanding of family dynamics because every conflict we have ever mediated was very much like stepping as a stranger into a family feud. Therefore, we begin sharing what we have learned about family dynamics by looking at the gift of a child, that little person whose psychic slate is initially untouched by socialized behaviors.

A Child's Gift

Childhood, the tender age during which we are taught to compete and fight, is the age in which the need for peacefully resolving conflicts is born. Thus, as facilitators we must understand how life, which today may seem like deadly grapple to many people, replaces childhood innocence and creative possibilities through the tutelage of parents, peers, schools, culture, and society.

To the Indian poet Rabindranath Tagore, "Every child comes with the message that God is not yet discouraged of man."[1] Each child offers his or her parents and society another chance to learn the meaning of love, to explore the boundaries of selflessness, to rediscover the possibilities of innocence, and to help us define who we are. Each child is a holy canvas on which we paint our loves and our fears, our joys and our sorrows, and a thousand other perceptions we hold to be ourselves.

According to Buckminster Fuller, American architect and inventor, "Every child is a genius but is enslaved by the misconceptions and self-doubts of the adult world and spends much of his or her life having to unlearn that perspective."[2] Thus, each child becomes the outward manifestation of the inner, adult self, for in the children of the world we see ourselves reflected. We, who are an imprint of our parental templates, have become the templates who will imprint ourselves on our children. And what can we give them? "There are only two lasting bequests," according to Hodding Carter, "[that] we can hope to give our children. One of these is roots; the other wings."[3]

To this end, Dr. Edward Bach penned a beautiful paragraph on the ideal essence of parenthood:

> Parenthood is a sacred duty, temporary in its character and passing from generation to generation. It carries with it nothing but service and calls for no obligation in return from the young, since they must be left free to develop in their own way and become as fitted as possible to fulfill the same office in but a few years' time.[4]

As children, we are molded in the template of our parentage, our peers, and our social environment, just as our parents were similarly molded. Too often the result is that the precious gift with which each child comes into the world—innocence mirrored in spontaneous joy, aliveness, and creativity without preconceptions or limitations—is not recognized, not acceptable, and not accepted.

Our innocence, which manifests itself as unbounded imagination, is stolen from us, often quietly and unobtrusively, through all sorts of external pressures to conform, because we need to fit in rather than be something new, challenging, and exciting. Yet it still seems to us that life is intended as a process of learning, a grand adventure, rather than a terror to be survived.

Nevertheless, however we turn out as adults, we are our family. And, unless we consciously choose otherwise, we take our family with us wherever we go, through our personal philosophy and through our behavior.

We Take Our Family with Us

Taking our family with us emotionally and psychologically is an important notion to understand as a mediator because we are inescapably our families to some degree. It is quite likely that the clearest thing participants bring to the arena of conflict is their familial upbringing. They are so entangled in their familial heritages that they seldom can separate their dysfunctional behaviors from the ecological and social principles over which they fight. Helping the combatants make this distinction is our task as mediators.

A word of caution is necessary here. While the behaviors exhibited by the disputants toward one another are often condemnable, the person perpetrating the behavior is doing the very best he or she is capable of at that moment and must be accepted with compassion—never condemned as a person.

It is not our intent to delve into a clinical discussion of family systems; excellent books on the subject are available. A brief overview of some dysfunctional familial dynamics is provided, however, because, as Mother

Teresa says, "In the home begins the disruption of the peace of the world."[5] Understanding dysfunctional familial dynamics is therefore critical to good mediation.

Dysfunctional Family Dynamics Lead to Ongoing Destructive Conflict

Dysfunctional behavior often leads to conflict, and thus it is absolutely necessary for us, as mediators, to understand dysfunction since the more dysfunctional a person is, the more inclined he or she is toward conflict. Mediation is therefore a process by which we help the combatants to break their dysfunctional cycle of destructive behavior consciously so they can resolve their conflict. To be a good mediator, however, we must work seriously on resolving *our own dysfunctional behaviors.*

Only when we are free of our own dysfunctional familial patterns can we really be open to the humility, spontaneity, and creativity demanded by the mediation process. Only then can we offer the understanding, insight, and empathy necessary to lead and communicate effectively. Each person's story is the same in principle, but differs in detail.

First, know thyself. Mediation is a skill that is critical to our success as environmental leaders and caretakers. But how are we to learn to help others if we are unaware of our own dysfunctional behaviors? Carol, for example, has participated in an advanced leadership program that emphasized the self-awareness and personal development, which are critical to gaining the skills for both mediation and negotiation.

Learning about your personality is a good start, but discerning how you are perceived by others and how to modify your own dysfunctional behavior is much more valuable to you as a mediator. If, for instance, you find yourself in conflicts that leave you wondering how you got there, then we strongly suggest that you consider furthering your personal growth. Becoming self-aware is one way to grow beyond the child and family situation of your past and become the psychologically mature adult you truly wish to be.

We are the strengths and the weaknesses of our upbringings because we all go through similar dynamics in various forms as we come into, grow up in, and leave our families. We thus tend to repeat the patterns—whether they are functional or dysfunctional—over and over again unless we consciously break an unwanted cycle. To break a dysfunctional cycle, one must first understand homeostasis.

Homeostasis Is Designed to Hide Dysfunction

It is critical that we, as mediators, understand homeostasis and homeostatic mechanisms because, just as each dysfunctional family has its own set of mechanisms, each party of combatants within a given conflict has its own. And each party's set is fashioned through an unconscious forging of the individual members' familial patterns into one collective pattern—that of the combatant party.

Homeostasis is the maintenance of a dynamic equilibrium within a system, such as a family. A family is a system governed by a set of rules that determine and control the interaction of its members in organized, established patterns. The family rules are a set of directives concerning what shall and shall not occur within and outside the family. Homeostatic mechanisms maintain the ongoing arrangement among family members by activating the rules defining each member's relationship to the whole.

My (Chris's) father, for instance, could not control the imperfections in his family no matter how hard he tried because they were really the imperfections he perceived within himself, which he transferred or projected onto the family. In turn, his perception of our imperfections triggered his abusive behavior, and his abusive behavior was the secret skeleton in our family closet.

My (Chris's) family probably appeared to be quite "normal" on the surface. Seen through knowledgeable eyes, however, which could have interpreted the symptoms I acted out as a child away from home, the red flag of abuse would have been readily apparent.

Dysfunction and homeostasis are therefore self-perpetuating, self-reinforcing feedback loops founded on coercion and fear. My (Chris's) father was abusive, and that would have drawn criticism. To avoid the criticism, we were all assigned roles to play, which kept the dynamic equilibrium in the family within acceptable bounds; this in turn kept the dysfunction within the family while giving the outward appearance of normalcy.

The roles we were assigned were to be the perfect son, daughter, wife and mother—according to my father's definitions. This was particularly important as far as his public image was concerned. If the homeostasis began to crumble, so would his perception of other people's perceptions of the family image, of his image, and that was an unacceptable threat to my father's sense of survival. And yet he did his level best under the circumstances of his abandonment at an early age and subsequent upbringing in an orphanage until the age of 15, when he was finally adopted.

At this same juncture stand the combatants in every environmental dispute, feeling an unacceptable threat to their survival. As prisoners of their familial upbringing, they are searching, albeit often unknowingly, for appropriate behavioral boundaries within which to feel safe.

Boundaries, the Silent Language

Boundaries are those lines of silent language that allow a person to communicate with others while simultaneously protecting the integrity of one's own personal space as well as the personal spaces of those with whom one interacts.

The language of boundaries transcends individual space to include familial space, cultural space, and even national space. Understanding personal boundaries during meditation among individuals of the same culture is difficult enough, but expanding that concept into a fluid working ability among different cultures is most difficult to accomplish. This is especially true in other countries, where mediation may be done through a translator in a language one can neither understand nor speak.

A simple way of looking at boundaries is the adage "good fences make good neighbors." As an example, consider cliff swallows, which attach their mud nests to such surfaces as the faces of cliffs, the sides of buildings, and the undersides of bridges. These enclosed, globular nests share common walls, which not only strengthen the nests but also keep the peace by preventing the inhabitants from peeking into each other's abodes. If, however, a hole is made in the common wall and the swallows can see each other, they bicker and squabble until the hole is repaired, which immediately restores tranquility.

A more complicated way of dealing with physical boundaries is to compare them to the home ranges and territories of animals. A home range is that area of the habitat of an animal in which it ranges freely throughout the course of its normal activity and in which it is free to mingle with others of its kind. A territory, in contrast, is that part of the home range of an animal that it defends, for whatever reason, against others of its kind. This defensive behavior is most exaggerated and noticeable during the breeding season of an animal.

How does this concept apply to us? Suppose it is Saturday morning, and you leave your home to take care of a few errands. You simply go about your business without paying much attention to what is going on around you or to the people you pass unless you happen to meet someone you know. In general, you are simply engrossed in what you are doing. When you have finished your errands, you start home.

The closer you get to your neighborhood, the more alert you unconsciously become to changes around you, such as the new people moving in two blocks away. This "protective feeling" becomes even more acute as you approach the area of your own home and notice a car with an out-of-state license plate parked in your neighbor's driveway. You get out of your car and immediately notice, perhaps with some irritation, that the neighbor's dog has visited your lawn again while you were gone. If your neighbor's dog had anointed someone else's yard with its leavings, you probably would have paid no attention.

The same general pattern extends into your home. Inside your home, how well you know someone and how comfortable you feel around them determine the freedom with which they may interact with you and your family and use your house. You are the most particular about your ultimate private space, your physical being.

For example, an unwanted salesperson may not be allowed inside your home. A casual acquaintance, on the other hand, may be allowed in the living room and to use the guest bathroom but is not allowed to wander about the house without permission. If one of your children's friends comes over, the friend may be allowed into the living room, kitchen, family room, guest bathroom, and your children's rooms (but only with both your and your children's permission) but are not allowed into your room or your bathroom. At times, even your children may not be allowed in your room without your permission or perhaps you in theirs.

As you return home after a Saturday morning of errands, the closer you get to your home, the more you notice what is going on and the more observant and protective you become. Inside your home, the closer you get to your own room, and beyond that to your physical person, which represents your ultimate territory, the more clearly and carefully you define your boundaries. The reverse is in effect, however, as you leave your room and go into the rest of your house or your neighborhood, which represents your home range.

Although this dynamic may function in a "normal" manner for strangers, it often becomes so blurred among the members of a dysfunctional family that personal boundaries, including the physical body itself, are violated. In some families, appropriate personal boundaries are all but absent. This dysfunctional trait is usually carried into the arena of environmental conflict.

It is therefore our task both to set the behavioral boundaries as rules of conduct, which not only are the infrastructure of society but also make the mediation process work, and to make sure that all participants understand and respect them. Understanding and respecting boundaries helps to build and maintain trust. This is critically important because interpersonal boundaries are an absolute social necessity of communication.

Let us look at a few concrete examples, beginning with the mediator. The most important interpersonal boundary for us as mediators to maintain is that of a guest at all times because we serve at the participants' behest. By staying within "guest boundaries," we are nonthreatening and can create and maintain a safe environment within which the participants can struggle to communicate. This means that we must never crack a joke or allow anyone else to do so because every joke is at the expense of someone or something, which can only be insulting.

One of the more important behavioral contracts that we make with the participants is to listen to one another without interrupting. If necessary, a "talking stick" is passed from person to person as they speak. The talking stick signifies the right of the holder to speak and the obligation of everyone else to listen in silence. This is imperative because waiting one's turn is part and parcel of civility and equality, both of which are prerequisites for a safe environment.

In our experience, ground rules are best developed and agreed on by the group. This agreement not only is important to maintain order but also is one of the first decisions that the group will make together. As such, it is important for us as mediators to recognize that the process of establishing ground rules may set the tone for all future group interactions. Examples of ground rules are the following:

1. Meetings begin and end on time.
2. One person speaks at a time (the talking stick example).
3. Listen respectfully when someone else has the floor.
4. Speak only for yourself.
5. Understand that everyone is "right" from his or her point of view—thus viewpoints are "right, right, and different," with difference being negotiable.
6. Value and respect all perspectives.
7. Treat everyone with respect.
8. No personal attacks are allowed.
9. Discuss issues, not positions.
10. Instead of dwelling on past failed efforts, focus on working toward a positive future.
11. If uncomfortable with a decision or direction, speak up.

These are merely examples, but it is easy to see how ground rules set the tone for the discussions and negotiations to come.

Although setting ground rules may sound fairly simple, learning to understand boundaries is often complicated by the various "coping mechanisms" through which we as children learn to survive and with which combatants attempt to quell their fears while dealing with one another. These mechanisms comprise a part of everyone's personality characteristics and as such are important for us to understand because they are often the key to unlocking the stubborn discord of conflict.

Coping Mechanisms: Unconscious Thoughts That Manifest as Recognizable Behaviors

Coping mechanisms, first deciphered and named "defense mechanisms" by Sigmund Freud, who developed psychoanalysis, begin as thought processes we devise to protect ourselves from that which we deem dangerous to our well-being. What begins as a thought manifests as a behavior when we are confronted with the perceived life-threatening circumstance from which the thought process was originally devised to protect us. If the combination of thought and action is successful, then we have devised a functional mechanism of survival, a coping mechanism, which increasingly becomes a self-reinforcing feedback loop every time it works as we expect it to work. As we begin to use it automatically, the thought process is relegated to our subconscious, and only the behavioral pattern is manifested.

Coping mechanisms therefore become the unconscious behavioral devices we learn to use to help us retain or regain control in uncomfortable situations. This really means we are trying to cope with a universe in constant change.

Coping mechanisms as a strategy for survival are often functional, positive, and entirely appropriate for a given circumstance when we develop them, but they eventually can and often do become outmoded and dysfunctional as circumstances change. Clinging to dysfunctional coping mechanisms when they fail to meet current or new situations in life can lead to a hardening of attitudes, a hardening of the heart, and create a rigidity that leads to destructive conflict.

Because dysfunctional coping mechanisms involve self-deception and a distortion of reality, they do not resolve problems; they only alleviate symptoms. Moreover, since they operate on a relatively unconscious level, they are not subject to the normal checks and balances of conscious awareness.

Coping mechanisms—we all have them. Although there is a vast array of coping mechanisms, only a few of the more common ones are discussed here. It is important that we, as individuals, consider those coping mechanisms that we use most and make an effort to recognize them—and control them—before they jeopardize our efforts. James Tamm and Ronald Luyet provide a list of 50 signs of defensiveness in their book, *Radical Collaboration* (p. 44).[6] According to Tamm and Luyet, "Defensiveness does not defend [one] from others but arises to protect us from experiencing our own uncomfortable feelings."[7] Carol has used this tool many times, both personally and as a teaching tool, to help students and colleagues identify their own defense mechanisms. Instead of the warning, "Don't do this at home," I strongly recommend that you take this list to work, to your spouse or partner, and to friends and explore with them your own defense mechanisms. I think you will see quickly that we all use many defense or coping mechanisms. This is not only a humbling experience but also a key to building the self-awareness needed to be an effective environmental mediator. Recognizing that we share the same or similar coping mechanisms is just one more reminder that we are all human and, as such, do the best we can at all times.

Keep in mind that the point of this discussion is *not* that coping mechanisms are bad or that we need to rid ourselves of our particular tactics for coping with life. Coping mechanisms are not clearly defined, separable behavioral patterns, but rather are overlapping behaviors, which grade into and out of one another almost at will. It is thus the awareness, the consciousness, with which we observe our behavior and that of others that is at issue. Therefore, we must ask ourselves with compassion and forthrightness: Does this behavior and its underlying motivation best serve my present needs in life?

We do not dwell on the coping mechanisms per se, but rather give brief examples to illustrate how they are used because they form the backbone of the thrust and parry of conflict. As such, it is absolutely necessary for us to understand coping mechanisms because the more functional a person is, the more inclined the person is toward peace; conversely, the more dysfunctional a person is, the more inclined the person is toward conflict.

Recognizing and understanding the language of coping mechanisms, especially dysfunctional ones, are vital in understanding a person's family dynamics and how that person deals with life. It is thus a critical step in understanding the dynamics of a conflict and how to help the combatants resolve their differences with dignity. As you read the following descriptions, you might think of examples from your own life and family upbringing.

Anger and Aggression

Anger and aggression are discussed together because anger is the emotion that triggers aggression as the act. Anger is a feeling of extreme displeasure, hostility, indignation, or exasperation toward someone or something. Anger is extreme fear or frustration violently projected outward and is synonymous with being upset, feeling a minor irritation or an intense rage. It is a temporary insanity that isolates us from the facts, from ourselves, and from one another.

In addition, we (you and I) are not angry for the reason or at the person or thing we think we are. We are always angry at ourselves for being afraid of circumstances and therefore feeling out of control, which has nothing to do with the person or thing at which we level our anger.

Unfortunately, this realization all too often follows my (Chris's) anger, which I have attempted to project onto someone or something else. I also find that a minor irritation is of the same category as intense rage because the dynamic is the same; it is only a less-intense reaction on the same continuum. I feel internal disharmony, which is fear of a circumstance in which I feel a loss of control, and I am angry about feeling afraid of the circumstance.

Unless we (you and I) fully understand this dynamic, we think we are really angry for the reason or at the person or thing at which we level anger. We therefore use our anger as a means of *not* having to deal with the circumstance that really causes our fear. This often happens at meetings between agency representatives and the public. The latter often hear things with which they disagree and over which they have no control. Instead of listening calmly, they get angry and start yelling. Chris has, in fact, mediated meetings at which participants have been so charged with emotion that they became red in the face, yelled, cursed, and physically shook with rage.

I (Carol) have had many experiences with anger and aggression. It seems to come with the territory when you are wearing the uniform of a federal agency. One example from when I worked in West Virginia comes to mind. An older coal miner, who was quite agitated, came to a meeting about his permit application within National Park Service boundaries. As soon as he was introduced to me, he shouted in anger, "The lights come on when you hit the switch, don't they? You have coal to thank for that!" Although I had little time to assimilate his verbal attack and respond to it, with sincerity I did the most respectful thing I could think of: I quietly thanked him.

The Golden Rule must always apply in situations dominated by anger and aggression. Treat others in the way you would like to be treated. The angry coal miner was probably afraid he would be denied his permit and so lose something most dear to him—his livelihood. Instead, I was able to deflect his anger and show him respect, in spite of his outburst. As a result, he sat down at the table and became a perfect gentleman for the remaining time we had together.

In the intensity of the emotion, people often feel that they are right in projecting their anger onto those who seem to be in control, those who have "taken" control away from them. In the grip of their anger, they do not perceive that they have a choice because they feel a loss of control, which they find terrifying.

Anger usually translates into aggression, which, as it is used here, is the habit of launching attacks, of being hostile. If we (you and I) show enough aggression toward a person or persons at whom we think we are angry, then we are coping with our fear by causing the person or persons to back away from the threatening energy. Through aggression, we think we can avoid having to deal with the circumstance over which we have no control and of which we are frightened.

All we have really accomplished, however, is to isolate ourselves from any understanding of the data and from the people who are presenting it.

If, on the other hand, we are patient, open minded, and gently ask questions, then we might be able to overcome our fear and in so doing realize that there are no enemies out there—only other people who, like us, are frightened of the unknown.

Appraisal

Appraisal is the act of evaluating something; of estimating its quality, amount, size, and other features; of judging its merits. As such, appraisal is an interesting coping mechanism in that it can effectively prevent forward motion. It is like being the traveler on the platform at the train station who is so afraid of missing the train that he spends all his time checking and rechecking the schedule. He is so preoccupied evaluating the schedule that he does not even see the train come and go.

Another example of an overappraiser is the shopper who goes to the grocery store to buy three items and has to read every comparative label in minute detail and then weigh and reweigh the data before making a choice. Thus, what would take most people five minutes to buy takes such an appraiser forty-five minutes.

Appraisers cope with their fear of criticism by checking, rechecking, and further rechecking the data; they are seldom willing to make a decision for which they may be held accountable. When in doubt, they conduct another study, but refrain, at any cost, from *saying* or *doing* anything until all the data are collected and have been carefully and properly analyzed. This, of course, will never happen, because even if all the data could be collected, the appraiser would still continue the analysis indefinitely.

Carol, as a mediator, has often dealt with appraisers and finds moving them forward to be a challenge. Over the years, I (Carol) have heard appraisers say things like, "We need more data" and "We need to wait for Joe," even if they have ten years of data and Joe really has nothing to contribute to the situation. The question is: How do you sort out the real needs of the participants from the appraiser's fear of accountability and criticism?

One such project was the reclamation of a mine that I (Carol) managed in Virginia. The unusual thing about this project was the fact that the appraisers were members of my own management team. None of them had experience in mine reclamation, and they resisted every step of the project, claiming they were "not comfortable" with it—a typical appraiser comment.

To move them forward, I dealt with them individually by providing examples of successful projects elsewhere, giving them the contact information for mine reclamation specialists, and by finding published studies and articles that detailed the benefits of reclaiming abandoned mines. In the end, I also applied some pressure because the funding for our grant had specific timelines, which had to be met. It was the combination of providing data and access to experts, coupled with the incentive to retain our funding, that finally moved them past the limits of their comfort zone.

Over the years, I (Chris) have met many people who appraise their life away. Although I find them exceedingly difficult to work with when decisions need to be made, I feel deep compassion for them because I remember times in my boyhood when I also was too terrified to make a decision, knowing I would be humiliated, beaten, or both, no matter what I did.

Defensiveness

To be defensive means to protect that which already is; to resist a new view, to resist the possibility of change, and to resist the truth about oneself. Defensiveness limits your growth in that you argue for your old self rather than taking a new look and embracing a new possibility. You defend the rut in which your old belief, your old behavioral pattern is stuck. You become defensive because at some level you know that what is being said is at least partly true, and if you acknowledge that truth, you will have to act on it, which means changing your stance, something you are loathe to do. Thus, you feel obliged to defend the old groove. After all, it is a comfortable, known entity, like home.

Defense as a coping mechanism takes planning. A planned life can perhaps be tolerated but cannot be fully lived.

> The mind engaged in planning for itself is occupied in setting up control of future happenings. It does not think that it will be provided for, unless it makes its own provisions. Time becomes a future emphasis, to be controlled by learning and experience obtained from past events and previous beliefs. It overlooks the present, for it rests on the idea the past has taught enough to let the mind direct its future course.
>
> The mind that plans is thus refusing to allow for change. What it has learned before becomes the basis for its future goals. Its past experience directs its choice of what will happen. And it does not see that here and now is everything it needs to guarantee a future quite unlike the past, without a continuity of any old ideas and sick beliefs. Anticipation plays no part at all, for present confidence directs the way.
>
> Defenses are the plans you undertake to make against the truth. Their aim is to select what you approve, and disregard what you consider incompatible with your beliefs of your reality. Yet what remains is meaningless indeed. For it is your reality that is the "threat" which your defenses would attack, obscure, and take apart and crucify.[8]

Denial

Denial is a refusal to recognize the truth of a situation; it is a contradiction, a rejection of what is. Although denial as a coping mechanism is part and parcel of almost all other coping mechanisms, it is also an entity unto itself.

Think, for example, of your mind as the honeycomb in a beehive and visualize yourself stuffing your unwanted feelings into an empty comb and sealing it so you will not have to deal with them—out of sight, out of mind. You are now effectively in denial of your feelings. The rest of your mind seems to be cleared of your discomfort. You are free to live, but only as long as you can continually mend the combs already filled and continually create more combs to accommodate future discomfort.

Denial is one of the most pervasive coping mechanisms in the world. It is such a simple device that it is probably the great-great-grandparent of all coping mechanisms. The following is a typical example of denial: Speaking intently and quickly, the dark-haired, green-eyed young woman explained she had been sexually abused by a relative from the time she was five years old until she was fourteen. Although she had two miscarriages, her parents still refused to believe her, which means they were denying that anything improper had taken place.[9]

Displacement

Displacement as a coping mechanism is used to shift the focus from that which is uncomfortable to that which is safe; it is often referred to as a "smoke screen." Chris has had attorneys for the federal government try to distract him with this tactic while he was under oath as an expert witness; they did not want him to complete his answer to a question they had asked because they were afraid of what he was saying, so they interrupted and asked a totally unrelated question. Recognizing this tactic, however, he always completed his answer to the first question and then answered the displacement question.

Another way to cope with fear of losing control is to displace the real reason with the use of time. Some people have their lives so tightly scheduled that they *do not have a minute to waste.* They confuse motion and time constraints with productivity. In this way, they control what they do, who they see, and how long they see them without ever having to take responsibility for saying: "I don't want to see you because you make me uncomfortable," or "I don't want to see so and so because I'm afraid that I might fail, which I cannot handle right now."

People use time to control those circumstances they wish to deal with and to see those people they choose to see for as long as they want to see them. At the same time, they are pleading a case for being innocently out of time—out of control—for those circumstances or those people with which they do not want to deal.

One retired man Chris knew was so afraid of dying that he displaced his fear onto time; consequently, he had no time to waste. The sad thing was that he was so conscious of his time running out that he did not enjoy what he did because he never had time to do it. He always had to get on to the next thing. He raced time around his prison cell—his fear of dying—and literally wore himself out before his *time* might have been up. His coping mechanism had become his unconscious agent of indirect suicide.

Filters

A *filter* is a device through which a substance (such as light, water, or thought) is passed to remove "unwanted impurities." In the sense of a coping mechanism, people filter out unwanted material as a way to *accept* and *understand* whatever they want to accept and understand. For example, have you ever tried explaining something to someone and had them hear only part of it, the part they *wanted* to hear?

Chris has often found this to be the case when he speaks to a group of people composed of the timber industry, environmental organizations, and land management agencies. They each hear what they want to hear in what he said, and they each address these different aspects of Chris's presentation during the question-and-answer period. The more polarized an audience is, the more predictable are the questions they are likely to ask and the responses they are likely to hear and accept.

At times, people live as though they are in a giant "safe" with filters to control what they see, what they hear, and what they feel. They thus hear only what they want to hear, see only what they want to see, and feel only what they want to feel. They can accept and understand that which they choose and do not have to move out of their comfort zone and be accountable in the world. This is what it means to "look at life through rose-colored glasses." Filtering is thus a common coping mechanism to hear and see "selectively," as exemplified in two of the three monkeys— hear no evil and see no evil.

Filters can be frustrating for the person who is trying to communicate with someone who does not want to hear what is being said. Yet we all filter information simply because we have different frames of reference. Speaking for myself (Chris), I always endeavor—and often fail—to lay aside my filters so I may become educated in the sense that the poet Robert Frost meant when he wrote: "Education is the ability to listen to almost anything without losing your temper or your self-confidence."[10]

Projection

Projection is a casting forward or outward of something. As a coping mechanism, it means the externalization of an inner thought or motive and its subsequent behavior, which is then attributed to someone else.

> ... and Aaron shall lay both his hands upon the head of the live goat, and confess over him all the iniquities of the people of Israel, and all their transgressions, and all their sins; and he shall put them upon the head of the goat, and send him away into the wilderness. ... The goat shall bear all their iniquities upon him to a solitary land; and he shall let the goat go in the wilderness.[11]

In biblical times, on the Jewish day of atonement, Yom Kippur, all the transgressions of the Jewish people were heaped (projected) onto the back of a "scapegoat," which was then driven away into the wilderness, "taking" all the people's transgressions with it. Projection as a coping mechanism thus has a long-recognized history.

Just as an empty movie projector casts only light, you can project onto other people only what you think about yourself because without thought, there is nothing to project. Thus, you see in others what you both consciously and unconsciously see in yourself—nothing more, nothing less.

As such, judgment, the projection of that which you see in yourself, is the projectile you cast outward in the word *should*—you should do this, you should do that. "You should" is thus a common attitude of the opposing sides in a conflict.

In reality, however, should is the stuff of someone else's standard of operation, of someone else's concept of right and wrong, of what you should or should not be or do. Someone else's should is only yours if you choose to accept it. On the other hand, you can choose to ignore another person's should, and then it has no effect.

Projection is a common coping mechanism. When understood as such, projections can be enlightening. You can, for example, tell almost immediately how participants feel about themselves by the kinds of projections they level at their opponents.

Rationalization

To rationalize in the sense of a coping mechanism is to devise self-satisfying but inauthentic reasons for one's own behavior. For example, you have been told to do something in your job with which you do not agree ethically. If you do not comply, however, you will lose your job—a real possibility in these days of corporate/political administrations. Therefore, you rationalize that you can do more good working for change on the inside of the agency or company, by compromising your beliefs, than you can by getting yourself fired for sticking to your principles. In so doing, you intellectually rationalize acceptance of the order and comply with it, but you have simultaneously committed the ethical honesty of your feelings to the prison of repression. Thus, you have murdered a vital, creative part of yourself.

The most commonly used rationalization is lack of control: "I can't." *Can't* means that whatever it is, it is beyond your control. Therefore, you are not responsible for your behavior. What you are really saying when you say "can't" is: "I will not, I choose not to, I am afraid to," or some similar declaration.

This rationalization probably came about because not knowing the answer to a question is not acceptable in our society. "I don't know" is reinforced as an unacceptable answer from grade school through college, the military, the workplace, and life in general. In fact, when you think about it, the statement, "Ignorance is no excuse under the law," is saying the same thing. Not knowing is not okay.

I (Carol) can sometimes "rationalize something endlessly," especially when it concerns a situation that did not go well. This was first brought to my attention while attending the Federal Law Enforcement Training Center. My assigned partner and I were given a scenario to conduct a "car stop" on a vehicle. We made the stop, and as all scenarios go at the training center, it resulted in my partner getting killed. As we got back in our patrol car, stressed out and upset, I began to rationalize, "If only I'd stopped earlier," "If only I had pulled up farther," "Maybe we should have … , " on and on. As I rambled on, my partner screamed at the top of her lungs, "Shut Up!"

I was not only taken aback but also her shout literally stung my ears. I started to think about what I said and why she was so upset at me (I did not dare utter a word). This was the first time I had realized that I used this as a coping mechanism. I think about that moment now when I hear myself saying those same things (repeatedly) and even hear her shouting at me to shut up. So I do. Being aware of our own coping mechanisms is the first step toward controlling them, a much-needed skill as a mediator.

Repression

Repression can be thought of as a one-way, spring-loaded valve into your unconscious. Any thought or emotion that causes you anxiety passes through this one-way valve, building tension in the coiled spring as it does so. Once trapped in the unconscious, neither the thought nor the emotion is allowed to reappear in your awareness. It might be expressed as follows: Homer really wanted to slug his brother for having offended Alice, but that would not have been acceptable at the party. So he clamped his jaws together and clenched his fists as he stalked from the room, tamping down his anger—putting a lid on it—so it would not erupt unacceptably. He repressed his emotions. Without an acceptable "safety valve" for releasing tension, energy continually builds in the spring until Homer will one day "blow up" unexpectedly and badly hurt his brother over some trivial matter.

Chris has seen this coping mechanism in agency personnel. On being ordered to do things for the good of the agency, things that violated their moral sense of what was right, they repressed their emotions to keep their jobs rather than maintaining the integrity of their beliefs, even if it meant resigning. The moment they retired, however, they attacked the agency with all the pent-up vehemence and bitterness of those long-repressed emotions.

Resistance

To resist is to work against, to fight off, to oppose actively. Resistance is not bad in and of itself. It is simply a conservative, stabilizing tendency, which keeps an individual from overstepping limitations too quickly and rashly.

Problems arise when your resistance to change becomes overreactive, obsolete, or maladaptive—in a word, dysfunctional. Then you are unable to express your potential or to meet your goals. Resistance, in the dysfunctional sense, is one of the most commonly used coping mechanisms to ward off change, to avoid the responsibility of moving forward, of participating in life.

Resistance is like swimming directly against the current of a large, swift river. A swimmer in such circumstances becomes worn out, despite a maximum effort, and is carried downriver by the overwhelming, persistent strength of the current and sometimes drowns. If, perchance, the swimmer is strong enough and determined enough just to stay even with the current, it soon becomes apparent that, while the current does not tire from the effort of flowing, the swimmer tires from the effort of swimming. Thus, the current ultimately carries the swimmer away—the tired carried away by the tireless.

Circumstances are the river of life, and change is its current. The individual swimmer can choose to resist the current, become fatigued, and perhaps drown, or can choose to flow with the current and, with patience, learn the skill necessary to cross the river easily. Herein lies the secret of the statement, "To be in control, one must give up the desire to control." Only when you give up trying to control life can you master navigating its current.

Today the pace at which change is occurring is unprecedented in our history. Increasingly, we feel like we have lost control, and this sense of loss often results in repressed anger and resistance. Carol once sat in a field office supervisors' meeting; two individuals from the same office bemoaned their staff. They complained that their staff was so negative that they refused to do their assignments, and that they were incorrigible (their words).

It was obvious to me (Carol) at the time that the supervisors were the problem. Albeit the agency was going through major changes in how it did business, how could they expect their staff to be optimistic or even positive if the messages their leaders passed to them were so negative? Would I want to work for these two? Would I, as a staff member of theirs, feel safe in this environment? I learned a lot from those two, and I still to this day work hard to communicate with my staff about change in as positive a tone as I can muster. It is not always positive news, to be sure, but I know that if they see me accepting the change rather than resisting it, and still surviving, then I know that they will be more resilient and more able to do the same.

That which you resist persists in the degree to which you resist it, and you become like that which you resist. It cannot be otherwise. What you resist is a lesson in life not learned, and life seems to persist in its lessons until you learn them.

Social psychologist Marsha Sinetar said in essence that resistance is a subtle inner device urging us to "back away" from the difficulties and demands of life. Psychoanalyst Carl G. Jung stated it a little differently: resistance "begets meaninglessness."

We find, however, that resistance serves two purposes in life, one positive and one negative. A feeling of resistance is positive when it is your inner voice telling you that what you have been asked to do really goes against your deepest sense of principles. In this case, you can feel good honoring your resistance.

On the other hand, there are times when you simply do not want to do something that needs doing. Then, your resistance works against you. You may end up with a terrible headache because your resistance is like driving a car by stepping on the gas pedal and the brakes at the same time with equal pressure.

Standards and Judgment

A standard is an acknowledged measure of comparison for qualitative and quantitative value, a criterion or a norm. We each have a standard against which we measure how things around us fit into our comfort zone. Our standard is therefore our basis for judging a person, situation, or thing as right or wrong, good or bad, comfortable or uncomfortable. It is not necessarily an accepted norm of social morality, however, because each person's standard is solely their own mental landscape of acceptability and has no validity for anyone else.

One's standard of judgment can be so narrow and biased, however, that it is self-defeating because it blinds the person to the truth. Consider the twelve-member committee for admissions to a prestigious prep school in New York, which voted unanimously to exclude a particular thirteen-year-old boy. The rejection was not surprising because the boy's academic record contained marks from failing to barely passing in almost every subject except English. In addition, his teachers' comments about his behavior ranged from "lazy" to "rebellious." After its decision, the committee learned that it had just passed judgment on the scholastic record of young Winston Churchill.[12]

I (Chris) believe everyone—myself included—does the level best he or she knows how to do at all times, and I seriously doubt any of us live up to our own standards for ourselves. If this is true, where is *the* standard as a true basis for judgment?

> Judgment, like other devices by which the world of illusions is maintained, is totally misunderstood by the world. It is actually confused with wisdom, and substitutes for truth. As the world uses the term, an individual is capable of "good" and "bad" judgment, and his education aims at strengthening the former and minimizing the latter. There is, however, considerable confusion about what these categories mean. What is "good" judgment to one is "bad" judgment to another. Further, even the same person classified the same action as showing "good" judgment at one time and "bad" judgment at another time. Nor can any consistent criteria for determining what these categories are be really taught. At any time the student may disagree with what his would-be teacher says about them, and the teacher himself may well be inconsistent in what he believes. "Good" judgment, in these terms, does not mean anything. No more does "bad."[13]

All we can judge is *appearances*. There is nothing else. An appearance is an outward aspect or an outward indication. Judgment is the process of forming an opinion or evaluation by discerning and comparing.

Because people are afraid of deviations from their standard, they cope with their fears by remaining the same while trying to control circumstances so other people will have to risk change. If the "other" people are unwilling to change, they become enemies, who are judged as not being okay, even inferior, because they do not live up to a certain standard. There are no enemies out there, only people frightened of change, of losing control, of being powerless, and are thus mistakenly rejected by their fellow human beings.

I (Chris) was a bachelor in the mid-1970s, and everything in my house was just so. Everything had a place and was in its place—always. I was so rigid with my standard of housekeeping that I was often uncomfortable with someone else's.

One day a friend of mine called and said he needed a place to live and asked if I knew of any. Without thinking, I said, "Yes. I have an extra room. Come and live with me." That was the beginning of the end. I did not know that I was about to get an education. He moved in with his dog, horse blankets, bridles, saddles, tools, rifles, and even his periodic girl-friends. My nice, neat, orderly, quiet, simple life was an instant shambles because in those days my friend seemed to be utter chaos looking for a place to unravel.

Yet this was one of the best things that ever happened to me. I could not "correct" my friend, as it were, no matter how hard I tried—and believe me, I tried. So I eventually joined him. He, in his mid-twenties, taught me, at the age of forty, how to play. He helped me to relax my standards and live a little. He became my personal counselor in overcoming my workaholism and my perfectionism. He gave me an irreplaceable gift, the ability to seize the moment and live it to the fullest.

Victimhood

Feeling like a victim of anything is a helpless, hopeless feeling, a feeling of being somehow violated. Being a victim of abuse is a violent, confusing, and overwhelming experience. One of the major aspects of being a victim is the experience of having little or no control over events. Something happens to you, and you feel powerless to do anything about it. In fact, implicit in the word *victim* is to be at the mercy of events, or of a circumstance or person; essentially to be in a position in which you have no control over what happens to you.

To use being a victim as a coping mechanism, therefore, is difficult at best for a mediator to handle because it is usually an unconscious act that is readily denied. After all, who would be a victim by choice? Although the following definitions seem to be relatively clear-cut, they are intellectual and leave much unsaid.

There are many definitions of victim, but three general ones will suffice for our discussion of victimhood as a coping mechanism: (1) one who is harmed by or made to suffer from an act, circumstance, agency, or condition; (2) a person who accidentally suffers injury, loss, or death as a result of a voluntary undertaking—a victim of their own behavior; and (3) a person who is tricked, swindled, duped, or taken advantage of.

One thing to notice about these definitions is that the victim suffers from a loss of control and is dealt a cruel blow by life. This image of having lost control makes playing a victim an easy way to get out of having to accept responsibility for having made the choice that put you in the circumstance of being the victim in the first place. Most of us probably play the victim at some point in life to cope with the feeling of being humiliated for not possessing control. What our society is telling us, in our own minds at least, is that it is not okay to be human, to err, that loss of control is somehow a terrible weakness.

Nevertheless, to understand and accept the premise of life-affirming mediation requires not only an understanding of coping mechanisms but also acknowledging each person's capacity for rational thought.

The Capacity for Rational Thought

It is critical that we, as mediators, work from the premise that all people possess the potential for rational thought (rational logic). To attain it, however, they must first work their way through the barriers of existing irrational thoughts (emotions that give rise to a sense of logic that is irrational—*especially fear*).

It is thus necessary to understand the meaning and relationship of two words: emotion and logic. As used here, emotion is a state of feeling, such as joy, anger, or fear, that is centered in the individual's sense of self. Emotion is the energy that drives us, that gives us values and feelings. Whereas anger and fear produce an irrational sense of logic, joy is a positive emotion and fosters rational logic. Rational logic is the mechanism that allows us to understand the emotions contained in our values. Logic allows an individual to understand that he or she is part of an interconnected, interactive system in which the governing principle of cause and effect is impartial.

Because the inviolate, biophysical principles that govern the universe are rational, Nature, which obeys these principles, is rational. We as a part of Nature must therefore possess the potential for rational thought, but we also possess—and often focus on—irrational thought and so imperfectly understand the rationality of Nature.

That notwithstanding, unless we believe that the people with whom we work possess the potential for rational thought, we are powerless to bring about peace short of total human annihilation because we cannot negotiate with another person as long as we are convinced that our counterpart's thinking is irrational. A cardinal principle of mediation and the power to act with confidence is the belief that the people with whom one works possess the potential for rational logic. This means one must believe the people have the potential to honor their feelings while thinking clearly, accept their individual power, and possess the desire for peace. Only then is it possible to reach accord with them.

When thinking is rational, based on the impartial principle of cause and effect, the group we are working with can become dedicated to the proposition that no person shall abuse another, that all members shall defend the rights of each member, and that each member shall defend the rights of all members. This is possible because a rational person tends to seek peace, which in turn can lead to the organized enactment of a shared vision for the future.

Rational thought can be tested through its converse. Namely, if one does not believe in the rational nature of another person, then one believes it is impossible to negotiate with the person. If one does not believe that rational people ultimately desire peace, then one cannot negotiate confidently toward peace with one's opponent. If one cannot negotiate with one's opponent, one is powerless to achieve peace, and if one cannot organize around rational thought, then the principles of peace cannot move from the minds of people into the actions of society.

By the time Chris is normally asked to mediate the resolution of a conflict, however, the people involved have usually reached a place of such psychological pain, such feelings of fear and rage, that a sense of hopelessness prevails. Under such circumstances, it is often difficult for them to think clearly and therefore direct much attention to dealing with the real causes of their emotions.

Although emotion and logic appear to be mutually exclusive, both are valid because they are different and not substitutable. For example, emotions (either negative, such as pain, fear, and despair, or positive, such as love, compassion, and joy) must be validated and the former transcended before the impartial logic of the whole systemic picture can be accepted. Thus, negative emotions can be brought to logic only when all parties feel safe enough to be open and honest—when love, trust, and respect can ultimately prevail, when "a gentle answer turns away wrath."[14]

A major problem in the world today is the apparently irreconcilable split between faulty logic based on repressed emotions[15] and rational logic based on the impartial consequence of cause and effect, which is reached when the emotions are accepted, validated, understood, incorporated, and transcended. If not transcended, the faulty logic of unbridled, negative emotions can become violence and moral chaos.

Only when negative emotions are transcended can they can give the insight, the inner vision necessary to reach rational thought, that which allows one to perceive the world as an impartial system based on cause and effect. If we, as mediators, choose to accept our own inner struggles toward rational thought, we can help others to do the same just because we have the courage to make that choice.

Everyone Is Right from a Personal Point of View

We now come to the notion of right versus wrong, again based on perceived similarities and differences. Society is composed of individual human beings much as the compound eye of an insect is composed of individual facets, each of which is slightly different in structure but equally important to the total vision of the eye. Each facet has its own light-sensitive element; each has its own refractive system, and each forms but a portion of the image.

As there are as many points of view in the compound eye of an insect as there are facets, so there are as many points of view in a society as there are people. Although everyone is right from a personal point of view, no one person has the complete image, and no one is *totally right*.

We all sense things differently when we see, hear, touch, taste, and smell; because we sense things differently, we understand them differently. In addition, our senses are variously effective under ever-changing circumstances. Our individual brains coordinate and integrate our individual sensing, producing an individual awareness. Through communication, our manifold, individual degrees of awareness are coordinated and integrated into a collective awareness. And it is through our senses that we become aware of the complementary nature of the "otherness."

It is precisely because we each have our point of view, established after we have considered the data and have reached a conclusion, that I (Chris or Carol) cannot convince you of anything. But, from a point of communication, I must accept what you think you heard, and you must accept what I think I said. Such acceptance is important because for me to convince you that I am right, I must simultaneously convince you that you are wrong. You will resist, of course, first because I have assaulted your dignity and second because you *are* correct from your interpretation of "your" data just as I am from my interpretation of mine.

For example, I (Chris) once held a postcard up in front of an audience and asked them to describe it and then tell me what it was. I got a surprising number of different answers. The interesting thing about it was that no one got a description one hundred percent correct from a factual point of view—only from his or her point of view. Moreover, there was some contestation regarding who was correct.

Although I cannot convince you that you are wrong without somehow attacking your dignity, I can give you new data, which *raises the value* of your making a new decision based on new information. In this way, I can be patient and give you the space that allows you to change your mind if you so choose while maintaining your dignity intact.

The question is, then, Who is right when we are all right from our own points of view? If everyone is right, then who is wrong? Because no one is wrong, we cannot argue any case based on "right" or "wrong." Right or wrong is always a human judgment dealing with appearances, not reality, which means that if I think I am right, I must "win," and if I win, I must be right. You, on the other hand, are clearly wrong because you "lost," and you lost because you are clearly wrong. Thus, each side becomes committed to winning agreement with its outlook and is not even in a position to contemplate another possibility under the competitive illusion of winners and losers.

For example, I (Carol) was once assigned to a wildfire near the boundary between "my" national park and a military base. Our fire crew reported to the scene to assist the civilian crew of the military with their efforts to suppress the fire. The incident commander was someone I had known for some time. He had been involved in several previous engagements with us and fought us on every step we would take to suppress a wildfire, even when the fires were in the national park. He would be even more difficult had we been on "his" military base.

When we arrived, I could see from his facial expression and agitated pacing that he literally hated the sight of us. I could almost see heat radiating off him. What ensued then was a battle of right and wrong; he now had his chance to be right. Despite the fire raging all around us, he was more focused on putting us in the wrong than in putting out the fire. Fortunately, his supervisor arrived and forced him to go sit in the cab of the pumper truck while the supervisor took over as incident commander. As we began to organize ourselves to cut a fire line, I could still see him sitting in the truck seething. We can get nowhere when each of us takes the immovable position that the other side is wrong—we get stuck.

Everyone loses, however, when issues are "settled" by judgments of right or wrong because everyone appears to be right from a personal point of view. This really is no different from a world at war in which each nation, each army, each person is sure God is on its side.

The duality of right versus wrong does not have to exist. There can instead be a continuum of "rightness" in which some are a little more right than others. Such a continuum is predicated on our individual lack of knowledge owing to our own limited perception of possible outcomes. Since we do not know for sure who is more right than whom, we must in fairness accept that everyone is right from a personal point of view, and each point of view is different—not wrong, only different, regardless of what the discussion concerns. The notion of "wrong" is therefore unacceptable in resolving a conflict.

If we are to survive the present upheavals of social evolution, we must be willing to accept the notion of *right, right, and different*. Wrongness in the classical, combative, human sense must become a relic of the past if we are to treat others as we ourselves would like to be treated. Only then can any issue be *resolved* in such a way that each side retains its dignity, and society can progress with some semblance of order into the future.

We find the duality of rightness or wrongness of almost everything to be so pervasive that the notion of right, right, and different is exceedingly difficult to get across in a society that stresses judgmental values as the wisdom of its norm. If we insist on the duality of right versus wrong, we will always be in competition with one another. If, on the other hand, we can agree that everyone is right from a personal point of view and that each point of view is only a different perception along the same continuum, we will be able to coordinate and cooperate with one another and together raise the level of our social consciousness to the benefit of all generations.

Acceptance of Circumstances Offers
the Choices of What Might Be

Choice equals hope. Choice and hope are the ingredients of human dignity. Dignity means living in peace, free of fear. Our most important choice in overcoming fear and violence is learning to accept a circumstance, whatever it is, as it is. In talking about acceptance, Mother Teresa says that if God puts us in a palace, to accept being in the palace. By the same token, if God puts us in the street, to accept being in the street. But, she says that we are not to put ourselves either in a palace or in the street; we are simply to accept whatever circumstance is presented to us at the present moment.

Unconditional acceptance of circumstances is perhaps the most difficult lesson with which I (Chris) struggle daily. I cannot, for example, control a circumstance, but I can choose to control how I respond to it and what my attitude will be. In that choice lies my freedom from fear because I recognize that I have a choice, and I have it now. Thus, by giving up trying to control things outside myself, I am in better control *of* myself and can choose how I want to respond to any given circumstance.

In the last analysis, we have a choice. We always have a choice, *and we must choose*, much as we might wish this paradox to be otherwise. If you do not like the outcome or if you err in your choice, you can choose to choose again. You are not, therefore, a victim of your circumstances but rather a product of your choices and your decisions based on those choices.

What in a conflict is your choice? Your choice is to control your attitude, as manifested through your behavior. You are thus responsible for your behavior, and therein lies the potential resolution of any dispute—to raise the value of changing your attitude and thus your behavior for the common good.

Our task as mediators is to help the parties understand that attitudinal and behavioral change is the key to the resolution of their dispute. If one or both of the parties want something, it is up to them to decide how they must behave to enhance the possibility of achieving their goals.

The more people are able to choose love and peace over fear and violence, the more they gain in wisdom and the more we all live in harmony. This is true because what we choose to think about determines how we choose to act, and our thoughts and actions set up a self-reinforcing feedback loop, a self-fulfilling prophecy that becomes our reality and our truth.

Choice is the tool with which we, as people, make ourselves who we are. It is here that we must recognize, amidst the myriad choices daily confronting us, that as we think so we create and so we become, either on the material plane or on the spiritual plane. And we are either freed by our creations (those born of love) or imprisoned by them (those born of fear).

The choice is ours, for we have free will in our thoughts and actions, which means that each day, with pen in hand, we write and rewrite, edit and reedit our autobiographies. Choice is thus the clay with which we daily mold and remold our character until the day we look into the mirror of our souls and see the cumulative reflection of our many choices, which have manifested as irreversible consequences beyond our control. But for now, we can still choose what we might be in that future time.

References

1. Rabindranath Tagore. Quotations. http://www.brainyquote.com/quotes/authors/r/rabindranath_tagore.html (accessed February 6, 2010).
2. Buckminster Fuller. Quotes. http://docs.google.com/viewer?a=v&q=cache:GJJx8PgsnEMJ:www.accelerated-learning.info/files/Quotes.pdf+Buckminster+Fuller+%22every+child+is+a+genius&hl=en&gl=us&sig=AHIEtbTyhXT5GdvK69UqbQgD7V3Vztj9Mg (accessed February 6, 2010).
3. Hodding Carter. Quotes. http://thinkexist.com/quotation/there_are_two_lasting_bequests_we_can_give_our/13675.html (accessed February 6, 2010).
4. Edward Bach. *Heal Thyself.* C.W. Daniel Company, Essex, England (1931).
5. Mother Teresa. http://www.goodreads.com/quotes/show/191239 (accessed March 12, 2011.)
6. James W. Tamm and Ronald J. Luyet. *Radical Collaboration: Five Essential Skills to Overcome Defensiveness and Build Successful Relationships.* HarperCollins, New York (2004).
7. Ibid., p. 30.
8. Bach, *Heal Thyself.*
9. M. Durrant. Therapy with young people who have been the victims of sexual assault. *Family Therapy Case Studies,* 2 (1987):57–63.
10. Robert Frost. http://www.quotedb.com/quotes/714 (accessed March 12, 2011.)
11. Leviticus 16:21–22. *The Holy Bible,* Authorized King James Version. World Bible Publishers, Iowa Falls, IA.
12. T.J. Fleming and A. Fleming. *Develop Your Child's Creativity.* Association Press, New York (1970).
13. *A Course in Miracles. Manual for Teachers.* Foundation for Inner Peace, Tiburon, CA (1975), p. 26.
14. Proverbs 15:1. *The Holy Bible* .
15. (a) Donald Ludwig, Ray Hilborn, and Carl Walters. 1993. Uncertainty, resource exploitation, and conservation: lesson from history. *Science,* 260 (1993):17, 36; and (b) Chris Maser. *Global Imperative: Harmonizing Culture and Nature.* Stillpoint, Walpole, NH (1992).

6

Communication: The Interpersonal Element

Introduction

Ideally, mediation revolves around understanding and sharing emotions and knowledge, both of which grow from and are a reflection of social experience. Emotions and knowledge are shared through communication, which is the very heart of conflict resolution and must be treated with the utmost respect. Just as dishonest or careless communication tells much about the people we are listening to, so does good communication. Good communication means respect for both listener and speaker because one must first listen to understand and then speak to be understood.

Communication is perhaps one of the most difficult things we do as human beings, yet it is simultaneously one of the most important things we do. We are creatures who must share feelings, senses, abstractions, and concrete experiences to know and value our existence in relation with one another. Communication, or language, is the way we share the very core of our relationships. Our existence revolves around it, and without it, we have nothing of value.

Language as a Tool

Although communication involves far more than mere words, we are concerned only with words here. Words are symbols for the things we experience; therefore, the more accurately a chosen word builds a bridge to our common ground, the easier it is to get in touch with one another, stay in touch, build trust, and ask for and receive help.

In this sense, semantics is more than quibbling over words; it reveals both our thought patterns and our consciousness of cause and effect. It is the conveyance of concepts, perceptions, personal truths, trust, and a shared vision for the future. Like every linguistic creation, language can empower or limit, depending on whether we see it as a set of labels describing some preexisting, unchangeable reality or as a medium with which to articulate a new reality—a sustainable way of living together on and with Earth.

Our task as a mediator is to create a safe place in which common bonds can be built, maintained, and strengthened through good communication, or a clear, concise use of language. Just as any relationship requires sensitive, honest, and open communication to be healthy and grow, so are relationships in the mediation process forged, maintained, and improved when feelings and information are shared accurately, freely, and with tact.

The quality of communication is thus enhanced if simple rather than complex words are used. Picturesque slang and free-and-easy colloquialisms, if they are appropriate to the subject and if they do not offend the sensibilities of the participants, can add variety and vividness to the mediation process. But substandard English, such as grammatical errors and vulgarisms, not only detracts from the mediator's dignity but also reflects the mediator's attitude toward the participants' intelligence.

If the subject under discussion includes technical terms, the mediator must be sure to define each term clearly and concisely so that all participants know exactly what is meant by it. It is also best to use specific rather than general words. In addition, to ensure clarity, short to medium-length sentences are best because, for most people, the spoken word is often more difficult to grasp than the written word, which can be read repeatedly and studied.

Recently, I (Carol) was at a meeting with a colleague who works primarily with the energy industry. In the course of our visit, my colleague said he had spent many hours facilitating meetings between their federal agency and a private energy company, only to find out more than halfway through their discussions that each was attributing a completely different meaning to the word *resources*. My colleague would say, "We need to be sure to take care of the resources on this project," meaning natural resources. And the energy representative would say, "We are here for the resource!" meaning specifically, in this case, the petroleum to be extracted. Needless to say, each side was confused regarding why no progress was being made on the project. The use of the words and how we define them are extremely important.

Quality communication requires constant, consistent practice. It is thus imperative that Carol and I continually monitor the words we use, their meanings, and their usage in our everyday speaking and writing. Every word must be valued, and any word that does not carry its weight must be discarded. We (Carol and I) must practice all day, every day because good communication comes primarily from good thoughts. By our thoughts, we (in the generic) privately define and by our actions we publicly declare who and what we are. British psychologist James Allen states this beautifully:

> A man's [and a woman's] mind may be likened to a garden, which may be intelligently cultivated or allowed to run wild; but whether cultivated or neglected, it must, and will, bring forth. If no useful seeds are put into it, then an abundance of useless weed seed will fall therein, and will continue to produce their kind.
>
> Just as a gardener cultivates his plot, keeping it free from weeds, and growing the flowers and fruits which he requires, so may a man tend the garden of his mind, weeding out all the wrong, useless, and impure thoughts, and cultivating toward perfection the flowers and fruits of right, useful, and pure thoughts. By pursuing this process, a man sooner or later discovers that he is the master gardener of his soul, the director of his life. He also reveals, within himself, the laws of thought, and understanding, with ever-increasing accuracy, how the thought forces and mind elements operate in the shaping of his character, circumstances, and destiny.[1]

A word spoken is thus the manifestation of a thought, whether positive or negative. Once spoken, it can never be withdrawn, despite an apology, because words are the public extensions of our private selves.

Good communication, a prerequisite for both teaching and learning, clears the way for shared, participative ownership of ideas as a means of building relationships within the mediation process. There are, however, a number of obligations that accompany good communication.

Because the right—and need—to know is basic in the mediation process, all parties must have equal access to pertinent information if a conflict is to be resolved. Here, we believe, it is better to err on the side of sharing too much information rather than risking someone being left in the dark. We say this because hoarded information subverts the mediation process through misrepresentation.

Everyone has a right to simplicity and clarity in communication and an obligation to communicate simply and clearly—especially a mediator. If I (Chris) cannot be simple and clear in what I say, then I do not understand the topic well enough to discuss it. Sometimes, for example, I have trouble expressing a concept while writing a book, giving a speech, or during the facilitation process. When this happens, I write an essay on the topic in a maximum of five double-spaced pages. And I work on it until I have got it down as well as I can. From that point, it is clearly in mind and flows easily whenever I need to discuss the subject.

I go to this length because I owe everyone truth and courtesy, although truth is often uncomfortable and at times a real constraint, and courtesy may be an inconvenience. Nevertheless, it is these qualities that allow communication to educate and liberate us.

I am obliged to practice discrimination in both what I say and what I hear, which means that I must respect my own language through its careful usage. I must acknowledge and accept that muddy language means muddy thinking, and muddy thinking means muddy language. I must therefore always remember that my audience (the parties in the dispute) may need something special from me, such as an extraordinary amount of patience and clarity while they struggle to communicate.

Language is the most profound tool Carol and I have as mediators because it both educates and liberates. Teaching and learning underlie mediation literacy and action. Mediation literacy is the "why" the process does what it does, and action is the "what" it does. With this in mind, we can use language to help the parties engaged in a mediation process to free themselves from their bonds of conflict. To allow the parties to liberate themselves, however, our communication must be based on sound reasoning, compassion, detachment, and sometimes on silence.

The Use of Silence in Communication

A mediator must learn to appreciate the power of silence in communication. Most people are profoundly uncomfortable with silence and feel compelled to speak, including many mediators who possess the need to direct, control, and intervene in the process and so destroy it. Silence, when allowed to flow unimpeded through indeterminate seconds and minutes, draws people out, causing them to engage both uncomfortable circumstances and one another.

For example, some years ago a small group of ranchers in central Oregon asked me (Chris) to help them articulate a vision statement for grazing livestock on public lands, one that would allow them to continue using public lands if they lived up to it. I agreed, but said that I could only help them if they could tell me why they wanted to be ranchers. Silence. They had no answer. They had never thought about it. So I took out the book I was reading, sat down, and became engrossed in it.

After agonizing over the question for a couple of hours, one of the ranchers approached me and said: "Ahh … , Chris, ahh … , I guess it's the way of life that I love."

"Okay," I replied, "let's call it lifestyle. What's it worth to you? How much are you willing to change your attitude and behavior concerning your use of public lands to maintain your chosen lifestyle?"

With these questions answered, the ranchers drafted their vision statement. Now, years later, they not only are grazing their livestock on public lands but also are model ranchers. One of them traveled around the United States speaking to other ranchers about what he learned.

It was their agony in the two-hour silence that finally drew out the answer they needed to find, and the answer was theirs—not mine. Had

I in any way helped them with the answer because I was uncomfortable with the silence, it would have been my answer—not theirs—and it would have been useless to them. As it turned out, the answer raised the value of being ranchers. They felt like the first-class citizens they are, and because they act accordingly, people listen when they speak.

The Need to Be Heard

Although one may not think of it as such, listening is the other half of communication. Communication is a gift of ideas; therefore, the other person can give you a gift of ideas through speaking only if you accept the gift through listening. The spoken word that falls on consciously "deaf ears" is like a drop of rain evaporating before it reaches Earth. Intolerance of another's ideas belies faith in one's cause.

The watchword of listening is *empathy*, which means imaginative identification with, as opposed to judgment of, the person's thoughts, feelings, life situation, and so on. The more a mediator can empathize with a person, the more that person feels heard, the greater the bond of trust, and the better you (as mediator) can understand the situation. This means, however, actively, consciously listening with a quiet, open mind, without forming a rebuttal while the other person is speaking. Such listening is an act of love, and anything short of it is an act of passive violence.

Some years ago, I (Chris) was on a television program in which the intent was to discuss the issue of ancient forests in the Pacific Northwest. An elderly lady on the program tried in vain to be heard, but the moderator consistently ignored her. Even after we were off the air, she tried again to tell the moderator how she was feeling, but he continued to ignore her. In the end, just to be heard, perhaps only by herself, she spoke aloud to no one; she spoke into space. She may as well have been alone in the world.

I (Carol) experienced a similar situation while deployed to the Gulf oil spill. While attending an open forum on the new private (non-British Petroleum) reimbursement process for businesses (such as those involving fishers, hotels/travel, and tourism) impacted by the spill, a woman approached the podium and demanded to know how local residents, who were not able to enjoy their beaches, were going to be made whole. It was clear that she was emotionally affected by the oil spill. The moderator did listen, but then pointed out that damages were being awarded for monetary losses only. If she could prove that she had suffered a monetary loss, she could file a claim. Although the handling of this situation was done properly, in a technical sense, the look of defeat and sorrow on the woman's face as she left the room demonstrated that empathy would have been a much better approach to her concerns. She also felt that no one was listening.

Not listening is an act of violence because it is a purposeful way of invalidating the feelings—the very existence—of another person. Everyone needs to be heard and validated as a human being because sharing is the bond of relationship that makes us "real" to ourselves and gives us meaning in the greater context of the universe. We simply cannot find meaning outside a relationship with one another. Therefore, only when we (in the generic) have first validated another person through listening as an act of love can that person really *hear* what *we* are saying. Only then can we share another's truth. Only then can our gift of ideas touch receptive ears.

All we have in the world as human beings is one another, and all we have to give one another is one another. We are each our own gift to one another and to the world; we have nothing else of value to give. We cannot give our gift, however, if there is no one to receive it, if there is no one to hear. Therefore, if we listen—really listen—to one another and validate one another's feelings, even if we do not agree, we can begin to resolve our differences before they become disputes. But to listen well and to speak well, it is important to consider the basic elements of communication.

The Basic Elements of Communication

Communication occurs when one person transmits ideas or feelings to another or to a group of people. Its effectiveness depends on the similarity between the information transmitted and that received, a common frame of reference.

The communication process is composed of at least three elements: (1) the sender, someone speaking, writing, signing, or emitting the silent language of attitude or movement; (2) the symbols used in creating and transmitting the message, sounds of a particular and repetitive form called spoken words, particular and repetitive handcrafted signs called written words, a particular arrangement of musical notes called melody, and facial expressions, hand motions for the deaf, touch for the blind, and generalized "body language" for the sighted; and (3) the receiver, someone listening to, reading, or observing the symbols. These elements are dynamically interrelated and that which affects one influences all.

Suppose Carol has something she wants to convey to you. She tries sending her thoughts through the air as intelligent noise for you to pick up with your receivers, your ears. You must then translate the sounds back into your thoughts, which simulate her thoughts, as you understand them. And you think you know what she said? She cannot even accurately tell you what she meant because there are seldom words with which to express clearly the nuances of thought. How, for example, can she really say, "I love you." What does that mean? She can feel it, but there simply are no words to describe the feeling.

Communication is thus a complicated, two-way process, which is not only dynamic among its elements but also reciprocal. If, for instance, a receiver has difficulty understanding the symbols and indicates confusion, the sender may become uncertain and timid, losing confidence in being able to convey ideas. The effectiveness of the communication is thus diminished. On the other hand, when a receiver reacts positively, a sender is encouraged and adds strength and confidence to the message. Let us examine how the three elements work.

Sender

A sender's effectiveness in communication is related to at least three factors. First is facility in using language, which influences the ability to select those symbols that are graphic and meaningful to the receiver.

Second, senders, both consciously and unconsciously, reveal their attitudes toward themselves, toward the ideas they are transmitting, and toward the receivers. These attitudes must be positive if the communication is to be effective. Senders must indicate that they believe their message is important and there is a need to know the ideas presented.

Third, a successful sender draws on a broad background of personal, accurate, up-to-date, stimulating, and relevant information. A sender must make certain that the ideas and feelings being transmitted are relevant to the receiver. The symbols used must be simple, direct, and to the point. Too often, however, a sender uses imprecise language or technical jargon that is nonsense to the receiver and thus impedes effective communication.

Symbols

The most basic level of communication is achieved through simple oral and visual codes. The letters of the alphabet, both spoken and written, constitute such a basic code when translated into words, as do common gestures and facial expressions. But words and gestures only communicate ideas when combined in meaningful wholes: speeches, sign language, sentences, paragraphs, or chapters. Each part is critical to the meaning of the whole.

Ideas must be carefully selected if they are to convey messages that receivers can understand and give a *response*. Ideas must be analyzed to determine which are best suited for starting, carrying, and concluding the communication and which clarify, emphasize, define, limit, or explain the context—all of which form the basis of effective transmission of ideas from the sender to the receiver.

Finally, the development of ideas from simple symbols culminates in the selection of the medium (such as hearing, sight, or touch) best suited for their transmission. In the mediation process, however, a variety of media (hearing, sight, touch, and at times smell and taste) makes for the most effective communication because it relates to the widest range of experiences.

Receiver

A basic rule of mediation is that it is Carol's and my responsibility as mediators to be clear, concise, and relevant, and because communication is a shared responsibility, the receiver must do his or her best to understand. We know communication has occurred when receivers respond with an understanding that allows them to change their behavior.

To understand the communication process, it helps to appreciate at least three aspects of receivers: their abilities, attitudes, and experiences, which often, and in many hidden ways, relate to their familial upbringing. First, it is important to discern a receiver's ability to question and comprehend the ideas transmitted. We can encourage a receiver's ability to question and comprehend by providing a safe atmosphere that welcomes such participation.

Second, a receiver's attitude may be one of resistance, willingness, or passivity. Whatever the attitude, we must gain the receiver's attention and retain it. The more varied, interesting, and relevant we are as mediators, the more successful we will be in this respect.

Third, a receiver's background, experience, and education (often extremely diverse in a group situation) constitute the frame of reference toward which the communication must be aimed. Carol and I assume the obligation of assessing the receiver's knowledge and of using it as the fundamental guide for effective communication. For us to get a receiver's response, however, we must first reach them, something a loss of words makes increasingly difficult with younger generations.

Changes in the *Oxford Children's Dictionary*

Every human language—the master tool representing its own culture—has its unique construct, which determines both its limitations and its possibilities in expressing myth, emotion, ideas, and logic. One of the greatest feats of humanity is the evolution of written language—those silent, ritualistic marks with their encoded meaning that not only made culture possible but also archive its history as part of its cultural commons.

The relative independence with which cultures evolve creates their uniqueness both within themselves and within the reciprocity they experience with one another and their immediate environments. Each culture, and each community within that culture, affects its environment in a specific way and is accordingly affected by the environment in a particular way. So it is that distinct cultures in their living create culturally designed landscapes, which in some measures are reflected in the myths they hold and the languages they speak. As such, language is the medium with which the condition of the human soul is painted.

The artist, using words to convey the colors of meaning by mixing them on a palette of syntax, composes the broad shapes of a cultural story line. Then, by matching the colors of words to give expression to ideas, the artist adds verbal structure, texture, and shades of meaning to the story. In doing so, the verbal artist paints a picture or portrait as fine as any accomplished with brush, paint, palette, and canvas; with camera and film; or with musical instruments and mute notes on paper. In addition, a verbal picture often outlasts the ravages of time, which claim those of paint on canvas, imprints of light on photographic paper, or musical instruments that give "voice" to mute shapes.

So what does it say about Western industrialized society when the latest edition of the *Oxford Junior Dictionary* has omitted words of historical significance pertaining to Nature and culture to make way for greater modernity, including such "technobabble" as *BlackBerry, blog, voice mail,* and *broadband*?

Yet, according to Vineeta Gupta, head of the children's dictionaries at Oxford University Press, changes in the world are responsible for these alterations. "When you look back at older versions of dictionaries, there were lots of examples of flowers for instance," she said. "That was because many children lived in semi-rural environments and saw the seasons. Nowadays, the environment has changed." Several criteria were used to select the 10,000 words and phrases in the *Junior Dictionary*, including how often words would be used by young children.[2] However, as Elaine Brooks points out, "Humans seldom value what they cannot name."[3]

Nature words deleted from the Oxford Junior Dictionary *include*: acorn, adder, almond, apricot, ash, ass, beaver, beech, beetroot, blackberry, bloom, bluebell, boar, bramble, bran, bray, brook, budgerigar, bullock, buttercup, canary, canter, carnation, catkin, cauliflower, cheetah, chestnut, clover, colt, conker, corgi, cowslip, crocus, cygnet, dandelion, doe, drake, fern, ferret, fungus, gerbil, goldfish, gooseberry, gorse, guinea pig, hamster, hazel, hazelnut, heather, heron, herring, holly, horse chestnut, ivy, kingfisher, lark, lavender, leek, leopard, liquorice, lobster, magpie, melon, minnow, mint, mistletoe, mussel, nectar, nectarine, newt, oats, otter, ox, oyster, panther, pansy, parsnip, pasture, pelican, piglet, plaice, poodle, poppy, porcupine, porpoise, poultry, primrose, prune, radish, raven, rhubarb, spaniel, spinach, starling, stoat, stork, sycamore, terrapin, thrush, tulip, turnip, vine, violet, walnut, weasel, willow, wren.

Cultural words taken out of the dictionary: abbey, aisle, allotment, altar, bacon, bishop, blacksmith, bridle, carol, chapel, christen, coronation, county, cracker, decade, devil, diesel, disciple, duchess, duke, dwarf, elf, emperor, empire, goblin, manger, marzipan, monarch, minister, monastery, monk, nun, nunnery, parish, pew, porridge, psalm, pulpit, saint, sheaf, sin, vicar.

Words put in: allergic, alliteration, analogue, apparatus, attachment, bilingual, biodegradable, block graph, blog, boisterous, brainy, broadband, bullet point, bungee jumping, cautionary tale, celebrity, chatroom, childhood, chronological, citizenship, classify, colloquial, committee, common sense, compulsory, conflict, cope, creep, curriculum, cut and paste, database, debate, democratic, donate, drought, dyslexic, emotion, endangered, EU, Euro, export, food chain, idiom, incisor, interdependent, MP3 player, negotiate, square number, tolerant, trapezium, vandalism, voice mail.[4]

Here the challenge is that ideas, which depend on words to convey, breed awareness ⇒ understanding ⇒ consciousness ⇒ choices ⇒ initial adaptability ⇒ decisions ⇒ actions ⇒ trade-offs ⇒ irreversible consequences ⇒ and so on. When, therefore, words are omitted from the cultural lexicon, the art of language is diminished, as is the ability to understand the biophysical systems that support the growing technological isolation from one's natural environment.

Some languages, as exemplified, are simply being eroded through the conscious substitutions of words, whereas others cease to exist altogether. Although language is not something we generally think of as becoming extinct, languages are disappearing all over the world, especially the spoken-only languages of indigenous peoples. As languages vanish, so do the cultural variations of the landscape they allowed, even fostered, because a unique culture cannot exist without the uniqueness of its language to protect its history and guide its evolution.

While it probably took thousands of years for the different human languages to evolve, it can take less than a century for some of them to disappear. As languages become extinct, we lose their cultural knowledge along with their perceptions and modes of expression. Because language is the fabric of culture and the living trust of our identity, when a language dies, the demise of the culture that gave it birth is imminent.

What is lost when a language becomes extinct? How many potential answers to contemporary problems, how much ancient wisdom, will be lost because we are losing languages, especially obscure, indigenous ones, to "progress"?

With the loss of each language, we also lose the evolution of its logic and its cultural myths and rituals—those metaphors that give the people a sense of place within the greater context of the universe—because language represents unity within and through time. Temporal unity is the language of memory, those images of experience stored in the human psyche and passed forward from generation to generation in the form of stories, myths, and rituals. Therefore, each time we allow a human language to become extinct, we are losing a facet of understanding, a facet of ourselves—the collective memory of a people archived in their language, a memory that is part of the human hologram, our collective commons of the human experience. As a global society, we are slowly making ourselves blind to our relationships with one another, the universe, and ourselves—which is augmented by *Nature deficit disorder* in the children of today.

Nature Deficit Disorder in Children

Everyone will likely agree that children today spend most of their time "plugged in" to a game system, a computer, or other electronic device. I (Carol) spent most of my time growing up outdoors, making mud pies, catching fireflies, and playing baseball. According to Richard Louv (author of *Last Child in the Woods: Saving Our Children from Nature Deficit Disorder*), "Nature deficit disorder describes the human costs of alienation from nature, among them: diminished use of the senses, attention difficulties, and higher rates of physical and emotional illnesses."[5] Children today spend hours plugged in to various electronic devices. The causes of ADHD (attention-deficit/hyperactivity disorder) are not all known yet, but recent studies have shown that for each hour of television a preschooler watches per day, the child's risk of developing concentration problems and other symptoms of ADHD by age 7 increases by 10 percent.[6] Even when these children do spend time in "nature," it is usually not free-play time, but scheduled or structured time, such as at soccer games or other sports.

Parents contribute to this shunning of the outdoors by instilling fear of the outdoors in their children. How many children are allowed to walk to school or play at a nearby park alone? Do we let them get dirty and truly play, or complain about them ruining their clothes? Do we encourage free play in the natural environment or buy the sports utility vehicle with dual video players in it? And, the bigger question, how are we, as environmental trustees, to communicate the value of our natural resources to a new generation that has not experienced nature?

And it is not only new generations who lack a connection to nature. While I (Carol) was teaching biology at a community college, I required students to participate in a field trip. Each class went to a park about 30 minutes away and spent the morning taking samples of macroinvertebrate insects in a small stream. A short hike down a well-established trail led to the open field, where we donned our chest waders and entered the stream. We had a great morning of stream sampling, and as our field trip came to a close, a student pulled me aside. A woman in her early fifties, she said she wanted to thank me for "forcing" her to go on the trip. She had not slept any of the previous night and debated calling me to cancel (and accept an F for the activity that day). When I asked her why she would do that (she was an excellent student), she replied, "I was terrified." She was so afraid that there might be bugs, spiders, or animals—or that she would get hurt—her complete fear of the outdoors left her nearly paralyzed at the thought of it. Yet she was so grateful and so proud of her accomplishment that, having completed the trip, she was beaming with pride as she told me her story. "I did it!" she said, "I really did it!" I was truly humbled by this experience. It reinforced the concepts we have discussed. I had no idea how different my experiences were from some of my students, and I was thereafter much more aware of the barriers some feel toward nature.

The bottom line is that the less time our children (and our peers) spend connecting with and learning to appreciate the natural world, the more difficult our jobs as environmental trustees, conflict mediators, and human beings will become. We no longer have a society with a shared experience of nature. As a result, our jobs as environmental conflict mediators have become much more complex and challenging.

Barriers to Communication

The nature of language and the way in which it is used often lead to misunderstandings and conflict. These misunderstandings stem primarily from three barriers to effective communication: (1) the lack of a common experience or frame of reference, (2) how one approaches life, and (3) the use of abstractions.

Lack of a Common Experience or Frame of Reference

The lack of a common experience or frame of reference is probably the greatest barrier to effective communication. Although many people believe that words carry meaning in much the same way as a person transports an armful of wood or a pail of water from one place to another, words *never* carry precisely the same meaning from the mind of the sender to that of the receiver. Words are vehicles of perceptive meaning. They may or may not supply emotional meaning as well. The nature of the response is determined by the receiver's past experiences surrounding the word and the feelings it evokes.

Feelings grant a word its meaning, which is in the receiver's mind, and not in the word itself. Since a common frame of reference is basic to communication, words in and of themselves are meaningless. Meaning is engendered when words are somehow linked to one or more shared experiences between the sender and the receiver, albeit the experiences may be interpreted differently. Words are thus merely symbolic representations that correspond to anything people apply the symbol to—objects, experiences, or feelings.

Thus, a sender must differentiate carefully between the symbols and the things they represent, keeping both in as true a perspective as possible. The truth of a perspective (the interpretation of an experience) is based on the degree to which a person is functional or dysfunctional, which is largely determined by the functionality of one's family of origin. It is also based on the degree to which a person has grown not only beyond his or her dysfunction but also in the breadth and depth of personal individual life experiences. Taken altogether, this translates into generalized personality traits.

Generalized Personality Traits

In a sense, generalized personality traits are an amalgamation of the dominant coping mechanisms with which one navigates life. They thus become the essence of one's interpretation of life experiences and the springboard of one's personal capabilities. These traits, which we each possess to a greater or lesser degree, are not cut and dried, but rather are overlapping tendencies with varying shades of gray. Nevertheless, they can be substantial barriers to communication.

For example, some people can take ideas seemingly at *random* from any part of a thought system and integrate them; these people have mental processes that instantly change direction, arriving at the desired destination in a nonlinear, intuitive fashion. Others can think only in a *linear sequence*, like the cars of a train; these people have mental processes that crawl along in a plodding fashion, exploring this avenue and that, without assurance of ever reaching a definite conclusion. If the random thinker is also at ease with *abstractions* but the linear sequence thinker requires *concrete* examples, their attempts to communicate may well be like two ships passing in a dense fog.

Then there is the *introverted* person, who (appearing self-possessed, even aloof) processes things internally, navigates life's path more or less alone, and has few friends over a lifetime. An *extroverted* person, on the other hand, is outgoing, mingles easily with other people, requires the presence of people to be happy, processes things through mutual discussion, and has a constant string of friends. An introvert works well alone behind the scenes, whereas an extrovert works well with people out front. In addition, there are four other traits, which can be summed as fatalist, exasperator, appraiser, and relator.

A *fatalist* is the consummate victim who feels powerless in the face of an all-powerful system or life itself and is forever suffering a loss of control. To this person, the operational word is *can't*. A fatalist, resigned to his or her lot in life, is often barely functional and requires a tremendous amount of energy even to reach zero on the scale of enthusiasm—energy sucked from whoever will give it. Just as soon as a person stops propping up the fatalist, however, the fatalist plunges below zero again.

Although fatalists want to be rescued, they resist any attempted rescue at any cost. Here we, mediators, must be wary. The only one who can rescue a person is the person in need of rescue, and only the person knows when he or she is ready for self-rescuing.

Nevertheless, fatalists are good technicians. They tend to be most comfortable with simple, clear instructions about which they do not have to think. Having said this, it is critical to understand that fatalists are usually paralyzed by having to bear responsibility. They work well behind the scenes, are usually patient with details, and may even accept monitoring the progress of an activity, provided they do not have to accept any responsibility for its outcome.

An *exasperator*, on the other hand, must be the center of attention and is deeply invested in so being. Here, the watchword is *control*. Some exasperators go to great lengths to command attention and be in control of whatever they are involved in doing. They tend, for instance, to be good at "one-liners," know "all" the jokes, are often the life of the party, and will argue any and every side of an issue, even changing sides in midstream, rather than acquiesce.

Exasperator personalities are as persistent as a bulldog. Rather than agree, they will say, "Yes, but ... ," just as long as someone will try to show them another way of thinking about something or another possible outcome.

Chris finds it best to acknowledge openly and freely the exasperator's point of view, the supposed position of power, which does not mean that he necessarily agrees with it. Once exasperators feel they have exerted their power and have been appropriately recognized, they can relax, and everyone can get on with the process of resolving the conflict.

Once an exasperator has an idea in mind, however, he or she gets impatient for action and, throwing caution to the wind, often barges ahead without getting adequate data or listening to other sides of an argument. On the flip side, if something needs to get done, done well, and completed on time, give it to an exasperator because the exasperator will move Heaven and Earth to show off his or her prowess.

While an exasperator often "knows it all," an *appraiser* wants facts, facts, and more facts. An appraiser seems to be uncertain in the world and wants to make sure that all the data are in, examined, weighed, reexamined, and reweighed before any decision is made. Such caution demands much patience on the part of a mediator because an appraiser often seems to hold the forward motion of the process in abeyance, regardless of how many data are at hand.

In Carol's experience, appraisers are often the ones who say they "don't feel comfortable" moving forward, "need Joe's input," or simply "need more data" to make a decision. Here it is prudent to refer constantly to such data as are available and to relate such data to the process and its potential outcome. If data are needed, ask an appraiser to obtain them, and you will likely get the best there is—and lots of it.

Then there is the *relator*, the person who is vitally concerned with what others will think and will go wherever the political wind blows. The relator seldom seems to know who he or she is as an individual and seems to have ideas only in relation to personal acceptability to others. Such a person changes his or her mind often and gives away personal power to whoever asks for it.

Since success or failure is not an event but rather the interpretation of an event, successes or failures of relators are determined by what everyone else thinks because they are constantly comparing themselves to those around them and internalizing what they are told by others. Unfortunately, we (in the generic) usually lose in the end when we compare ourselves to others because we tend to select someone we admire and then find our differences to be deficiencies, even liabilities.

Relators, in Chris's experience, are subject to getting their feelings hurt easily and often. This is perhaps the major way in which they try to control uncomfortable circumstances because it causes most people around them to "walk on eggshells."

In working with relators, it is best to refuse to accept their power, even when it is offered. Instead, ask them what they think and how they feel in an effort to draw them out. Done gently and patiently, this can work well.

Relators are generally excellent with public relations because they are sensitive to how others feel and work hard to win approval. They thus have a good sense of how to market an idea.

There are also product-oriented thinkers, symptomatic thinkers, and systemic thinkers. A *product-oriented thinker* is a person oriented to seeing only the economically desirable pieces of a system and seldom accepts that removing a perceived desirable or undesirable piece can or will negatively affect the productive capacity of the system as a whole. This person's response typically is, "Show me; I'll believe it when I see it." To such a person, mediation is usually seen as an immediate problem-solving exercise.

In my (Chris's) experience as a mediator, the more a person is a product-oriented thinker, the more reluctant the person is to change. This type of individual sees change as a condition to be avoided because he or she feels a greater sense of security in the known elements of the status quo, especially when money is involved. But, as Helen Keller once said, "Security is mostly a superstition. It does not exist in Nature. Life is either a daring adventure or nothing."[7] (Conversely, the more of a systems thinker a person is, the more likely he or she is to agree with Helen Keller and risk change on the strength of its unseen possibilities.)

A product-oriented thinker is likely to be a rural resident who is very much concerned with land ownership and property rights and wants as much free rein as possible to do as he or she pleases on his or her property, at times without regard for the consequences for future generations. The more of a product-oriented thinker a person is, the greater the tendency to place primacy on people of one's own race, creed, or religion, as well as on one's personal needs, however they are perceived. The more of a product-oriented thinker a person is, the greater the tendency to disregard other races, creeds, or religions, as well as nonhumans and the sustainable capacity of the land. Also, the more of a product-oriented thinker a person is, the more black and white one's thinking tends to be, as illustrated in the following example:

> The wimpy [sic] comments by Mike Mitchel in Sunday's "Rural Issues" were disturbing. As the head "honcho" and decision-maker for a BLM [Bureau of Land Management] office, he said things like, "We just follow the regulations and enforce them. ..." Also, "We have our regulations and have no choice."
>
> That's typical bureaucratic arrogance, and a cop-out. Those regulations didn't come down the mountain on stone tablets. They are the product of a well-funded lobby in Washington, D.C., that represents those who are "saving us" from the horrible ranchers, miners and farmers of Nevada.
>
> He says the land will restore itself in 15 or 20 years if we change grazing practices. Restore itself for what? So some manicured marshmallow-butt from Washington can start up a cattle ranch on abandoned land? Get real! Nevada ranchers are on the land now! The BLM should help them do what they do best, or get the hell out of the way. I'm not to [sic] smart, but I recognize typical Sierra Club rhetoric when I hear it.
>
> As the song goes: When will they ever learn?[8]

Symptomatic thinkers, by analogy, are ones who go to their doctor because they do not feel well. In turn, their doctor tells them that they must get more exercise and lose 20 pounds, to which they respond, "Can't you just prescribe a pill? I don't want to change my lifestyle." If, on the other hand, we modern humans are to live with any measure of dignity and comfort, the symptomatic rationale embedded in our contemporary lifestyles must give way to a systemic approach that recognizes and accepts the reciprocal interactions among all aspects of social-environmental sustainability worldwide. Granted, this sounds like a daunting task, yet in our view it is paramount to human survival. Our hope is to encourage the acceptance of this challenge and to make the case that a more life-enhancing path exists than the dismal course we are now following toward a predictable culmination of great suffering and widespread deprivation.

A symptomatic thinker reminds me (Carol) of a superintendent for whom I once worked. When I presented him with the fact that an endangered plant species was found on the edge of the proposed site of the new visitor center at the park, he replied, "Can't you move it? It's just a plant."

In contrast to product-oriented and symptom-oriented thinkers, *systemic thinkers* tend more toward a systems approach to thinking. A systems thinker sees the whole in each piece and is therefore concerned about tinkering willy-nilly with the pieces because they know such tinkering might inadvertently upset the desirable function of the system as a whole. A systems thinker is also likely to see him- or herself as an inseparable part of the system instead of apart from and above the system. A systems thinker is willing to focus on transcending the issue in whatever way is necessary to frame a vision for the good of the future.

A systems thinker is most often an urban dweller who is likely to be concerned about the welfare of others, including those of the future and their nonhuman counterparts. Systems thinkers also tend to be concerned with the health and welfare of planet Earth in the present for the future. And they readily accept shades of gray in their thinking.

There are still other generalizations that can be made, such as people who are visually oriented as opposed to those who respond to sound or touch. In addition, these traits come in a variety of combinations, which indicates how different and complex people can be in response to their life experiences. These differences and complexities naturally carry over into people's patterns of communication. None of these patterns is better than any other as far as the mediation process is concerned; each is only different and needs to be understood.

In the end, having incorporated all of the familial pieces within ourselves in one way or another—both functional and dysfunctional—we (in the generic) go out into the world and take our families with us. How we grow up thus determines how we approach life.

As I (Chris) finally broke the cycle of dysfunction within myself, I learned something that is critical to resolving conflicts of any kind: The more a person is drawn toward peace and an optimistic view of the future, the more functional (psychologically healthy) an individual is. Conversely, the more a person is drawn toward debilitating destructive conflict, cynicism, and pessimism about the future, the more dysfunctional (psychologically unhealthy) an individual is.

Making Language Real

Recognizing and understanding the nuances of how people use language is a vital clue to one's personality dynamics. Such understanding is critical in altering the dynamics of a conflict and in helping combatants to resolve their differences with dignity.

Concrete words refer to objects a person can directly experience. Abstract words, on the other hand, represent ideas that cannot be experienced directly. They are shorthand symbols used to sum up vast areas of experience or concepts that reach into the trackless time of the future. Albeit they are convenient and useful, abstractions can lead to misunderstandings.

The danger of using abstractions is that they may evoke an amorphous generality in the receiver's mind and not the specific item of experience the sender intended. The receiver has no way of knowing what experiences the sender intends an abstraction to include. For example, it is common practice to use such abstract terms as *proper method* or *shorter than*, but these terms alone fail to convey the sender's intent. What exactly is the "proper method"? It is shorter than *what*?

When abstractions are used in mediation, they must be linked to specific experiences through examples, analogies, and illustrations. It is even better to use simple, concrete words with specific meanings as much as possible. In this way, the mediator gains greater control of the images produced in the receiver's mind, and language becomes a more effective tool.

Since I (Chris) mediate the resolution of environmental conflicts, I endeavor to get the participants physically out of the comfortable conference room and into the field, where we can wander through the area of conflict and discuss it. I can thus transform the abstractions of the conference room into concrete examples of the field, which one can see, touch, smell, hear, and, if necessary, taste.

For example, I was asked to mediate a better understanding between a local mill owner/logger and the personnel of the U.S. Forest Service in the state of Colorado. The mill owner had recently purchased a large, expensive piece of logging equipment that was more efficient in harvesting trees than were the men who used to work for him, who the machine had replaced. The problem was that the huge piece of equipment was severely compacting the fragile soils of the mountainous forest, to the ecological detriment of the sustainable productive future of the forest. But the mill owner did not understand the ecological effects he was causing.

I spent two days with the Forest Service folks and the mill owner. The first day was spent in the conference room, where I showed slides of how forest ecologists at that time thought a forest functioned both above and below ground. The audience was asked to explore the consequences of long-term management decisions on both the native forest ecosystems and their human culture. Much of the discussion on the first day was a maze of abstractions to the mill owner, no matter how simply I explained the data, because he had no frame of reference for what happened below ground.

The second day was spent in the forest in the area where the logging was taking place. We discussed the concepts and data from the first day as we examined and discussed the actual soil condition in the uncut forest and compared it to the area just logged. Throughout the discussion, which included digging in and examining the soil to establish a common frame of reference, I related our observations to the abstract notions of the day before.

By midafternoon, yesterday's abstractions became today's concrete examples to the mill owner, and he began to understand what the Forest Service folks had been trying to tell him. Finally, much to my surprise, he turned to the forest supervisor and said that he had never really understood the consequences of his actions on the forest and on his young son's options to log if he so chose. He said that while the piece of equipment was more efficient and cost-effective than the men who used to work for him, it was compacting the soil so much that the forest might have trouble coming back. He said he realized that by making a little more money now, he might be costing his son the opportunity to log in the future, and he owed his son that chance. Thus, he thought that he should sell the piece of equipment and rehire the men.

In another case, I was asked by a forest supervisor in Minnesota to conduct a two-day workshop on the ecological value of old-growth forests. The supervisor had one district ranger who saw only dollar signs when he looked at the big, old trees and resisted anything that prevented him from cutting them as fast as possible. The problem was that the forest supervisor had established an old-growth committee throughout the entire forest to create a long-term, forestwide management plan for the old-growth component of the ecosystem. For the committee to be effective, however, it had to include a representative from every district, but this particular ranger refused to assign anyone from his district to the committee.

Folks from throughout the forest and I spent the first day in a conference room, where I showed slides of how a forest functions above and below ground. I emphasized the role of large-woody material, such as whole, old-growth trees that fell onto the forest floor and ultimately decomposed into the forest soil. Again, this was a day of general discussion of people's perceptions and frames of reference. As such, it was riddled with abstractions for some of the people, including the ranger.

Knowing this, I took the group into the field the next day, where we explored the abstractions of the first day in the concreteness of touchable examples. The ranger was quiet most of the time, appearing skeptical at best. Partway through the afternoon, however, he went up to the forest supervisor and said, "I never thought about a forest like this. I still don't understand everything I've heard, but I want to be on the old-growth committee myself."

This, again, was for me a totally unexpected outcome, but it illustrates the power of the mediation process to raise a person's level of understanding and thus the person's consciousness of cause and effect. When mediation is done in the way we (Carol and Chris) practice it, the process protects people's dignity and so makes it easier for them to change their thinking because they feel themselves to be in a venue of psychological safety.

Inability to Transfer Experiences from One Situation to Another

Another major barrier to communication is the inability to transfer the outcomes of experience from one kind of situation to another. The potential ability to transfer results of experiences from here to there is influenced by the breadth of one's experiences. Every group represents a vast array of experiences, some broad, others narrow.

Experiential transfer, however, is critical to understanding how ecosystems and their interconnected, interactive components function, including the bridge between a community and its surrounding environment. It is also a necessary ability in resolving environmental conflicts, whereby potential outcomes can be projected to a variety of possible future conditions.

When participants cannot make such transfers for lack of the necessary frame of reference, they find many of the ideas to be abstractions, whereas others, with the required experience, feel them to be concrete examples, based on their accumulated knowledge. This is where analogies are useful.

To make sure that my (Chris's) analogy will be understood, I ask the participants if they are familiar with the concrete example I propose to use in helping to extend the their frame of reference to include the abstraction. If I am talking about the value of understanding how the various components of an ecosystem interact as a basis for the apparent stability of the system, I may use the following examples:

1. *What happens when just one part is removed?* A helicopter crashed in Nepal some years ago, killing two people. A helicopter has a great variety of pieces with a wide range of sizes. The particular problem here was with the engine, which is held together by many nuts and bolts. Each of these nuts and bolts has a small, sideways hole through it so that a tiny "safety wire" can be inserted; the ends are then twisted together to prevent the tremendous vibration created by a running engine from loosening and working the nut off the bolt.

   The helicopter crashed because a mechanic forgot to replace one tiny safety wire that kept the lateral control assembly together. A nut vibrated off its bolt, the helicopter lost its stability, and the pilot lost control. All this was caused by one missing piece that altered the entire functional dynamics of the aircraft. The engine had been "simplified" by one piece—a small length of wire.

Which piece of the helicopter was the most important at the moment of the crash? The point is that each part (structural diversity) has a corresponding relationship (functional diversity) with every other part. They provide stability only by working together within the limits of their evolved potential in biology or designed purpose in mechanics.

2. *What happens when a process is "simplified"?* The newly elected mayor of a city, whose budget is overspent, guarantees to balance the budget; all that is necessary, in a simplistic sense, is to eliminate some services whose total budgets add up to the overexpenditure. This analogy represents the *symptomatic* approach to problem solving, which is always simplistic. What would happen, for example, if all police and fire services were eliminated? Would it make a difference, if the price were the same and the budget could still be balanced, if garbage collection was eliminated instead?

The trouble with such a simplistic view is in looking only at the cost of and not the function performed by the service. The diversity of the city is being simplified by removing one or two services, without paying attention to the functions performed by those services. To remove a piece of the whole may be acceptable, provided we know which piece is being removed, what it does, and what effect the loss of its function will have on the stability of the system as a whole.

Once I am sure that the participants are following the analogy, then I can help them transfer the concept to the abstraction. As the principle of transfer becomes clear, the abstraction begins to take on the qualities of a concrete idea, and the barrier to communication is dissolved. Removing such barriers is important if the mediation process is to fulfill its greatest potential for safeguarding social-environmental sustainability.

References

1. James Allen. *As a Man Thinketh*. Grosset & Dunlap, New York (1981).
2. Koeret van Mensvoort. Children's Dictionary Dumps "Nature" Words. http://www.nextnature.net/?p=3110 (accessed May 29, 2009).
3. Elaine Brooks. Eco Child's Play. http://ecochildsplay.com/2009/02/02/nature-words-dropped-from-childrens-dictionary/ (accessed May 29, 2009).
4. Words deleted and added to the *Oxford Junior Dictionary* have been compiled from Children's Dictionary Dumps "Nature" Words.
5. Richard Louv. *Last Child in the Woods: Saving Our Children from Nature-Deficit Disorder*. Algonquin Books, Chapel Hill, NC (2008).
6. J.M. Healey. Early television exposure and subsequent attention problems in children. *Pediatrics*, 113 (2004):917–918.
7. Helen Keller. http://thinkexist.com/quotation/security_is_mostly_a_superstition-it_does_not/10997.html (accessed February 24, 2011).
8. Don Costar. No need to change grazing practices. Letters to the editor. *Reno-Gazette Journal*, Reno, Nevada (January 13, 1995).

7

The Process Is the Decision

Introduction

The process of mediating the resolution of a destructive conflict is the *decision* for the combatants. For this statement to be valid, however, mediation must be freely sought and accepted, and I (Carol or Chris) must be mutually acceptable to all parties as their mediator. In addition, because people change their positions most easily when their dignity is intact, it is the mediator's task to make the process as gentle and dignified as possible.

Further, for the process to work, everyone involved must understand and accept that the primary responsibility for the resolution of a conflict lies with the parties themselves. They must reach agreement voluntarily, which means that the mediator must protect each party, to the extent possible, from any pressure that may jeopardize a voluntary decision to resolve the disagreement.

There is yet another ingredient in the milieu of mediation that must be accounted for prior to reaching agreement between or among parties. Namely, the mediator must earn the respect and trust of the people involved and simultaneously help them find faith in themselves; today's trust enables the future by forgiving the mistakes we all make while growing up. Through such forgiveness, we (in the generic) free one another to perform in the present for all generations through the environment of trust. In addition, the mediator's behavior must foster faith in the process itself, which is a major step toward success.

Faith in the Process Is Belief in the Outcome

Faith, which is belief without evidence, keeps the dreamers dreaming, the doers doing, and the process flowing. If the mediator has faith in the outcome of the facilitation process, it fosters the participants' faith in it as well. That notwithstanding, however, I (Chris) must have faith in the process because I never know what is going to happen or what the outcome may be. "Faith," says Indian philosopher and poet Rabindranath Tagore, "is the bird that knows dawn and sings while it is still dark."[1]

Throughout history, some of greatest thinkers adopted faith as a principle, the description of which appeared in the writing of St. Augustine:

> *Understanding follows faith*. We do not believe what we are already able to understand, but attempt to understand that in which we have faith. … The fact that knowledge, or understanding, does not come before faith means inevitably that faith entails risk. The risk entailed in faith is of a very special sort; it involves no calculation. … The emphasis in faith is on the willingness to risk, not on the chances of losing your wager.[2] (italic in original)

I (Chris) learned faith while planting peas as a young child. After I planted my peas, I immediately began wondering if they were growing, so I would dig some of them up to see. Sometimes I even dug them up more than once a day. Those that I dug up too often died, but those I left alone long enough or those I failed to find germinated and grew. I could then see them coming up through the soil. I did not know what went on in the soil because I could not see, but I learned that if I was patient, the seeds would grow, and that each pea seed would grow only a pea plant— a profound lesson in faith.

Most of us, without even thinking about it, place an extraordinary amount of faith in taxicab drivers to get us safely where we are going. I (Chris) have had many and varied experiences in taxis in such different places as New York City; Washington, DC; Cairo, Egypt; New Delhi, India; Tokyo, Japan; and Paris, France. I have actually gone through Cairo and Tokyo with my eyes closed, and in Paris, my wife, Zane, dug holes in my hand with her fingernails as the driver wove in and out of howling, bumper-to-bumper traffic at kamikaze speed. Yet I have never been in an accident in a taxi.

I also fly a lot, and I have faith in the whole concept of an airplane. That huge gadget actually gets off the ground, stays in the air, and lands in some predictable manner. In addition, it usually ends up where I am told it will. What is even more amazing is that it most often gets to the appointed destination on or about the time I am told it will, and I have not had a pilot run out of fuel yet. I have, however, had some interesting experiences flying.

In another vein, have you ever looked closely at leaf buds on a tree in winter? I (Chris) am still awed that inside the frozen buds are miniature leaves just waiting for spring to release them from bondage. I find the same miracle in the seeds of a flower. Each seed has already present, hidden within its coat, all the radiant colors of the flower, like an artist's paint stored in tubes, and I can imagine what the flower will look like when it blooms. Yet, if my lack of faith causes me to break open either bud or seed, I destroy the miracle.

In all these instances, I had faith in the outcome. I have risked my life in taxis and airplanes based on faith in the outcome of my venture. I also have faith that trees will continue to leaf out each spring and that flowers will continue to bloom, each in its own time.

We do a thousand things each day armored with our past experience of their having worked but with no direct evidence that they will work again, although we have faith that they will work as before. Yet how often have you heard someone say: "I'll believe it when I see it," rather than, "I'll believe it until I see it, and then I'll know it."

We (in the generic) live by faith all the time. Even the practice of science is based on faith: faith in the questions posed, faith in the procedures used, faith in the data collected, and faith in the interpretation of the data. I (Chris) remember, for example, testifying before an administrative tribunal in Toronto, Canada, in 1991, regarding forestry practices in the Province of Ontario.

I spent two days explaining, based on more than twenty years of research, my interpretation of forested ecosystems and how they function. On the third day, my cross-examination began by a criminal lawyer hired by the timber industry. At one point, she wanted to challenge my data with a number of other studies, which she contended would refute my findings.

"My data are my truth," I said, "and I will not allow it to be compared to other data. My truth needs no defense, but it might need explanation."

At that point she hissed, "You mean to tell me that you expect the tribunal to accept your data on faith?"

"But of course," I replied. "They either accept my data on faith, or they accept someone else's on faith. I don't know what the correct answer is, nor does anyone else. Whatever data the tribunal accepts will of necessity be accepted on faith."

"Yes, but," began the lawyer, "I still think ... "

The chairwoman of the tribunal interrupted. "I agree with Mr. Maser," she said. "You have made your point, now please proceed."

Someone once said that it is not the load that wears you down; it is the way you carry it. The way we each carry our load depends on our understanding and acceptance of faith as the guiding principle of life. We must have faith in something greater than ourselves because self-knowledge comes through struggle with things unseen, things that help us understand not only ourselves but also the struggles of others. Life, after all, is a matter of faith, not of sight.

The same is true of the mediation process. It only works with both active participation and faith in the primacy of the process.

The Primacy of Process

A *process* is the functional interaction of two or more components and is the necessary sequence of steps toward a desired outcome—the product. But first you need to know what outcome you want. Then you need to focus on the process with a consistent, constant, disciplined effort. If you focus only on the outcome, you destroy the process, as clearly stated in Thomas Merton's translation of Chuang Tzu's classical poem:

> When an archer is shooting for nothing he has all his skills.
> If he shoots for a brass buckle, he is already nervous …
> The prize divides him.
> He cares.
> He thinks more of winning than of shooting—and the need
>   to win
> Drains him of power.[3]

The story of the brass buckle is often applicable in life. My (Chris's) grades in college, for example, were mediocre, including my first term in graduate school, for which I barely qualified. I was so worried about maintaining a B grade point average (the brass buckle) that I could not study (shoot my arrows well). I was so worried about the outcome that it was my entire focus.

One day I decided that I was not going to make it in graduate school anyway, so I decided to forget about grades. I would just go to school while my money lasted and concentrate on learning what I wanted to know. It was only then that learning became an exciting process. Once I became focused on the process of learning and forgot about the grades, I never got below a B average again.

Years later I had another poignant lesson about the relationship between process and product. While working in the U.S. Department of the Interior, Bureau of Land Management (BLM, as it is usually called), I was ordered to go to Washington, DC, to brief the staff of the director of the BLM about the results of our research. I was being given an opportunity to speak, and I wanted my audience to hear what I had to say. Therein lay the problem.

I was single in those days, and I thought of myself as a "wildlife biologist," which meant I had to uphold the image of an underpaid martyr for the cause. Since I had never been in the "big time" or gone to Washington,

DC, as I was now suddenly ordered to do, I asked my friend Jack Thomas about the "big city."

Toward the end of our discussion, Jack asked:

"What are you going to wear when you speak to the director's staff? Do you have a $200 suit?"

"No," I snapped, "I don't have a $200 suit, and what's more I'm not going to get one. I'm going to wear my biologist clothes. After all, I'm going there to talk to them, not to put on a fashion show!"

"Do you really want them to hear you," Jack asked, "or just look at you?"

"To hear me, of course," I growled in righteous indignation. "How I look has nothing to do with what I say."

"True," he said, "but they have to get past how you look before they can hear what you say."

At some level in my being, I knew he was right, but I didn't know why. Yet I could not just give in, so I said, "I'll think about it," and left his office.

That evening I grudgingly took stock of my clothes. Except for a few drab, almost worn-out shirts from Sears, the rest of my clothes were from the Salvation Army, where I had figured out that I could get $250 worth of clothing for $17.50. Besides, what difference would it make if I wore a blue denim shirt with green and brown plaid pants that were three inches too short as long as I was clean and sounded intelligent? Furthermore, I had my good army shoes. True, they were twenty-five years old, but no one would notice the holes in the soles if I kept my feet on the floor.

As soon as Jack got to the lab the next day, he called down to my office. "Maser, come up here."

I went upstairs to his office.

"Have you thought over what you're going to wear to DC?" he demanded.

"Yes," I answered.

"Well, what have you decided?" he asked indignantly. "Do you want to be heard or just stared at?"

"Heard," I said flatly.

Jack picked up his telephone and rang Marion's number. Marion, our head secretary and business manager, was a wonderful, understanding woman.

"Marion," said Jack, "Maser's going to fun city next week, and he needs a $200 suit. Will you please take him to town and get him some DC clothes?"

"I'd love to!" she replied.

Because two people cared enough to take the time and had the patience to walk me through one of my blind spots, I was in fact heard in Washington, DC. The director's staff might not have liked what I had to say, but I was heard.

Jack taught me an important lesson. If I want a particular outcome, such as being heard, I must go through whatever process or take whatever steps are necessary to achieve that outcome. In this case, it meant wearing the appropriate clothing, even if I did not agree with it or even like it. It meant that I had to make a choice, and that I had to accept the outcome of that choice. Thus, the clothing I wore in Washington, DC, determined the staff's perception of me. My appearance became their truth not only about me as a person but also about what I said. It was, after all, my choice—and my outcome.

Perception Is Truth; Facts Are Relative

The Indian spiritual leader Mahatma Gandhi said: "A votary of truth is often obliged to grope in the dark."[4] Our collective challenge, therefore, lies in our blind spots, not in our vision. Unlike correcting a blind spot in the rear view of an automobile, which can be rectified simply by adding a different kind of mirror or a supplemental one, we cannot correct our personal blind spots so easily. To correct them, we must grow in our perception and in our acceptance of what is. *Perceive* means to seize wholly, to see all the way through. Perception is thus the act of seeing in the mind, of understanding.

For Socrates, true knowledge was more than a simple inspection of facts, although the last can provide important information. Rather, true knowledge was the power of the mind to understand the enduring elements that remained after the facts disappeared. While our perceptions grow and change as we mature, not everyone's perceptions mature at the same rate, which accounts for the widely differing degrees of consciousness with respect to cause-and-effect relationships. This disparity is neither good nor bad; it simply means that each of us has different gifts to give at different times in our lives as we see truth differently.

Truth is absolute; perceptions of truth are relative. Therefore, facts, which are perceptions of truth, are relative and thus *some version of the truth*, but not "The Truth." Consider the following statement: The world functions perfectly; our perception of how the world functions is imperfect. People assume this statement to be true because it accepts "universal laws" (both biophysical and spiritual) as absolute truth. But what are those laws? How do they work? We do not know because our perception is constantly changing as we increase the scope of our knowledge.

Trying to understand the universal laws is the essence of science. Yet, even having worked as a scientist for more than twenty years, I (Chris) would not know a "scientific truth" if I stepped on one because my perception of how the universe works is constantly changing. A "scientific fact"—in the conventional sense—is therefore a fact only by consensus of the scientists, which means that a scientific fact or "truth" is only an approximation of what is. It represents our best understanding of reality at a particular moment and is constantly subject to change as we learn.

Nevertheless, perception *is* learning because cause and effect are always connected. Gandhi reached this conclusion when he said:

> At the time of writing I never think of what I have said before. My aim is not to be consistent with my previous statements on a given question, but to be consistent with truth as it may present itself to me at a given moment. The result has been that I have grown from truth to truth; I have saved my memory an undue strain; and what is more, whenever I have been obliged to compare my writing even of fifty years ago with the latest, I have discovered no inconsistency between the two.[5]

Gandhi was consistent in his changing perceptions of what the truth was at different stages in his life. He grew from truth to truth as his vision cleared, and he could see greater and greater vistas. He said that if one found an "inconsistency" between any two things he wrote, the reader "would do well to choose the latter of the two on the same subject."[6]

As I (Chris) have grown, I am increasingly struck by the way my perception of "what is" continues to unfold. I see the world anew; I perceive it differently. My reality is therefore different, and I am increasingly capable of responding to what is without making a value judgment because, as British physician Edward Bach says, "The knowledge of Truth also gives to us the certainty that, however tragic some of the events of the world may appear to be, they form but a temporary stage in the evolution of man."[7]

The accepted definitions of truth are only modifications of the definitions of perception. Truth as a human understanding resides in everyone's heart, and it is there one must search for it. Although we must each be guided by truth as we see it, no one has a right to coerce others to act according to their own view of truth. In the end, our "detector of truth" is our inner voice. Thus, there is no magic in the perfection of hindsight; it only points out that we did not listen to our inner voice when it spoke the first time.

The truth of the human mind is relative and therefore but a perception of that which is true. If our perception of a truth were in fact *the truth*, we would find no such thing as a *half-truth* or *some version of the truth*.

Truth is perfect understanding of that which is. It is neither the spoken nor the written word, although these may have a ring of truth to them. Truth cannot be defined; it can only be experienced and lived. The following is a case in point:

> Environmentalists and native Indians have banded together to launch an unprecedented attack on the industry's forest practices.
>
> Their campaigns against MacMillan Bloedel [Company] in Moresby Island in the Queen Charlottes and against B.C. Forest Products in the Stein Valley in southwestern British Columbia, among others, have focused much unwanted attention on forestry.
>
> The industry [mainly MacMillan Bloedel] launched a multimillion-dollar public relations campaign last year to counter the lobby by environmentalists and Indians.
>
> Ray Smith, MacMillan Bloedel's president, says the industry began its campaign, which includes television commercials stressing his company's commitment to the environment, because "the Industry's side of the story wasn't being told."
>
> Smith says he, like the environmentalists, feels sad when stately 400-year-old trees are felled.
>
> "But they serve a magnificent purpose too."[8]

I (Chris) have been in British Columbia, and I have seen mile after mile of back-to-back clear-cuts made by the MacMillan Bloedel Company. (You can also see it in a book titled *Clearcut: The Tragedy of Industrial Forestry.*[9]) Understand that what I see is what I experience, and what I experience becomes my truth. What you see is what you experience, and what you experience becomes your truth.

The environmentalists and the Aboriginal Canadians were upset by what the company had done to the forest—through their own experience of what the company had done, not by what they *think* it had done. What the company said in its multimillion-dollar public relations campaign could not alter what the people experienced.

Much of British Columbia had already been deforested, and the evidence was clearly visible. Nevertheless, the company was trying to tell the people that what they had experienced on the landscape was not what they really experience when they look at mile after mile of often-unstable logging roads and square mile after square mile of back-to-back clear-cuts. No amount of defense on the part of the company could hide the evidence.

Here it must be made clear that the only "facts" in the world are the result of things we can see—observable, quantifiable events. For example, the fact that glaciers are melting all over the world is a fact. It not only is measurable but also has been measured. That is irrefutable. Now, why the glaciers are melting, what role humans have played in the melting, and what it means for our collective future is another question—one based on an interpretation of the observable facts. These interpretations are arguable based on an individual's perception of the world and how things within it function.

When you and I defend something, it is because we feel attacked, and we feel attacked because at some level we are dealing with a personal untruth. All our defense does is call attention to our untruth, uneasiness, and lack of harmony because truth ignored becomes a predator.

In British Columbia, therefore, it was the citizens' perceptions of MacMillan Bloedel's *motives*, as expressed across the landscape through its deeds and the attitude with which those deeds were performed that were being called into question. No public relations campaign could change that. Thus, while the company may have succeeded within the realm of its motives, it failed in the public's perception of land trusteeship, in part because the visible effects of such massive clear-cut logging could not, to the public, be reframed in positive environmental terms.

Reframing the Issue

Although our educational systems in the United States—beginning with parents and ending with universities—stress the positive, they usually teach in terms of the negative. What does this statement mean?

Suppose your neighbor lives along a busy street and has a little boy named Jimmy. Your neighbor is concerned about Jimmy because of the increasing automobile traffic in the neighborhood.

One day, Jimmy's mother says to him, "Jimmy, *don't go* into the *street*." The directive words (those telling Jimmy what to do) are "don't go" (a confusing contradiction), but the operative words Jimmy hears are "go street." To him, "don't" is an abstraction, whereas "go street" is a concrete directive. So he goes into the street and gets hit by a car.

What Jimmy's mother really meant and needed to have said was, "Jimmy, *stay in* the *yard*." Then the directive words (the ones telling Jimmy what to do) would have been "stay in" (clear and concise with a singular meaning), and the last word Jimmy would have heard was "yard" (again, clear and concise with a singular meaning). He would therefore have remained in the yard and would still be alive.

This example illustrates that, having been raised trying to make positive statements out of negative ones, we spend most of our lives trying to move away from the negative, unwanted circumstance—and we cannot. We can only move *toward* a positive, desired situation.

Let us look at an example from the Northwest Territories of Canada. A few years ago, I (Chris) was asked to help a band of Aboriginal Canadians create a vision for some 800 square kilometers of forest for which they had to draft a management plan that was acceptable not only to them but also to the Canadian territorial and federal governments.

After we had gone through the educational part of the workshop (how forests, streams, and rivers function and how humans can fit into the processes), we went into the forest, where I instructed the participants to sit down and be silent for twenty minutes. I told them to listen to the forest and feel its heartbeat, something they acknowledged never having done. Afterward, we discussed how they were feeling, what they were thinking, and what the experience had meant to them. Then, with a much-heightened awareness of their forest and its cultural significance, we went back to the conference room, where I asked them what their vision of the future was, what they wanted their forest to look like.

> *"We don't want it to look like B.C.," was the answer. (B.C. is the abbreviation for British Columbia, which in the northern part, just south of the border with the Northwest Territories, is laced with gigantic clear-cuts to which the Aboriginal Canadians objected. Although I did not, on this occasion, ask them why they did not like the clear-cuts, questions about participants' negative feelings are often instructive. They can help both a mediator and the participants themselves more fully understand the emotions behind a particular point of view.)*
> *"I appreciate what you're saying," I replied. "So what do you want your forest to look like?" I queried again.*
> *"We don't want it to look like it does south of the border," was the reply.*

After two or three more such exchanges, I realized that the participants did not know how to frame their vision, their desire for the future, in a positive statement. All they could do was try to move away from the perceived negative.

I thus spent considerable time helping them reframe the negative into a positive by asking a series of questions.

> *"What is your staple diet?"*
> *"Moose" was the reply.*
> *"What kind of habitat do moose need?"*
> *"Willow and birch thickets."*
> *"When do you hunt moose?"*
> *"In the late summer and autumn."*
> *"Do you have any medicinal plants that are important to you?"*
> *"Yes, such and such."*
> *"Where do they grow?"*
> *"In this kind of place and that kind of place."*

"I notice that birch bark is used to make various domestic objects. Are birch trees
important to you?"
"Yes."

The exchange continued. Finally, I asked if anything had been omitted or forgotten. A few things came to mind.

While I was asking these questions and the participants were responding, someone was writing both questions and answers on a large flip chart. The filled sheets were then fastened to the walls of the room. After completing this initial phase of reframing, the participants forgot about the clear-cuts in British Columbia and began focusing on the cultural requirements that needed to be translated into their forest plan.

After taking the ideas from the sheets on the walls and crafting an outline, then sentences and paragraphs, the final prose was distilled into a vision statement and a series of goals (discussed at length in Chapter 10). Through the simple process of questions and answers, the participants' negative fears were translated, by the participants themselves, into a shared vision and goals for the positive future of their forest and hence their culture.

To further the translation process and help the Aboriginal Canadians learn how to do it, I asked a member of their community (whom they selected) to sit next to me in front of the group. His purpose was twofold: (1) He was my "cultural attaché," the person I relied on to make sure that I did not inadvertently breach cultural etiquette; and (2) it was his responsibility to learn the process of helping the community reframe negatives into positives.

As the process continued, I increasingly gave the responsibility to him until, in the end, all he needed was a gentle coaching here or there. In this way, the focus was taken off me and placed on him as he learned how to lead his people through the process. This gave him an indispensable skill for the community while making me dispensable. The outcome was an acceptable management plan of the people, by the people, and for the people—of all generations.

There is great power in learning to reframe negatives into positives. In so doing, the participants not only understand the conflict from another vantage point but also understand that much of the confusion in communication comes from trying to move away from unwanted negative circumstances. Trying to move away from a negative situation precludes people from saying what they really mean because they are focused on what they do not want. As long as people express what they do not want, it is virtually impossible for them to figure out what they *do* want. It is thus the mediator's continual task to aid the parties in reframing their negative fears into positive potentials, which helps them begin to see conflict as a learning partnership.

References

1. Rabindranath Tagore. Rabindranath Tagore quotes. http://thinkexist.com/quotes/rabindranath_tagore/2.html (accessed on March 16, 2010).
2. James P. Carse. *The Silence of God*. Macmillan, New York (1985).
3. Thomas Merton. *The Way of Chuang Tzu*. New Directions, New York (1965).
4. Louis Fischer. *The Essential Gandhi: An Anthology of His Writings on His Life, Work, and Ideas*. Random House, New York (1962).
5. Richard Attenborough. *The Words of Gandhi*. Newmarket Press, New York (1982).
6. Ibid.
7. Edward Bach. Heal thy self. In: *The Bach Flower Remedies*. Keats, New Canaan, CT, 1997.
8. Associated Press. British Columbia wood companies face challenges. *The Sunday Oregonian* (August 7, 1988).
9. Bill Devall (ed.). *Clearcut: The Tragedy of Industrial Forestry*. Sierra Club Books/Earth Island Press, San Francisco (1993).

8

Conflict Is a Learning Partnership

Introduction

When combatants can perceive and understand conflict as a learning partnership, it is much easier for them to ask their perceived adversary, "Will you please help me to sort out this problem?" And when they get the answer, it is rarely threatening. Through asking for help, they often find some terrified, repressed part of themselves looking back at them through their "adversary's" eyes.

In a sense, mediating the resolution of an environmental dispute is much like being a therapeutic counselor. To understand what this means, we recommend reading Chapter 14 in a work by Corey, from which the following quotation is taken: "Since counselors are asking people to take an honest look at themselves and to make choices concerning how they want to change, it is critical that counselors themselves be searchers who hold their own lives open to the same kind of scrutiny."[1]

It therefore falls on us (Carol and me) to treat the mediation process as a learning partnership, which means that *we* must also be open to learning. If we are not willing to learn, we cannot teach because teacher and student are one and the same. Transformative mediation is thus an assembly of students and teachers who agree to learn with and from one another, with the mediator acting as an invited guide throughout the process.

A Mediator Is at All Times a Guest and a Leader Simultaneously

A mediator must be a guest at all times in the process as well as the leader. As such, Carol and I, as mediators, must learn to lead. Before we can learn to lead, however, we must learn to follow. The act of leadership demands humility, whereas the outcome of leadership demands grace. This is one way of saying that we are responsible for our conscience, and everyone else is responsible for his or hers. Thus, while we may, through our mediation process, help people to change their views, we cannot judge the way in which they do so.

Leadership Is the Art of Being a Servant

True leadership is concerned primarily with mediating someone else's ability to reach their potential as a human being. Leadership comes from the heart and deals intimately with human values and human dignity. We must lead by example, as Francis Bacon noted when he said, "He that gives good advice, builds with one hand; he that gives good counsel and example, builds with both; but he that gives good admonition and bad example, builds with one hand and pulls down with the other."[2]

A leader knows and does what is right from moral conviction, usually expressed as enthusiasm, which causes people to want to follow with action. Essentially, a leader is one who values people and helps them transcend their fears so they might be able to act in a manner other than they were capable of doing on their own.

Leadership has to do with authority, which is control, or the right or power to command, enforce laws, exact obedience, determine, or judge. Two kinds of authority are embodied in this definition: that of a person and that of a position.

The authority of a person begins as an inner phenomenon. It comes from one's belief in one's higher consciousness, which acts as a guide in life when one listens to it: "As a man thinketh in his heart, so is he."[3] In contrast, a person who has only the authority of position may have a socially accepted seat of power over other people, but *power can exist only if people agree to submit their obedience to authority*. A person who holds a position of authority, yet does not live from the authority within, can only manage or rule as a dictator—through coercion and fear—but cannot lead.

A leader's power to inspire followership comes from a sense of authenticity because the leader has a vision that is other-centered rather than self-centered. Such a vision springs from strength, those universal principles that govern all life with justice and equity, as opposed to the relatively weak foundation of selfish desire. It is the authenticity to which people respond; in responding, they validate their leader's authority.

Managerialship, on the other hand, is of the intellect and pays minute attention to detail, to the letter of the law, and to doing the thing "right" even if it is not the "right thing" to do. A manager relies on the external, intellectual promise of new techniques to solve problems and is concerned that all the procedural pieces are properly accounted for, hence the epithet "bean counter."

Good managers are thus placed at a disadvantage when put in positions of leadership because all such people can do is rise to their level of incompetence and remain there, in which case an ounce of image is worth a pound of performance. Similarly, a leader placed in the position of managerialship is equally inept because the two positions require vastly different skills.

A good mediator, however, must be both an effective leader who guides the mediation process and an effective manager who keeps it running smoothly. By way of example, think of driving a herd composed of a hundred head of cattle.

There are three basic positions in driving cattle: point, flank, and drag. The person riding point is the leader, the one out front guiding the herd. The flankers, or people riding along the sides of the herd, manage the herd by keeping it moving in the desired direction while preventing individuals from leaving the herd. "Riding drag" means to keep the cattle at the rear of the herd moving at a given speed while preventing individuals from dropping out of the herd. Being a mediator is like being a single person who simultaneously must be riding point, flank, and drag because he or she is responsible for moving the whole herd safely from one place to another.

As a leader of the mediation process, one must be the servant of the parties involved. Servant leadership offers a unique mix of idealism and pragmatism.

The idealism comes from having chosen to serve one another and some higher purpose, appealing to a deeply held belief in the dignity of all people and the democratic principle that a leader's power flows from commitment to the well-being of the people. Leaders do not inflict pain, although they often must help their followers to bear it in uncomfortable circumstances, such as compromise. Such leadership is also practical, however, because it has been proven repeatedly that the only leader soldiers will reliably follow when risking their lives in battle is the one who they feel is both competent and committed to their safety.

Carol's and my first responsibility, therefore, is to help the participants examine their senses of reality, and our last responsibility is to say thank you. In between, we not only must provide and maintain momentum but also must be effective. Beware! Most people confuse effectiveness with efficiency. Effectiveness is doing the right thing, whereas efficiency is doing the thing as expeditiously as possible, although at times it may not be the right thing to do.

When the difference between effectiveness and efficiency is understood, it is clear that efficiency can be delegated, but effectiveness cannot. To us, effectiveness is enabling others to reach toward their personal potential through the mediation process. In so doing, we leave behind a legacy of assets invested in other people.

We are also responsible for developing, expressing, and defending the participants' civility and values. Paramount in any mediation process is good manners, respect for one another, and an appreciation of the way in which we serve one another. In this sense, civility has to do with identifying values as opposed to following some predetermined process formula.

For a participant to lose sight of hope, opportunity, the right to feel needed, and the beauty and novelty of ideas is to die a little each day. For us to ignore the dignity of the mediation process, the elegance of simplicity and truth, and the essential responsibility of serving one another is also to die a little each day. In a day when so much energy seems to be spent on mindless conflict, to be a mediator is to enjoy the special privileges of complexity, ambiguity, diversity, and challenge.

As auto manufacturer Henry Ford once said, "Coming together is a beginning; keeping together is progress; working together is success."[4] In the end, it is the collective heart of the people that counts; without people, there is no need for either leaders who mediate or mediators who lead. Lao Tzu, the Chinese philosopher, said of a good leader (mediator), "A leader is best when people barely know he exists, when his work is done, his aim fulfilled, they will say: 'We did it ourselves.'"[5] Such is servant leadership, and such is our goal. To achieve our goal, we must make the mediation process safe enough for people to trust it and willingly give up their hidden agendas.

Hidden Agendas

It is a mediator's responsibility to make the process safe enough that all hidden agendas are placed on the table; otherwise, they can destroy the essence of mediation. A hidden agenda occurs when a person holds back the information about what they really hope to gain from the process. Hidden agendas vary, and only two are discussed here as examples. The first has to do with the hidden agenda of a mediator and the second with that of a participant.

Mediator

I (Chris) was recently part of a national committee dealing with grazing fees on public lands. Our charge was to advise the secretaries of both the Department of the Interior and the Department of Agriculture on how to structure the grazing fee incentive program.

Fairly early in the two-and-a-half-day meeting, the Secretary of the Interior joined us for most of a day. It soon became clear that he wanted a particular outcome, and that he had a definite timetable. This was bad enough in and of itself, but what was worse was that the two mediators knew what he wanted and were doing their level best to covertly push us in that direction. I had the distinct feeling, as did others, that the mediators were trying first and foremost to please the Secretary of the Interior by getting as close as possible to what he wanted as quickly as possible.

The facilitators' hidden agenda became clear on the first day. Whenever someone expressed personal feelings about the issue of grazing and range condition in general, a necessary part of the process, the facilitators did their best to cut that person off and return to the strictly structured, carefully controlled, predetermined mediation format. We were not allowed to deal with our senses of value, either individually or collectively. There were thirty of us who, for the most part, were complete strangers when the meeting was first called to order; thus, we never really got to know one another.

I, as a participant, ended up not trusting the facilitators' intentions and not liking the way I was treated. Consequently, I would not choose to work with them again. They appeared to be strictly product oriented in a self-serving way. Although I do not know what they hoped to gain, my intuition at the time told me it was further employment.

Participant

Some years ago, I (Chris) was asked to participate as an independent observer in a consensus group. At least thirty points of view were represented because at least thirty people, in addition to the mediator and myself, were present. During the two-day meeting, I interpreted three general "collective" views, two of which represented a long-standing battle over whether to cut the water catchment of a particular city. Because I knew nothing about the conflict, even though it had been alive for some years, I had no vested interest in it and could therefore see the collective views. Let us examine my interpretations of them, one at a time.

> *View 1:* A most sincere elderly lady, who had lived in this city all her life, had been told in the third grade that the water catchment of the city, covered with virgin old-growth forest, was her national heritage and would never be cut. Now she found people from a land management agency clear-cutting "her water catchment," and she felt betrayed. Where the third-grade teacher got the notion of an inviolate national heritage is moot. The lady, joined by her son, thought the land management agency should cease and desist all cutting and road building in the water catchment forever. On this she was adamant.
>
> *View 2:* The conservation groups that were represented were unanimously opposed to further logging and roading of the water catchment because the virgin old-growth forest created and protected the pure quality of the water supply of the city.

View 3: The people from the land management agency saw the old-growth timber as an economic commodity that had to be cut and milled or there would be an irreparable economic loss because the old-growth forest would fall down and rot—an unthinkable economic waste.

All three views, each with a stake in the water catchment, played the consensus game with a hidden agenda. The hidden agenda each side was trying to conceal from the others while acting innocently open minded became obvious as the mediation process unfolded. Although the hidden agendas were never admitted, much less openly laid on the table, they were covertly defended whenever someone got too close to the truth—a sure sign that all was not as it appeared. Let us examine each hidden agenda.

View 1: The elderly lady and her son had become rather prominent as distributors of a small newsletter to the group of conservationists interested in saving the old-growth forest of the water catchment. If the lady and her son won their point of view, they would disappear into the oblivion from which they came; with the issue resolved, the other folks would turn to new issues. Thus, whenever reconciliation seemed possible, the son categorically refused to accept anything that had the appearance of moving the problem toward solution. His hidden agenda seemed to be to keep the issue alive and thereby forestall the feeling of rejection through loss of importance and thus loss of identity.

View 2: The conservationists were committed to saving the old-growth forest (trees). Each time the people from the land management agency conceded a point that would benefit water quality but not save the trees, the conservationists had to find a new point from which to argue, one that sounded valid with respect to clean water and did not mention trees.

View 3: The people from the land management agency were committed to cutting the timber for economic reasons. They thus submitted to the procedure, but with the knowledge of the authoritative position and final decision on their side.

Where did we go from here? First, each person was right from his or her point of view, from the personal interpretation of the data. Second, no one in the room really understood consensus. Consensus does not mean something will be enacted; it means that the parties agree to agree on something. And the agreement the participants ended up with was that something needed to be done, which is where they started.

The mission was doomed to failure because *no one* disclosed a real agenda. Why not? They withheld their agendas because there was a lack of trust in the process. After all, the mediator was an employee of the land management agency represented in the dispute, in addition to which the agency both paid for and hosted the session. Without being an impartial third party who had earned the participants' trust, the mediator could neither lead nor teach, even by example.

Rethinking the Use of *Consensus*

Some people consider the word *consensus* to be a negative word. It means that "everyone agrees" with the direction a group is taking, which is often not the case. Dr. Hans Bleiker, founder of the Institute for Participatory Management and Planning, suggests that the term *informed consent* should be considered the ultimate outcome of our mediation efforts, rather than seeking "consensus" from a group of participants. He defines *informed consent* as "the grudging willingness of opponents to go along with a course of action that they are actually still opposed to."[6] It means that, as mediators, we hope the participants will accept the decision that is made, even if they do not agree with it 100 percent, but nevertheless feel they can live with the decision and support it.

There are going to be times, however, when consensus is just not possible. To proceed in those cases, one could obtain the consent of each participant to move forward, despite their inability to reach agreement, because it is best to move forward rather than make no decision or take no action. The "Bleiker life preserver" is a four-step thought process used to guide a group toward informed consent. In brief, it consists of the following four statements:

1. This is a serious problem (or an important opportunity) that just has to be addressed.
2. This group (or agency) is the right entity to address it. In fact, it would be irresponsible for you/them, with the mission that you/they have, not to address it.
3. This approach is reasonable, sensible, and responsible.
4. We do listen; we do care. (Everyone has heard your concerns, and we do care about making the right decision.)[7]

I (Carol) have found the Bleiker life preserver to be helpful when a group is "stuck" and cannot move forward because one or more members feel that reaching consensus is not in their self-interest. In those cases, seeking informed consent has been an invaluable tool in the mediation process.

Mediator as Teacher

Whether one realizes it, a mediator is a teacher in that learning is a change in behavior as a result of an experience, which is the purpose of transformative mediation. Most people who seek mediation have fairly definite ideas about what they want from the process, and they will learn from any activity that tends to further their purposes. Because previous experience conditions a person to respond to some things and to ignore others, it is imperative that the mediation experience is made relevant to the desired outcome, namely, that the parties learn to reconcile their differences and work cooperatively with one another. To accomplish this, some elements of learning must be understood.

The Foundation of Learning

If an experience challenges the learner; if it requires involvement with feelings, thoughts, and memory of past experience; and if it necessitates physical activity, it is more effective than an experience in which all a person has to do is deal with abstractions or commit something to memory. Each person approaches a task with preconceived ideas and feelings and may have these ideas changed for a variety of reasons as a result of experience. The learning process may therefore include the following elements simultaneously: verbal, conceptual, perceptual, emotional, and problem solving.

Learning is multifaceted in still another way. While learning a subject at hand, people learn other things as well. They develop positive or negative attitudes about mediation, depending on their experience with the process. They may, for example, learn greater self-reliance under the guidance of a skillful mediator. Such incidental learning may have a great effect on a person's total development, hence the transformative nature of mediation.

The effectiveness of learning is based on a person's emotional reaction in that learning is strengthened when accompanied by a pleasant feeling and diminished when associated with an unpleasant one. It is thus better to tell the parties involved in the mediation process that their problem, although difficult, is within their capability to understand and resolve. Having said this, however, it is incumbent on us, as mediators, to keep our word. Therefore, whatever learning situation is encountered in the mediation process, it must contain elements that affect the parties positively and produce such feelings as self-worth, success, freedom, clarification, and empowerment—all of which enhance learning.

Part of the foundation of learning is primacy, the state of being first, which often creates a strong, almost unshakable, impression. This means that what we teach through the mediation process must be right the first time. For the parties, it means that the learning must be right the first time because "unteaching" and "unlearning" are far more difficult than teaching and learning. It is thus critical that the first experience be positive and functional, for everything that follows is predicated on this first experience. Part and parcel of this first experience is the notion of intensity because a vivid, dramatic, or exciting experience teaches more than a routine or boring one.

How People Learn

Learning comes initially from perceptions directed to the brain by one or more of the five senses: sight, hearing, touch, smell, and taste. Psychologists have determined experimentally that "normal" individuals acquire about 75 percent of their knowledge through sight, 13 percent through hearing, 6 percent through touch, 3 percent through smell, and 3 percent through taste.[8] Learning occurs most rapidly, however, when information is received through more than one sense.

Nevertheless, real meaning can only come from within a person, even though the sensations evoking these meanings result from external stimuli. People therefore base their actions on the way they believe things are.

Factors Affecting Perception

Learning is a psychological problem, not a logical one. Therefore, the mediator must organize the process to fit the psychology of the participants. As long as a person feels capable of coping with a situation, each new experience can be accepted as a challenge; if, on the other hand, a situation seems overwhelming, the person feels unable to deal with it and perceives a threat. Mediation is thus consistently effective only when those factors influencing perceptions are recognized and taken into account as positively as possible.

Among the factors affecting perception are: (1) basic necessity; (2) self-concept; (3) timing, opportunity, and time; and (4) recognizing an element of threat. *Basic necessity* is a person's need to maintain and enhance the organized self. The self is complete in that it is a physical and psychological combination of a person's past and present experiences, as well as future hopes and fears. A person's most fundamental, pressing necessity is perceived to be perpetuating this identity of *self*, which in turn affects all perceptions.

Just as the food one eats and the air one breathes become part of the physical self, so the sights one sees and the sounds one hears become part of the psychological self. We are psychologically what we perceive.

As a person has physical barriers that prevent dangerous things from harming the physical being, such as flinching from a hot stove, so a person has perceptual barriers that block those sights, sounds, and feelings thought to pose a psychological threat. Helping people to learn thus requires finding ways to aid them in developing different perceptions in spite of their dysfunctional coping mechanisms. Since a person's basic necessity is felt to be self-maintenance, the mediator must recognize that anything asked of a party, which may be interpreted as imperiling the self, will be resisted and denied. Here a thought by Henry Wadsworth Longfellow is apropos: "If we could read the secret history of our enemies, we should find in each man's life, sorrow and suffering enough to disarm all hostilities."[9]

Self-concept, or how one pictures oneself, is a powerful determinant in learning. A person's self-image, described in such terms as "confident" or "insecure," has much influence on one's total perceptual process. If a person's experiences in the mediation process tend to support a favorable self-image, one is more likely to remain open to subsequent experiences. If, on the other hand, a person has negative experiences, which threaten their self-concept, there is a tendency to reject additional participation.

The people in the mediation process who view themselves positively are less defensive and more readily internalize and assimilate their experiences. But those with negative self-concepts activate their psychological barriers, which tend to keep them from perceiving and may actually inhibit their ability to implement that which is perceived in a functional manner.

Timing, opportunity, and time are necessary to perceive and learn. Learning depends on perceptions, which precede those perceptions to be learned. Timing is thus important because a person may not be ready to learn certain things without prior experience. Assuming the timing is right, one requires both the opportunity and the necessary time to accommodate the experience of learning. In addition, the amount of time necessary to learn a given thing differs from person to person.

Finally, *fear* adversely affects one's perception by narrowing the perceptual field. People confronted with a threat tend to focus their attention on the perceived danger, which reduces their field of vision to a fraction of its potential. Anything a mediator does that is interpreted as threatening makes the already frightened person less able to accept a new experience by adversely affecting their physical, emotional, and mental faculties.

Insights

Insights involve grouping perceptions into meaningful wholes, or systems thinking. *Evoking insights is a mediator's main task*; therefore, it is essential to keep each person constantly receptive to new experiences and to help each person realize and understand how a given piece relates to all others in the formation of patterns. Understanding the way in which each piece may affect the others and knowing the way in which a change in any one may affect changes in all others is imperative to true learning. Although insights almost always occur eventually, effective mediation can speed the process by teaching the relationship of perceptions as they occur, thus promoting the development of transformative insights in the mediation process.

Motivation

People in a mediation process are like all other workers in that they want a tangible return for their efforts. If such motivation is to be effective, the participants must believe their efforts will be positively rewarded. Such rewards, whether they are the furtherance of self-interest or group recognition, must be constantly apparent during the mediation process.

Although many lessons with obscure objectives will pay off handsomely later, a person may not appreciate this immediately. If motivation is to be maintained, therefore, it is important to make the participants aware of applications that are not immediately apparent.

Mediators often inadequately appreciate the desire for personal security and comfort. All participants want secure, pleasant conditions and states of being, even under the most trying of circumstances. If they recognize that what they are learning can promote this goal, their interest is easier to attract and hold.

Along these lines, psychologist Abraham Maslow's hierarchy of needs is helpful in understanding this point. Although Maslow's hierarchy of needs is given in the shape of a pyramid, we can visualize the same concept by picturing a stepladder with a wide base and a narrow top. Beginning with the first rung from the bottom are the basic physiological survival needs, such as air, water, food, and shelter. On the second rung are the needs for safety, security, stability, structure, order, limits, and law. The third rung deals with belongingness and love, which express themselves in the need for roots, origin, being part of a social group, and having a family and friends. The fourth rung encompasses self-esteem, which manifests itself in the need for strength, mastery, competence, self-confidence, prestige, status, and dignity. The fifth and highest rung is self-actualization, which is the inner driving need to become all that one can be by knowing truth, justice, beauty, simplicity, and perfection.[10]

Notice how far up the ladder (the fourth rung) one must go before dignity is mentioned. Notice also how many external product-oriented needs must be met before a person feels enough in control of the conditions of life to "afford" a sense of dignity.

Fortunately, there is within each person engaged in a task the belief, however small, that success is possible under the right conditions. This belief can be a most powerful motivating force. A mediator can best foster such motivation by introducing perceptions based solidly on experiences that are easily recognized as achievements in learning.

A majority of people seem to have trouble transferring abstract concepts from one situation to another, as previously discussed. Therefore, concrete examples are important and can be supplied through the use of appropriate analogies, which help participants transfer a commonly understood experience to a foreign situation. For example, a human community can be used to explain how an ecosystem functions. Once the basic principles are understood in a human context, they can be transferred to a forest, grassland, or an ocean, always coming back to the human community as a touchstone. In addition to using good analogies, a wise mediator constantly relates the objectives of the lesson to the participants' intentions and necessities and thereby builds on the participants' natural enthusiasm.

The relationship between a mediator and participants has a profound effect on how much the participants learn and change. Carol and I must create as safe and gentle an environment as possible through our own demeanor to enable participants to help themselves.

The following generalizations about motivated human behavior may be helpful:

1. Work is as natural to people as are play and rest. Work that is a source of satisfaction will be voluntarily performed, but that which is perceived as a form of drudgery or punishment will be avoided if possible.

2. A person will exercise self-direction and self-control in the pursuit of goals to which he or she is committed.

3. A person's commitment to his or her goals is directly related to the perceived reward associated with their achievement.

4. A reasonably functional person learns, under the right conditions, to both accept and seek responsibility. Ambivalence and shirking responsibility are not inherent in human nature, but rather are usually consequences of dysfunctional experiences during childhood and negative, unsafe experiences in life.

5. The capacity to exercise a relatively high degree of imagination, ingenuity, and creativity in the resolution of common problems is a widely distributed human trait.

6. Under the conditions of modern life, the intellectual potentialities of the "average" person are only partially used.[11]

Carol and I accept these assumptions and see vast, untapped potentialities in participants. The raw material lies waiting; its release is partly in our hands and partly in those of the participants.

The Fallacy of Rescuing

Over the years, I (Chris) have been in many situations in which either an individual person, such as the previously discussed fatalist, or a whole group wanted to be rescued. When someone wants to be rescued, the person inevitably wants a quick fix, with me doing all the work.

I have experienced two major problems with this notion. First, the person who ostensibly wants to be rescued will continually fight any effort to be rescued. To this person, wanting help to change sounds good, but the person is not ready to give up the long investment in his or her current situation. The person is getting some kind of value out of it, even if unconsciously.

The second problem is that, even if I could and would rescue someone, my efforts would be of no value. For example, while in Japan in 1992, I spent much time looking at forestry problems and discussing what I saw with Japanese foresters, prefecture mayors, and others. It was clear that the plantations of larch trees, put in by the Americans following World War II, not only were a mistake but also were sick and needed to be replaced with native forest.

After I got home, a Japanese gentleman wrote to me and asked me to plan a forest for a particular area that could be grown for a thousand years. I told him "No." I said that if I, as an American, were to plan a forest for the Japanese, I would be giving the Japanese an American forest planned in America by an American; it would be of no value to them culturally because it would be my forest, planned for me, and based on my own sensibilities. I did say, however, that I would *help* the Japanese plan a forest in Japan for themselves. Then it would be Japanese planning their own forest, with their own species, for their own culture. Only then would the forest be of any value to them.

The point is that each person or group of people must struggle with and through their own processes if they are to derive anything of value from them. Even if I could rescue someone (go through the person's growth process for him or her), I would not. To do so would be stealing the person's struggle to grow and whatever value the person would have derived from it. Besides, that which is not earned is casually tossed aside because the person, not having earned it, finds in it no value. It is thus a mediator's ever-present responsibility to define—through clear boundaries—his or her relationship with the participants while mediating the resolution of a dispute.

The role of the mediator is comparable to the difference between "coaching" and "mentoring" as the terms are used in teaching organizational leadership. I (Carol) recently began coaching several individuals through an agency-based leadership program. It has been an enormously satisfying, yet humbling experience. Coaching involves helping a person arrive at what he or she values and hopes to achieve—to encourage the person, ask questions, be present, and mirror what we hear back to the person to assist him or her on the journey of personal development. A mentor, in contrast, is someone who gives answers, provides guidance, makes the connections, and takes a more active role in determining one's direction or actions. As mediators, we are, by this definition, coaches. We help participants find their own truths, express their true values, and find their own way on their journey toward dispute resolution.

A Mediator's Role in Participant Relationships

Helping to achieve good human relations is one of our (Carol's and my) basic responsibilities. To achieve such relations, we must consider the following points:

1. People gain more from wanting to resolve their own issues and learning in the process than from being forced to participate through such means as court directives.

2. Participants tend to feel secure when they know what to expect or what is going to happen. When they understand the benefits of what is taking place, they are more willing to move forward.

3. Each individual within a group of participants has a unique personality, which we must constantly consider. If, however, we limit our thinking to the group as a whole, without considering the participants as individuals, our efforts are directed toward an average personality—which fits no one.

4. If we give sincere praise or credit when due, we provide an incentive to strive harder. By the same token, insincere praise given too freely is valueless.

5. If a participant is gently briefed, in private, on erroneous assumptions and told how he or she might correct them, progress and accomplishment follow.

6. It is vital that our philosophy and actions are consistent. If a situation, such as being allowed to interrupt and speak out of turn, is acceptable one day but not another, participants become confused.

7. No one, including participants, expects us to be perfect. Nevertheless, the best way for us to win the trust and respect of participants is to admit mistakes honestly. If we try, even once, to bluff or cover up, the participants sense it quickly, and our behavior destroys their confidence in both the mediation process and us. Therefore, if in doubt about some point, we must freely admit it.

These are but a few of the many attitudes and reactions that help establish the kind of mediator-participant relations that promote resolving conflicts through effective learning. To accomplish this kind of learning, however, one must be present in the moment, every moment.

Mediation Means Total Participation

Being present—here and now—is the only way to participate in life, and effective mediation *requires* total participation. But, we (Carol and I) cannot be present if we are thinking about either the past or the future. It is therefore critical that we are totally focused on the present and keep the parties focused totally on the present during the entire process.

What is so important about being present? Have you ever noticed that the present is seldom quite right or seldom seems good enough? Yesterday is past and gone; you cannot change it—opportunities forgone are opportunities lost. Tomorrow is not here, and you have no idea, despite your aspirations, hopes, expectations, and predictions, what it will bring. In reality, tomorrow is something that is always coming, yet never arrives. The present, the here and now, is all anyone ever has. This is *everyone's eternal reality.*

Being present, in the sense of being mentally here, now, is a difficult concept, because there is no word that means mental presence as opposed to simple physical presence. Let us examine what being present means.

Suppose that, while driving, you are thinking about (remembering) the past, say the vacation you took last year. It was your first trip to the Bahamas, and you had a rough flight. The unexpected storm really frightened you, but once in the Bahamas, you had a marvelous time. You are flying to the Bahamas next month for your long-anticipated vacation, and you begin thinking about how much fun you had last year and you expect this year. Suddenly, out of nowhere, you have a vivid flash of the flight of last year and become afraid that the flight next month might be the same. In all of your reverie, you are either in the past or in the future, and now you are jerked into the present as your car sputters, and you coast to the side of the road out of gas. You were so busy thinking about the flight that you missed the gas station.

Being fully conscious in the present is important because fear is a projection of a past experience into the future. You cannot, therefore, be afraid in the present, in the here and now, because the present moment cannot be projected into the future; only the past can be projected into the future. What you really fear is the future, the fear of the unknown, the fear of being afraid—the fear of fear. Struggling to keep yourself in the present is thus a conscious choice you must make each time fear raises its ugly head.

Another reason for being in the present is to allow someone else in the present with you. I (Chris) sometimes think, for example, that I know what someone is going to say or how they are going to say it, whatever it is. I find this especially true if I do not want to hear either the answer or the tone of voice I *know* I will get. If I do not keep myself in the present, if I expect the person's old pattern of response, then *I limit* the person's ability to respond differently in the here and now because I simply do not hear it. I hear what I expect to hear, which justifies my expectation and imprisons both the other person and our relationship somewhere in the past. It also imprisons me in the past because all I accept and, therefore all I hear, is old business.

If we (in the generic) are not present with one another, our attempts to communicate can become frustrating experiences of talking either at or past one another because the present, the here and now, is all we have. It is thus a mediator's responsibility to bring the parties back to the present whenever they stray unnecessarily into either the past or the future. Such presence is a prerequisite for detachment and equanimity throughout the mediation process.

Detachment and Equanimity

Detachment from an outcome is total acceptance of what is without any desire to have something else, which is a critical concept in transformative mediation. Detachment is checking our ego at the door as we come into the room. This is, at best, difficult to learn, and I (Chris) have consciously struggled with it for over two decades.

When I (Chris) was younger, I was deeply upset by the clear-cut logging of the ancient forests in the Pacific Northwest, where I grew up. I would argue long and loudly about the need to save them and the greed and stupidity of those who wished to liquidate them. I tried to convince anyone and everyone that the forests needed to be saved. I was so rabid about my point of view being the right one that few people cared to listen unless they already agreed with me. Consequently, I became frustrated, cynical, and self-righteous, all of which only made matters worse. I became enraged at the *greedy bastards who were clear-cutting my forest,* but I never thought to ask them how they felt about the forests they were liquidating.

One day, as I was giving a passionate speech on the need to "preserve" the ancient forests of the Pacific Northwest, I suddenly felt the sword taken from my hand and a sense of peace come over me, a sense that was immediately reflected in the audience. Several people came up to me later and said they had never thought about it that way, and that what I said made sense. It was then I realized that to speak for the forests or for anything else, I had to change—not the people in the audience, but me. If I wanted people to listen, it was incumbent on me to change, to say what I had to say in a way that would allow them to hear. But how? I did not know how.

A few weeks later, I saw the movie *Gandhi*. Then I read a couple of biographies about Gandhi in which he was often quoted, and through his writings, he gave me the answer. I had to detach myself from the outcome, a truly difficult task.

If Gandhi was correct, in detachment lay acceptance of the outcome. Expectation is the attachment, the vested interest in the outcome, because people with expectations see themselves as the ones possessing the means of achieving the right and justifiable result. If, on the other hand, one acts willingly out of duty to a Higher Authority, one can act with detachment because the Higher Authority is acknowledged as the only one with the wisdom to justly govern the outcome.

If I am detached, I have no vested interest in the results of a given process, and I can treat all sides, all points of view, and all possible outcomes with equanimity. Equanimity is the kernel of peace in detachment just as surely as anxiety is the kernel of agitation in attachment.

For example, a person who has worked passionately for a cause may suddenly have the insight that passion placed before principle is a house divided against itself, which so divided cannot long stand. Because of this new understanding, the person now becomes focused on the principle as a process and becomes detached from the passion—the desired result. The reaction of their peers most often is: "How can you give up the cause? We've believed in it for so long."

Attachment to the cause has for these people become life itself, their very identity, as discussed under "Hidden Agendas." Therefore, even as they ostensibly fight to "win," they cannot afford to win because if they were actually to resolve the issue at the heart of their cause, they would have to find a new identity, something most people are loath to do.

We, as professional biologists, often fall into the trap of "fighting for the cause." For example, I (Carol) have frequently worked with colleagues who were violently opposed to any type of development on the landscape. This could take the form of new homes, industrial facilities, new schools—anything and everything. And, while I agree that habitat fragmentation is destructive to fish and wildlife populations, if I am completely opposed to a project, such as a new housing development, I often find myself excluded from the final decision. This unwillingness to detach from the issue has resulted in millions of acres of habitat lost. If, on the other hand, I enter such a process with the hope of a good outcome for both the community and the fish and wildlife habitat, the process is typically very different. Instead of being pushed aside early in the process, I have found myself working through the issues side by side with the developers and the community—and nearly always obtaining an outcome that has some benefit to the species I care about. For me, the outcome has been inevitably better when I detached myself from a "cause" and focused, instead, on the values that first brought me (and the other participants) to the table.

If a mediator is truly detached from the outcome, the mediator will find equanimity to be his or her touchstone. Equanimity, the effect of detachment, is reflected in the calm, even-tempered, and serene personality of one who is simply open to accepting what is. Such a person can perform mediation without the need or the expectations of approval or a predetermined outcome. Such a person acts out of peace.

In turn, the peaceful action allows others to see an alternative way of perceiving something because no one is trying to convince them of anything. They are given the ideas and the space to consider them. Then, if they so choose, they can change their minds in privacy while retaining their dignity intact.

The one who is detached is part of the principle and is therefore part of the resolution or the transcendence of the problem. On the other hand, one becomes part of the problem when one is attached to a point of view and its necessary outcome. Detachment and equanimity serve to make the mediation process safe enough to permit the expression of anger, which can be defused. We (Carol and I) keep it focused on us, where it has no effect.

As a Mediator, You Must Be a Sieve, Not a Sponge

Anger, as previously stated, is fear violently projected outward from a person onto another person or an object. But I (in the generic) am *not* angry for the reason or at the person or thing I think I am. I am angry at myself for being afraid of circumstances and therefore feeling a loss of control, which has nothing to do with the person or thing at which I level my anger.

That notwithstanding, people must be able to vent their anger in safety during the mediation process because the anger is there, and it will go somewhere. It is therefore important that a mediator keep the anger focused on him- or herself, but as though the mediator is a sieve through which the anger simply passes because it is nothing personal.

For example, when a participant aims his or her anger at another participant, I (Chris) redirect that person's anger at myself by saying, "Excuse me, but I believe you were talking to me." The person can thus dissipate his or her energy, feel he or she has been heard, have personal fears validated, and become more receptive to other data and ideas. At the same time, I keep the mediation environment as safe as possible by preventing another participant from being directly attacked in front of everyone else. Because I know the individual is not angry with me, their anger has no effect on me.

I (Chris) remember meeting with the radical environmental group Earth First! in Arcata, California, some years ago. They had asked me to speak about old-growth forests and sustainable forestry. During my presentation, I pointed out that one must be careful not to become what one is against in confronting a perceived injustice with civil disobedience.

Some of the people did not understand what I meant, so I gave the example of combating violence with violence. "If I am treated with violence," I said, "and I therefore *react* with violence, how am I any different from my opponent? I am not. I have in attitude, behavior, and tactics become what I am against; I have become as my opponent."

At this point, the most militant individuals arose, yelling and swearing at me with such anger that my wife, who was in the audience, became terrified for my safety. Their rage was electrifying. Had I stopped any of it, taken any of it personally, or in any way defended myself against it, the situation would easily have gotten out of hand and become dangerous. Instead, I let it pass through untouched, and the militants all stormed harmlessly out of the room and did not return.

Because I did not *respond* to the anger, a number of people came up to me after I was through speaking. To a person, they said that they had not thought of violence in the way I had presented it and would reconsider their stance. If only one person had said that, it would have been well worth the blast of rage leveled in my direction.

If a mediator ever makes the mistake of taking someone's anger personally, of internalizing it, the mediator becomes like a sponge soaking it all up. Being a sponge for another's anger is not only detrimental to the mediator emotionally but also causes the mediator to become a major problem in the mediation process. At this point, the mediator can no longer function as a mediator because he or she now has a vested interest in (can no longer be detached from) the outcome.

As the mediation leader, I (in the generic) must bear, unflinchingly, all the abuses that the parties normally hurl at one another. In effect, a person, such as a mediator, who serves the people must pass the tests described in the eulogy that Senator William Pitt Fessenden of Maine delivered on the death of Senator Foot of Vermont in 1866:

> When, Mr. President, a man becomes a member of this body he cannot even dream of the ordeal to which he cannot fail to be exposed; of how much courage he must possess to resist the temptations which daily beset him; of that sensitive shrinking from undeserved censure which he must learn to control; of the ever-recurring contest between a natural desire for public approbation and a sense of public duty; of the load of injustice he must be content to bear, even from those who should be his friends; the imputations of his motives; the sneers and sarcasms of ignorance and malice; all the manifold injuries which

partisan or private malignity, disappointed of its objects, may shower upon his unprotected head.

All this, Mr. President, if he would retain his integrity, he must learn to bear unmoved, and walk steadily onward in the path of duty, sustained only by the reflection that time may do him justice, or if not, that after all his individual hopes and aspirations, and even his name among men, should be of little account to him when weighed in the balance against the welfare of a people of whose destiny he is a constituted guardian and defender.[12]

Such is the price of leadership—to be the keeper of everyone else's dignity.

As a Mediator, You Are the Keeper of Each Participant's Dignity

As I (Chris) understand dignity, its emotional foundation rests on the perceived ability to make choices, which in turn provides a sense of hope. As mediator, I am the keeper of each participant's dignity, which means I will protect their dignity so the participant can protect mine. Protecting one another's dignity is tantamount to making and keeping mediation as safe and gentle as possible. Being the keeper of the participants' dignity means there is no blame or guilt, only an opportunity to think differently.

I spoke some years ago at an annual banquet for the Florida Audubon Society in Tallahassee. The day after I spoke, I was on a panel with the supervisor of one of the national forests in the southeastern United States. His opening story exemplifies dignity as the ability to make choices and having some things of value from which to choose:

"I am concerned about what we are doing to our forests," he began. "I am concerned about what we are saying to one another. I think about it all the time. My nine-year-old son came home from school the other day in tears. 'What's wrong?' I asked."

"Dad," he replied "my teacher said you're destroying the forest. You're cutting it all down. What's going to be left for me when I grow up?"

The forest supervisor was trembling with emotion. I could feel his terrible pain, and because of his pain, I am not sure he was even aware of the audience as he spoke.

"I'm concerned," he said, "about what we're teaching our children in school. I'm concerned about what we're telling them about their future. I think about it all the time."

The forest supervisor's young son was asking his father: Where is my choice? Where is my hope? What will be left for me? What will give me a sense of well-being, of dignity, when I grow up?

And yet we in the United States are teaching the children of countries we smugly deem to be "underdeveloped," "developing," or "third world" that they are somehow "lesser" or "inferior" human beings than our children and we are. I (Chris) say this because, of the several facets reflected in the term *development*, we have chosen to focus on a very narrow one: the growth of personal materialism—a *standard of living*—through centralized industrialization, which we glibly equate with social "progress" and "economic health."

I (Chris) have over the years worked in a number of countries without giving much thought to the notion of "developed" versus "developing" or "underdeveloped," as some would put it, although I have spent time in each. During a trip to Malaysia some years ago, I was profoundly struck by the arrogance and the narrowness of such thinking. What we are really talking about is a degree of *industrialization*—and that is a different issue.

That said, Malaysia is the only place in which I have ever heard the people refer to their own country as "developing," as though they were lesser than developed countries and must somehow "catch up" to be equal—a notion of inferiority their children are learning indirectly. Moreover, they often apologized to me for being *lesser human beings* when they were about to ask me a question—and that included a university professor.

Our subjective feelings and human values govern our choices. Our so-called rational, objective intellect or our scientific knowledge or technological advances do not govern them. Remove the sense of choice that has to do with one's determination of one's own destiny and you remove hope as well, and human dignity withers.

Because dignity is closely tied to being in control, humiliation is the greatest enemy of dignity. Let us return to the government meeting I (Chris) spoke about in the discussion of hidden agendas. As I said, the facilitators were intent on meeting the Secretary of the Interior's agenda for grazing on public lands. To meet that agenda, they had to control the length of time each person spoke, especially on the last day. To do this, they made a big red paper flag with large yellow letters on it: BS (bullshit). Then, when they thought someone had spoken long enough and wanted to hurry the meeting along, one of them would wave the BS flag from the front of the room, in an attempt to humiliate the speaker into silence. What kind of example did they set? Was it a safe place for people with different values to come together? What did they do to the participants' trust and dignity?

Mahatma Gandhi once said: "It has always been a mystery to me how men can feel themselves honoured by the humiliation of their fellow beings."[13] I (Chris) have been humiliated in my life. I never felt that my loss contributed to anyone else's honor. I always felt robbed by humiliation because the person who humiliated me was trying to extract my obedience, make me lesser—always lesser—to gain my submissiveness to their control. And I do not want to be controlled; I want to be respected. I, like everyone else, need love and help, not criticism, judgment, and humiliation.

A young man taught me a wonderful lesson about humility and human dignity, a lesson I will always remember. It was a cold winter, and most of us kept fires going in our wood-burning stoves when at home. One day this young man's wife cleaned the ashes out of their stove. She put them into a paper bag and put the bag in the back of their pickup truck. What she did not know, however, was that some of the ashes were still hot. In fact, they were hot enough to catch the bag and other things in the back of the truck on fire and severely damage the interior of the pickup's canopy.

"What did you say to your wife about burning up your truck?" I asked, as if it were any of my business in the first place.

"Nothing," he said. "She was already humiliated. Why should I add to it? After all, she didn't do it on purpose."

That was not the response I had anticipated. People often get a lot of mileage out of other people's mistakes and proceed to flog them with embarrassment.

What would the world be like if we were all as kind and thoughtful as that young man? What would the world be like if we were all the caretakers of one another's dignity? Do you think we could resolve the problems for which the lack of human dignity is an obstacle in the healing of our global society? As a mediator, you have a chance to begin doing just that, healing society, but you must have a beginner's mind to see the oft-hidden opportunities.

Have a Beginner's Mind

To approach life with a beginner's mind, a mind simply open to the wonders and mysteries of the universe, is a gift of Zen. A beginner, unfettered by rules of having to be something special, sees only what the answers might be and knows not what they should be. The one who deems him- or herself to be an expert, on the other hand, is bounded by the rules that govern being an expert. Such a person acts as if he or she is special, the one who knows what the "correct" answer should be, yet is too often blind to what other answers might be. The beginner is free to explore and to discover, while the self-appointed expert grows rigid in a self-created prison.

Two women and one man on three different occasions, years apart, are excellent examples of having the beginner's mind. I (Chris) often use a simple, fun exercise, which requires nothing more than six wooden matches or six toothpicks, to help people understand that their imagination is as bounded as their blind acceptance of social convention and as free as their willingness to reach beyond such convention in seeking their soul's creative eye.

The instructions are simple: Sit at the table and make four equilateral triangles out of the six matches or toothpicks *without* crossing one over another. Rarely do people succeed because to accomplish this feat on the single dimension of the flat surface of a table seems impossible, which their mind quickly tells them, even as they struggle not to accept it. They think it must be possible because I told them to do it, but they cannot figure out how and eventually give up. There are, however, at least two ways to solve this problem, one of which had been unknown to me.

The way I had learned to solve the problem was to make one triangle on the flat surface of the table and then stand the other three bits of wood upright within the one, thus encompassing more than a single dimension. The other way is to break a match or toothpick and arrange them appropriately on the surface of the table.

The first time I saw the problem solved this way was at a workshop I was conducting to help wildlife biologists look beyond professional convention for answers to their management problems. During the workshop, one of the biologists came to me and said that his wife, who had accompanied him to the meeting, was interested in what I was talking about and asked if she could join us. "But of course," I said.

With the lady sitting at the table, I gave my usual instructions and then simply watched what happened. While all the men arranged and rearranged their matches to no avail, she put hers on the table and sat looking at them. Suddenly, a tiny smile crept over her face. Picking up the matches, she laid one down at an angle. Then she deftly broke one in two, laying each half across from the other on each side of the middle of the first match. Finally, she arranged the remaining four in a square to close the exposed sides. Although not perfect, she had four triangles.

"Well I'll be damned," was all I could say as she beamed at me from across the table.

Over the years, I continued giving my original instructions, wondering if anyone else would break a match. Finally, after more than two decades, a sixth-grade teacher looked at her matches for about thirty seconds, then looked up at me and asked: "Can I break the matches?"

"Yes," I answered, and then asked her, "How did you figure that out so fast?"

"Well," she replied, "any time I'm given limits, the first thing I do is check them to see if there's an alternative."

What a marvelous answer. How fortunate are her students. They have a rare teacher, one with a beginner's mind.

Even more recently I learned of yet a third way to solve the problem. I gave six toothpicks to a district ranger of the U.S. Department of Agriculture Forest Service, with the usual instructions. Seated at his kitchen table, he laid the toothpicks on the top of the table, looked at them for a few seconds while his young son watched, and then broke each toothpick in two.

The boy turned to me with a questioning voice and said: "He broke them."

"He didn't tell me I couldn't," replied his father as he made four equilateral triangles on the tabletop, with one piece left over.

What does breaking matches have to do with mediation? First, it demonstrates that most socialized individuals become stuck within their self-imposed limitations. Second, it shows that it is a rare socialized individual who has managed to retain a childlike beginner's mind.

Breaking matches is like going into mediation with little specific knowledge of the conflict with which you are about to deal. That way, you are as detached and unbiased as possible because you have only minimal, general information about the dispute prior to entering the arena. It is thus difficult to form opinions about who has done what or why because you do not know. You therefore remain open to possibilities—a beginner's mind.

Because I (Chris) purposefully know little about a conflict I am going to mediate, once in the process, I have each party in turn tell me its perceptions of the dispute. The exercise is for each party to educate me about the dispute from its understanding of the whole. As each explanation unfolds, not only does the side recounting it clarify its own understanding of its perceptions but also the other party (or parties) hears for the first time the whole of the other's story from the other's point of view. During this storytelling, I learn what the dispute is about because I hear it from different sides and am thus able to find common ground, differences, negotiable areas, quagmires, and hidden potential for resolution.

With a beginner's mind, it is easier for my intuition to preside equally with my intellect and open my creative space. This open space, which allows intuition the freedom to exercise its creative powers, is perhaps the greatest value of having a beginner's mind.

Because intuition is so important to the beginner's mind, it is necessary to examine it, albeit briefly. Intuition, the knowing beyond knowledge, has been widely accepted since ancient times as the forerunner of deep inner truth and creativity. It is generally characterized as an instantaneous, direct grasping of reality, the source of our deepest truths, the unquestionable knowing that we call "axiomatic."[14] Even John Stuart Mill, the pillar of the empirical method, stated that, "The truths known by intuition are the original premises from which all others are inferred."[15]

It is well known, for example, that Niels Bohr, Albert Einstein, Sir Arthur Eddington, Eugene Wigner, and Erwin Schrödinger intuited the principles of quantum physics, for which it is understood that the concepts of time, space, and the conservation of forces are based on intuitive insight, if not on faith. "Intuition," says Russian revolutionary thinker Pitirim A. Sorokin, "is more than a guide to truth; it seems also to be the ultimate foundation for our understanding of beauty and good because our aesthetic and moral judgments are based on deep subjective feelings."[16]

But intuition has been clouded by ambiguity and controversy for the last century or so and regarded as a meaningless by-product of unconscious processes. At best, modern academia often assumes it to be lucky guesses based on gut hunches, creative flashes, and momentary insights. At worst, academic scholars, who pride themselves on discovering logical, scientific solutions to difficult problems, see intuition as irrational concoctions of the unconscious mind, based on memories, habits of thought, social conditioning, or emotional predispositions.

Intuition is therefore implied to be unreliable, unscientific, irrational, and purely subjective with no foundation in measurable reality, which is a very different view from ancient times, when it was considered "the source of deep inner truth." It is, nevertheless, this latter meaning of intuition to which I (Chris) subscribe. I say this advisedly, based on years of unerring experience.

There is yet another value to having a beginner's mind: the freedom to be authentically oneself, which the intuitive/creative edge brings out and to which people respond.

Being Oneself

When all is said and done, it is most important just to be yourself, be authentically you. Being authentically yourself has two components: authenticity and being. Authenticity is the condition or quality of being trustworthy or genuine. Beyond any dictionary definition, authenticity is the harmony between what you think, say, and do and what you really feel—the motive in the deepest recesses of your heart. You are authentic only when your motives, words, and deeds are in harmony with your attitude—freedom from guile.

As Ralph Waldo Emerson noted, "Your attitude thunders so loudly that I can't hear what you say."[17] Your attitude is the visible part of your behavior, but your motives are hidden from view. When your visible behavior is out of harmony with your motives, your attitude points to a hidden agenda.

Being is more difficult to explain to the Western mind. The best explanation of "being" that I have found is in the books by Eckhart Tolle.[18]

When Zane, my wife, and I (Chris) took our morning walks in Las Vegas, Nevada, we saw spadefoot toads on the lawns, bunnies in the undeveloped lots, and occasionally a roadrunner, which is a marvelous bird in the cuckoo family. None of these animals went out of its way to please us, and yet we thrilled each day just to see them and to wish them well. They were just being, and in their "beingness" they brought us great joy. They did not have to do anything or be anything other than what they were doing and being.

Your mission as a mediator is simply to act as yourself and to give what you can to the best of your ability, one mediation at a time—no more and no less. To understand this concept fully, you would do well to see the movie called *It's a Wonderful Life*.

In the small town of Bedford Falls, so the story goes, lives a young man, George Bailey, who cannot wait to leave his hometown to see and conquer the world. But for one reason or another, he never leaves. Being altruistic in his outlook on life, he is other-centered and keeps passing by his chances to go to college and beyond.

Finally, however, facing bankruptcy just before Christmas, through no fault of his own, George decides that he is worth more to his family dead than alive because of his life insurance policy. He therefore tries to kill himself by jumping off a bridge into the river, but an angel, Clarence Oddbody, is sent to save him. Clarence, however, cannot convince George that his life has any value. Adamant that his life is worthless, George wishes he had never been born, and Clarence grants his wish.

To the townspeople, George never existed, so while he knows everyone, no one knows him. He sees how the town would have developed and how the people would have fared had he never been born. George finally sees and understands just how many lives the ripples of his actions have affected by his just being who he is—a simple man who never left his hometown, who never conquered the world. He was perfectly himself, and that was all God asked of him—just to act as himself and to give what he could to the best of his ability, one day at a time.

So relax and be yourself. In turn, your example will allow participants to be themselves and to respond to what you have to offer them even as you respond to what they have to offer you, which means that you will always be learning.

The Continual Learning Curve

As a mediator, you are always in school, with much to learn and no hope of learning it all. Nevertheless, you have a full and continuing responsibility to study disciplines involved in the disputes you mediate to improve your awareness, skills, and abilities. Above all, it is critical to work diligently on personal, unresolved familial matters. There is a perpetual need for personal growth for you as mediator to free yourself from unwanted psychological and emotional baggage.

The freer you are of your own dysfunctional baggage, the closer you are to having the all-important detachment and creativity of a beginner's mind. Along the way, you will find that you do not and cannot have all the answers. This not only is okay in and of itself but also is a blessing that perpetuates the wonder of discovery, especially for the parties with whom you are working.

Not Knowing an Answer Is Okay

Although ignorance is thought of as the lack of knowledge, there is more to it than that. Our sense of the world and our place in it is couched in terms of what we are sure we know and what we think we know. Our universities and laboratories are filled with searching minds, and our libraries are bulging with the fruits of our exploding knowledge, yet where is there an accounting of our ignorance?

Ignorance is not okay in our fast-moving world. We are chastised from the time we are infants until we die for not knowing an answer someone else thinks we should know. If we do not know the correct answer, we may be labeled as stupid, which is not the same as being ignorant about something. Being stupid is usually thought of as being mentally slow to grasp an idea, but being ignorant is simply not knowing the acceptable answer to a particular question.

My (Chris's) favorite answer to a question from an audience member is a purposeful "I don't know," which not only allows me to discover some heretofore hidden secret but also affirms that I neither am nor must I be in charge of the universe. In my ignorance, I find the incredible freedom to accept the frailty of what it means to be human, to be simply what I am.

The preoccupation of society with building a shining tower of knowledge blinds us to the ever-present, dull luster of ignorance underlying the foundation of the tower, from which all questions must arise and over which the tower of knowledge must stand. Each new brick in the tower of knowledge is born of a question that illuminates our ignorance. Yet ignorance, which often is seen as negative, is but a point along the continuum of consciousness, as are knowledge and the knowing beyond.

The quest for knowledge in the material world is a never-ending pursuit, but the quest does not mean that a thoroughly schooled person is an educated person or that an educated person is a wise person. We are too often blinded by our ignorance of our ignorance, and our pursuit of knowledge is no guarantee of wisdom. Hence, we are prone to becoming the blind leading the blind because our overemphasis on competition in nearly everything makes looking good more important than being good. The resultant fear of being thought a fool is one of the greatest enemies of learning.

Although our ignorance is undeniably vast, it is from the vastness of this selfsame ignorance that our sense of wonder grows. But, when we do not know we are ignorant, we do not know enough even to question, let alone investigate, our ignorance.

No one can teach another person anything. All one can do with and for someone else is to facilitate learning by helping the person to discover the wonder of his or her ignorance. By asking an appropriate question in an appropriate way, you may be able to help that person become aware of this ignorance in a given area without stealing the person's dignity.

A teacher is but a "midwife," as the Greek philosopher Socrates said, because once a person realizes his or her ignorance and begins in earnest to search for understanding, that person slowly comes to see that such understanding can only be drawn out from within. Understanding, after all, is the unique perspective of each and every person.

Success or Failure Is the Interpretation of an Event

It is critical for a mediator to understand that success or failure is the interpretation of an event and not the event itself. The Greek philosopher Epictetus hit the mark when he wrote: "Men are disturbed not by things, but by the view which they take of them."[19]

Success and failure are opposites of the same dynamic. They are merely degrees of magnitude along a continuum. The interpretation may be somewhat influenced, however, by who does the interpreting. Knowing what you want to get out of an event, you may interpret the outcome as a huge success, whereas others, whose perceptions of success demand a different outcome, may interpret the same event as a dismal failure.

How, then, do you measure success in mediation when you may not see a tangible outcome of the process? Were you either to hope for or to expect a certain outcome, you may not see anything that even closely resembles it. By seeking a certain outcome, however, you would have an attachment to the result and therefore bias it. So how do you succeed? You succeed by having no expectations and letting the process guide itself to the necessary conclusion.

Chris's Measure of Success

The following are three examples of my letting the process guide itself to the necessary conclusion.

Example 1

In January 1988, I mediated a group of about thirty people, including an Indian tribe, timber interests (corporate and private), Oregon and Washington Departments of Wildlife, environmental activists from several groups, county government representatives, local community people, and the U.S. Forest Service. The problem was a growing conflict of interests over a ten-year forest plan of the Forest Service. The fight boiled over into the local newspaper, with people criticizing and blaming one another through their letters to the editor. A total impasse was finally reached with the release of the Draft Environmental Impact Statement (Draft EIS) for the Umatilla National Forest.

At this point, Ralph Perkins (district ranger on the Walla Walla Ranger District) and Shirley Muse (chairperson of the Umatilla Forest Resource Council, a local conservation group) met and, with bulldog determination, decided to work together to resolve, out of court, the deepening crisis over the EIS. That is when I was invited to be the mediator.

I spent the weekend with a group of people, many of whom had been enemies through the newspaper but had never met face to face. The following February 8, 1994, letter by Shirley Muse reads in part:

> The primary objective of the workshop was to focus on interpersonal and philosophical foundations and the processes that provide the products on U.S. Forest Service lands. Chris Maser worked from the premise that before we could hope to settle land management issues out of court, we must shift our focus from a product only orientation to a process orientation. For two days we worked, first in small groups and then together in a large group, learning to set [a vision, goals, and] objectives and in the process learning to help each other define areas of agreement and areas that might need to be negotiated. The end product of the workshop was to begin framing a [vision] for the forest based on those areas of agreement. Chris wanted to create a workshop that would help us make a necessary shift in thinking and a change in the process in such a way that all parties involved might retain our dignity—the prerequisite for "winning."
>
> The sessions were based on mutual learning, sharing, defining fear, expectations, hidden agendas and values exercises. We dealt with change and paradigms and perhaps most importantly, with the concept of dignity in consensus groups. Strong points centered around listening actively—not listening is a form of violence and forming rebuttal is a defense mechanism. We shared a common concern for decisions in land management and recognized that the outcome of our work would in the end become a human judgment decision.
>
> With that beginning, the "Guiding the Course" group set ground rules, jelled the make-up of the group and began working together in an effort to develop a sound management plan for the Umatilla Forest.

Example 2

In June 1992, I spent time in Čergov, northeastern Slovakia, evaluating the condition of the native forest, which is primarily European beech with an intermixing of white fir. The group with which I worked had patterned themselves after the militant environmental activists Earth First!, and they were having trouble getting the Slovakian Federal Forest Service to listen to them. Although we had no formal meeting as such, I spent eighteen days with them, in their offices, homes, and the forest.

The native forest was being rapidly clear-cut and replaced with plantations of such nonnative species as Norway spruce, larch, and pine, which
are not biologically sustainable in Čergov. The biological errors of forestry
made in Germany, the United States, and Canada were all being repeated
in the forests of Čergov and for the same reasons—shortsighted, immediate, economic gain for areas outside the local communities.

Not only were local, native forests being liquidated through clear-cutting,
but also topsoil was being exported toward the distant sea through uncontrolled erosion. Within one hour after each thunderstorm, all the streams
and rivers fed by clear-cut slopes went from clear water to that which
looked like milk chocolate, as the soil of the forest was washed away.

Armed with what I had seen, we talked about many issues, including
peace versus violence, one of the main topics. I gave a slide presentation to
the Federal Forest Service, which, due to Communist rule, was about forty
years behind in scientific data. Finally, I wrote a report about our delib-
erations, which I presented at an international conference on the environment. The report was an outgrowth of what I had seen, our discussions,
and a series of recommendations for healing the forest.

Before I left, the chief of the Federal Forest Service said to me: "I don't
understand everything you said, and I can't accept everything you said.
But if I have learned one thing from you, Chris, it is that the forest is
sacred, not the plan."

If nothing else were to come from my trip, this was a great success
because it showed that I had earned the chief's trust and that he, after
forty years behind the Iron Curtain, still could—and had—changed some
of this thinking.

Some weeks after I returned home, I received a letter from the group
that had invited me to Slovakia stating that because the people agreed to
work peacefully with the Forest Service, the report (translated into Slovak)
circulated its way through the Slovakian Parliament. As a result, the group
was officially invited to work with the Federal Forest Service in revising at
least some parts of the forest plan.

Example 3

Dean Button called me from the East Coast in 2000 and asked if he could
use a mediation I had done as a case study for his doctoral dissertation
while at Antioch New England Graduate School. I agreed and suggested
Lake View, Oregon. The following passages are taken from Dean's 2002
dissertation: From the abstract:

> A case study of the Lake County (Oregon) Sustainability Initiative
> explores how a more multidimensional conceptualization plays out
> "on the ground." Local citizens are interviewed to learn how their
> engagement in a visioning process [which is de facto preemptive

conflict resolution] contributed to decision-making focused on revitalizing a steady declining rural economy based on logging and ranching on federally owned forest and rangelands. Representatives from national environmental organizations, federal land management agencies, and local citizens joined in a partnership to chart the future for Lake County that serves the multiple interests at stake there while also preserving a way of life that holds deep meaning and value for the ordinary citizens of Lake County. Lake County is discussed as a model for other communities to emulate.[20]

From the body of his dissertation:

Chris Maser's approach to sustainability reflects an usually high degree of *practical wisdom*. It is distinctive in that it emphasizes the intimate connection between the particulars of place and the more abstract and philosophical universals that are at the core of sustainability. However, Maser is not some detached philosopher concerned only with abstract ideals. On the contrary, he is trained as a zoologist with a long track record as a research scientist in natural history and ecology in forest, shrub steppe, sub-Arctic, desert, and coastal settings. Today he writes and lectures, works as a facilitator in resolving environmental disputes, leads groups in visioning processes, and acts as a mentor for those interested in pursuing sustainable community development.

When I asked Maser where I could go to explore his work with a community, he mentioned Lake County, Oregon, and suggested I contact the local program officer from Sustainable Northwest, the Portland-based, non-profit organization that was coordinating the sustainability initiative there. The Lake County Sustainability Initiative office in Lakeview provided access to the community and helped with introductions. I traveled to Oregon hoping to gain a more sophisticated understanding of how the particulars of Lake County brought practical wisdom to bear on the challenges of sustainable development that community faced.

Maser's involvement helped to steer the Lake County Sustainability Initiative in a very specific direction. Instead of focusing exclusively on the hard science related to degraded ecosystems—clearly a crucial element in any sustainability initiative, Maser encouraged the participants to assume a much larger and ultimately more challenging agenda. Maser addressed the group as they were about to spend a day in the forest, telling them: "I've had a love affair with science all my life, but I left active research so I could concentrate on this question: How can social questions and science be put together so the landscape and society can coexist sustainably?"

Here was a natural science "expert" acknowledging the importance of considering what the National Research Council, in its *Our Common Journey*, identifies as the core element of an emerging science of sustainability—this "small set of understudied research questions central to a deeper understanding of the interactions between society and the environment" (NRC, 1999:10). However, Maser went on to warn the group that science could not answer the questions they were gathered to address, saying: "You are struggling with *social questions.* Have the courage to answer them *socially.*"

As they prepared to embark on their journey, Maser counseled the group that the territory ahead would be full of the paradoxes one comes to expect in complex systems: "In this Information Age of ours, learn to doubt your knowledge and trust your intuition—it's your greatest gift. And you have to learn to honor your ignorance because that's where all wise questions come from. One of the most important things you can ever do is learn to ask a good question because a society evolves toward the questions it asks. So if you focus on wise questions, you'll move toward appropriate solutions."

Maser recalled, during our interview, that the group was struggling to verbalize their vision of where they wanted to go: "I said, 'Okay, now I want from each of you a one- or two-sentence statement of what you think this all means, what you want your community's future to be like.' They wrote. Some of them had to write a paragraph, but a vision statement has to be one or two sentences. ... The challenge is that most adults come from their heads. So, we went around the room and they read their statements, but each one was rejected—until they came to a girl who was a sophomore or junior in high school. (I had told them in the beginning that I wanted some children to participate. I wanted young folks.) When the young woman read her statement—which came straight from here (*refers to heart*), unadulterated—they all said, 'Yes! That's it!'"

This moment was singled out by several of the participants as one of the most memorable of the entire process. Months later, it was recalled with a mixture of incredulity and pride. Even some of the "old-timers," who expressed impatience with the emphasis paid to "process," had a noticeable shift in energy and enthusiasm when making the recollection.

An official with the Forest Service recalled: "They went through all kinds of gyrations at the meetings—identifying their mission and value systems, those kinds of things. Some of them worked and some of it was probably wasted energy—but the interesting thing is a lot of the stuff in here came from a couple of high-school kids. I was at that meeting, and what came out of those kids was really like a light went on to that committee! Gee! That's what we're really here for! That was of value to me. I thought, man! That's great! When the local kids see what they want out of their landscape—and they live here—not the adults—it's the kids. ... "

By asking participants to respond to questions of value, meaning, and social significance, and by helping them to create a decision-making environment in which they found it conducive to answer the questions, Maser's approach to sustainable development is an exemplar of a participatory process that successfully integrates scientific and policy expertise within the larger social context in which it is embedded. Those who engaged in the process were quick to acknowledge the power of this approach. One participant remarked: "As far as a facilitator, I don't think we could've found a better one. It's a real shame that there is only one Chris around. Why don't we have hundreds of them?"[21]

Dean Button, Ph.D.
Director of Program Development
School of Humanities and Social Sciences
Rensselaer Polytechnic Institute
Troy, New York

These groups represent the ultimate success, by my measure. They are carrying on with that which is important to them because I had left enough tools behind to make myself dispensable, which to me is the ultimate goal of mediation. The process and its outcome are theirs, and that is how it needs to be. If, however, I had expected or wanted perfect land use plans to emerge from these meetings, I would have failed because there is no such thing as a perfect plan, only noble intentions and a continuing process.

Carol's Measure of Success

The following are three examples of what I consider to be measures of success in my mediation experience:

Example 1

One of my first tasks on arrival at Prince William Forest Park, in Virginia, was to bring a fairly complex mine reclamation project to closure. The Cabin Branch Pyrite Mine had been abandoned in 1920 after an unsuccessful labor strike. The site remained heavily impacted by mining operations, particularly Quantico Creek, which ran through the site. A Section 319 grant from the Environmental Protection Agency had been approved, and the deadline to obligate the funding was fast approaching. Right away, I began to gather the participants for the project, which included the (1) Virginia Department of Mines, Minerals, and Energy; (2) National Park Service Divisions of Geologic Resources and Water Resources in Lakewood, Colorado; (3) National Park Service National Capital Regional Office; (4) Prince William Forest Park Superintendent and staff; (5) the permitting agencies (e.g., Virginia Marine Resources Commission, Virginia State Historic Preservation Office); and (6) the public.

As the approach to the reclamation project began to take shape, I developed an outreach plan and met with the media and park neighbors to explain the project. Numerous articles were published, and I personally guided park neighbors on tours of the site to explain our plans. Surprisingly, and possibly because of the advance media coverage, it was not the public who challenged the project, but rather the internal participants who were unfamiliar with the techniques and practices to be used in reclaiming the abandoned mine. From seed mixes to surface contouring, little was easily agreed on.

The contentiousness of the details demanded considerable mediation skill. Consequently, I spent a great deal of time and effort mediating between the Virginia Department of Mines, Minerals, and Energy staff and the National Park Service—the greatest challenge being that I still had to have a job in the end. There were times when individuals would storm out of the room in anger or would dress me down verbally over their disagreement with the seed mix or the kinds and placement of trees to be planted. One would not think that a simple project (compared to those I had completed in West Virginia) would be so difficult. Much of the problem was the lack of understanding of technical practices used in reclaiming old mines, as opposed to more natural, ecological techniques used in restoration of degraded land.

My role, therefore, was to educate the National Park Service scientists and staff, while maintaining the trust and respect of the expert reclamation technicians of the Virginia Department of Mines, Minerals, and Energy. Unlike many mediation experiences, this project had a tangible result—reclamation of the mine, which came to fruition in late 1995 after a great deal of effort. My measure of success, however, was not the completion of the on-the-ground project itself, but is found, instead, in a letter I received two years later from the Mineral Policy Center in Washington, DC, from which President Philip Hocker wrote:

> I've been hiking in the Park since my wife and I moved to the Washington area from Jackson Hole in 1987, and I've often hiked by the Pyrite Mine Site. I remember when it was a raw hillside with pools of orange water at the base. It's impressive to see the progress that has been made on reclaiming that site—and know it must have taken a lot of hard work on the part of Park staff to make it happen. Carol did a very capable job of explaining both the technical issues at the site, and also the administrative labyrinth that had to be traversed to get the project done. Please pass on our thanks to Carol—she did an outstanding job … and also really helped us move forward with our work.[22]

Example 2

In July 2010, I was deployed with the U.S. Coast Guard to the *Deepwater Horizon* oil spill. My role there was to serve as a liaison officer between Santa Rosa County, Florida, and the U.S. Coast Guard Incident Command Staff in Mobile, Alabama. The Incident Command Post in Mobile was directing management of resources, which included the beach cleanup crews and their equipment, as well as the "vessel-of-opportunity" oil-skimming fleets.

Local officials were angry that they had no control over these assets and rightfully so. At one point, oil was spotted approaching Pensacola Pass, which protects the mouth of Pensacola Bay, an ecologically sensitive area. It took six hours after reporting the oil to the Incident Command Post for someone to respond. Once some control was turned over to the county, things seemed to be a bit better, but the lack of trust between local and federal personnel remained a significant challenge.

As I worked with the local officials for the rest of my allotted time, I did my best to build trust and to be responsive to their needs. I did my best to treat them with respect and to value their professional expertise and knowledge. And, when I could not secure them the additional operational control that they wanted, I was open and honest in communicating the outcome, even though they may not have liked it. The measure of success in this case came at a time in late August, when my services as liaison officer were no longer needed. As Chris mentioned, one goal in mediation is to make oneself dispensable—once the day-to-day communication and operations were flowing smoothly, mediation was no longer necessary.

Example 3

When I first arrived at Prince William Forest Park, I faced a new challenge, that of working with one of our most influential neighbors, the Department of the Navy, Quantico Marine Corps Base. It became clear to me at our monthly Environmental Review Board meetings just how contentious the relationship between personnel on the base and my predecessor had been. Environmental Review Board meetings provided a forum in which to review all pending environmental projects on the base and obtain input from people whose programs might be affected. In this case, we were invited as adjacent federal landowners who might be affected by proposed projects.

At one of the first Environmental Review Board meetings, I requested that a map showing the park boundary be included in the environmental assessment for a proposed timber sale. The lieutenant colonel, who was serving as chair of the meeting, turned to me and began yelling and demanding to know who I was and by what audacity had I to "tell them what to do." With a quiet voice, I said respectfully, "Sir, an adjacent federal landowner must be included in any environmental compliance documents. This is a requirement of the National Environmental Policy Act." He did back down, but then this was a typical interaction with base staff when I arrived in my new job.

Over the next year or two, I worked closely with base staff, attending every scoping meeting for proposed projects on base that might affect the park. I treated base staff with respect and professionalism, provided them with my counsel in a reasonable and positive way, and kept my focus solely on those issues that were truly of concern. I also went out into the field with the staff personnel as often as I could to see project sites and to talk about "our" values and different management philosophies to find some common ground.

My predecessor, in contrast, had been openly critical of actions taken by base personnel on a wide range of activities, many of which had no influence on the park but represented more of a philosophical difference in how to manage natural resources. Therefore, I inherited a significant "trust deficit" with respect to the base staff.

I once attended a timber sale scoping meeting, where the biologist snarled at me as I entered the room saying, "Oh, we're in trouble now, the Park Service is here." A year or so later, the base staff and, in particular, the timber sales staff, really seemed to have responded to my efforts and began to propose much more environmentally sensitive projects (such as increasing buffer areas around streams). I therefore decided that I no longer needed to attend every scoping meeting.

The day after my absence from the first meeting, I received a call from a distressed timber sales biologist. "Is everything okay?" he queried. "You weren't at our scoping meeting yesterday!" I tried to explain that his proposal was great, that we were happy with their work, and that no comment from us was needed. In response, he said that he really needed me there because my approval of their projects was important to him and to his supervisor. I could not have predicted this turn of events, but I will always consider it an outstanding measure of success: From being seen as an obstacle to overcome to being considered a critical member of the team was an amazing transformation, one that taught me a lot not only about mediation but also about myself.

The Labels of Success or Failure

The labels of success or failure are usually assigned to the perceived outcome or product of an event rather than to the actual process of learning embodied in the event itself. Therefore, when you abdicate your right to interpret the event, such as a mediation process, success or failure becomes a judgment determined by others, which may be termed the "cultural trance" because the value of an individual's spontaneous creativity usually gets smothered by the prevailing social standards.

The cultural trance is the uncritical acceptance of all the *shoulds, oughts,* and *musts* thrust on us from childhood onward by myriad external sources. If you look to *others* for your self-esteem, success involves a visible accomplishment that "others" must approve. Lack of such visible accomplishment therefore is deemed a failure. Success means you do it yourself, and failure means you need help. Because success is usually measured in terms of how much money or power one has, failure is simply a measure of perceived lack. Success is a measure of being in control of circumstances, and failure is a measure of not being in control of circumstances.

The real success or failure in life, however, is whether you are doing what you really want to do in your heart of hearts. Mythologist Joseph Campbell calls it "following your bliss." If you are doing what you really want to do, regardless of material returns, then you have a success of the heart, no matter what anyone else thinks. Others can measure only the appearance of success based on *their* definition. Yet an apparent failure in the short term can prove a success in the long term. Failure can then be viewed as delayed or postponed success.

If, therefore, you allow others to define you, you allow them to determine your success or failure. If you accept failure on this basis, then the point at which you acquiesce is the point at which you are defeated.

One of my (Chris's) favorite stories is about Babe Ruth, the baseball player. Ruth had struck out two or three times in one game. When the game was over, a sports reporter asked him what he was thinking about as he struck out.

"Hitting a home run," he said.
"Well," asked the reporter, "how does it feel to fail?"
"I didn't fail," replied Ruth. "Every time I get a strike, I'm one swing closer to the next home run, and you know who has to worry about that!"

Babe Ruth had learned two very important lessons. The first was that to be a winner, he had to be willing to risk being a loser, and the degree to which he was willing to risk losing determined the degree to which he was ultimately capable of winning. Ruth was the home-run king only because he was first willing to be the strikeout king. We (in the generic) all have to be willing to be poor at something for a while so that, through practice, we can excel.

The second lesson was to be consistent in his efforts, which Winston Churchill put well when he said: "Success is going from failure to failure with enthusiasm."[23] The crowd in the bleachers did not bother Ruth. He smiled at them in the same, quiet way when they booed him as he did when they cheered him. Babe Ruth knew who and what he was, a champ.

Assisting Parties in Clarifying and Resolving Their Conflict

Being One Pointed

Because it is essential that the parties trust you as a mediator, you must be what the Buddhists call "one pointed." Being one pointed means that you are totally focused on what you are doing; it is therefore necessary to divest yourself of all diversions. To this end, you would be wise to sign and honor both a conflict-of-interest statement and a confidentiality statement pertaining to each and every dispute resolution that you facilitate.

If, in the process of mediation, you find nothing good to say about a comediator—remain silent. Discussion between and among mediators concerning any given case, but particularly an active one, is to be conducted solely in private. It is also imperative that you enter into a conflict being handled by another mediator or other mediators only after fully conferring with them and only after receiving everyone's approval, which includes all persons involved in the dispute.

Coping with Change

To assist parties in clarifying and resolving their conflict, you must understand the dynamics of change in both the ecological sense and the human dimension. This means you must be able to help the people understand and cope with change as a creative process to be accepted, lived with, and adapted to as an opportunity, rather than resisting change as a condition to be avoided. Change, after all, is a universal constant, and its effects, while unavoidable and always novel, can be purposefully guided to some extent.

You must also be well versed in both functional and dysfunctional coping mechanisms, homeostasis, and boundaries through having done personal work with your own unresolved familial issues. Such understanding is critical because how one copes with change is in large measure predetermined by childhood learning experiences.

When Potential Resolution Is in Violation of Public Policy or Law

At times, you may find yourself in a situation for which the parties moving toward an agreement are doing so contrary to public policy or in violation of the law. Since you have no right to impose standards of behavior on the parties, it may be ethically necessary for you to withdraw from the process. This is an important consideration because you are both legally and ethically without authority to enforce law or to act in any way as an agent of investigation or law enforcement. As soon as such a situation arises, you must consult with the proper authority, which in turn will recommend the action to be taken.

References

1. Gerald Corey. *Theory and Practice of Counseling and Psychotherapy*. 3rd edition. Brooks/Cole, Monterey, CA (1986).
2. Francis Bacon. Quotation. http://quotationsbook.com/quote/1246/ (accessed March 21, 2010).
3. James Allen. *As a Man Thinketh*. Grosset & Dunlap, New York (1981).
4. Henry Ford Quotes. http://thinkexist.com/quotation/coming_together_ is_a_beginning-keeping_together/146314.html (accessed March 21, 2010).
5. Stephan Mitchell. *Tao Te Ching*. Harper Perennial, New York (1992).
6. Hans Bleiker. Institute for Participatory Management and Planning. http://www.ipmp.com/about/ (accessed December 1, 2010).
7. Ibid.
8. Kenneth W. Estes and Robert Debs Heinl. *Handbook for Marine NCOs*. 4th edition. Naval Institute Press, Annapolis, MD (1996).
9. Henry Wadsworth Longfellow. Sensitivity. http://lhmci.com/study/qualities/sensitivity.html (accessed March 21, 2010).
10. Abraham Maslow. *Toward a Psychology of Being*. 2nd edition. Van Nostrand, Princeton, NJ (1968).
11. Ibid.
12. John F. Kennedy. *Profiles in Courage*. Harper & Row, New York (1961).
13. Louis Fischer. *The Essential Gandhi: An Anthology of His Writings on His Life, Work, and Ideas*. Random House, New York (1962).
14. Jeffrey Mishlove. Intuition, the source of true knowing. *Noetic Sciences Review*, 29 (1994):31–36.
15. John Stuart Mill. A System of Logic. http://www.marxists.org/reference/archive/mill-john-stuart/1843/logic.htm (accessed March 21, 2010).
16. Pitirim A. Sorokin. Excerpted from *The Crisis of Our Age*. http://www.intuition.org/sorokin.htm (accessed March 21, 2010).
17. Ralph Waldo Emerson. Ralph Waldo Emerson Quotes and Quotations. http://www.famousquotesandauthors.com/authors/ralph_waldo_emerson_quotes.html (accessed March 21, 2010).
18. (a) Eckert Tolle. *The Power of Now*. New World Library, Novato, CA (2004); and (b) Eckert Tolle. *A New Earth*. Plume, New York (2006).
19. Epictetus. http://quotationsbook.com/quote/4083/ (assessed on February 24, 2011).
20. Dean Button. Toward an Environmental Cosmology: The Power of Vision, Values, and Participation in Planning for Sustainable Development. Ph.D. dissertation. Antioch New England Graduate School, Keene, NH (2002).
21. Ibid.
22. To gain an insight into just how badly the area of the mine had been degraded over time, as President Philip Hocker saw it, read the first story, Cabin Branch Mine Orphaned Land Project, on this Web site: http://water.epa.gov/polwaste/nps/success319/Section319III_VA.cfm (accessed November 20, 2010).

23. Winston Churchill. The Courage to Fail. http://fbicgirls.com/index.
php?option=com_content&view=article&id=89:the-courage-to-fail&catid
=16:blog&Itemid=2 (accessed March 22, 2010).

Section II

The Legacy of Resolving Environmental Conflicts

9

Practicing the Mediation of Conscience

Introduction

Good conflict resolution is a meticulous practice in democracy. It is thus critical to understand something about democracy as a practical concept. Democracy is a system of shared power with checks and balances, a system in which individuals can affect the outcome of political decisions. People practice democracy by managing social processes themselves. Democracy is another word for self-directed social evolution.

Democracy in the United States is built on the concept of inner truth, which in practice is a tenuous balance between spirituality and materialism. One such truth is the notion of human equality, in which all people are pledged to defend the rights of each person, and each person is pledged to defend the rights of all people. In practice, however, the whole endeavors to protect the rights of the individuals, while the individuals are pledged to obey the *will* of the majority, which may or may not be just to each person.

The will of the majority brings up the notion of freedom in democracy. Nothing in the universe is totally free because everything is in a relationship with everything else, which exacts various degrees of constraints. Just as there is no such thing as a truly "free market" or an "independent variable," so are individual and social autonomy protected by moral limits placed on the freedom with which individuals and society can act. To this effect, author Anna Lemkow lists four propositions of freedom: "(1) An individual must win freedom of will by self-effort, (2) freedom is inseparable from necessity or inner order, (3) freedom always involves a sense of unity with others beyond differences, (4) freedom is inseparable from truth—or, put the other way around, truth serves to make us free."[1]

Lemkow continues:

> We tend to think of freedom as dependent on circumstantial or external factors, but these propositions point us inward, suggesting rather that freedom is a state of consciousness and ... depends on ourselves.

> Indeed it is something to be won, something to be attained commensurately with becoming more truthful, or more attuned to and aligned with the abiding inner, metaphysical, or moral order or law.
>
> Socio-political and economic freedom or liberty, in turn, would depend (at least in the longer term) on the predominant level of consciousness of the citizenry.[2]

Lemkow is positing that a human being is not completely free to begin with, but possesses the potential capability of self-transformation in the direction of fuller freedom. Beyond this, democracy requires respect for others and excitement in the exchange of ideas. People must learn to listen to one another's ideas, not as points of debate but as different and valid experiences in a collective reality. While they must learn to agree to disagree at times, they must also learn to accept that, like blind people feeling the different parts of an elephant, each person is initially limited by his own perspective. When these things happen, people are engaged in the most fundamental aspects of democracy and come to conclusions and make decisions through participative talking, listening, understanding, compromising, and agreeing.

In a democracy, *connection* and *sharing* are central to its viability because a democracy only works when it is being practiced. People are not required to separate feelings from thoughts concerning a topic. Their roles—as teachers, students, leaders, mediators, and followers—fluctuate within and across the issues. The importance of a democratic system lies in its connection to people's lives, their own experiences, and the real problems and issues they daily face. Practicing democracy can be thought of as education in and for life. And, because people have within them the seeds of greatness, as teacher Myles Horton says, "it is not a matter of trying to fill people up but rather of fulfilling them."[3]

The challenge, therefore, is to engage people in the democratic process, which is difficult when they confuse the government with the administration of the government or when the administration becomes so dysfunctional that people despair in their seeming inability to fix it. But then, a perfect government does not exist.

A just government must be founded on truth, not knowledge—something we in the United States have all too swiftly forgotten. To achieve such government, it must be based on service (where people are other-serving) rather than power (where people are self-serving). Therefore, environmental protection is only possible if the government is accountable to its people beyond special interest groups and political lobbyists.

We live in an increasingly complex society of intense competition and materialism. In such a society, people commit foul acts to gain power, through both positions of authority and financial success. People commit such acts while falsely expecting to benefit by them, thinking that such benefits will somehow bring happiness. But in the end, as Socrates warned, the guilt of the soul outweighs the supposed material gains. Thus, because people lack perfect knowledge and perfect motives, democracy must be continually practiced and continually improved through that practice.

Nevertheless, the *people* are the government, but they can govern only as long as they elect to use the constitutional system for empowerment. It is important to understand that empowerment is self-motivation. No one can empower anyone else; one can only empower oneself. One can, however, give others the psychological space, permission, and skills necessary to empower themselves and then support their empowerment. Beyond that, one can help in the process of empowerment and can increase the chances of success by recognizing another's accomplishments each step of the way. That is true democracy.

Therefore, in the case of the United States, where the government is of the people, by the people, and for the people, when the people empower themselves, they are the government, and it is the administration of that government that resides in Washington, DC—not the government itself. The administration becomes the government only when the people turn their power over to the administration and in effect say: I'm a victim and can't change the system or take care of me.

Democracy is a viable system because it rests on a self-reflective principle, that is, by inviting a constant reinterpretation of itself, it is always in a state of becoming, which continually interweaves it within the intimacy of life. For democracy to remain viable, it must be used because it is an interconnected, interactive system of balancing and integrating contrasting perceptions of data, fact, and truth. A working democracy is thus predicated on finding the point of balance through compromise in such a way that the rifts between opposites can be minimized and healed.

Compromise and the Point of Balance

Mediation is the way to compromise and the point of balance that resolves conflicts. The *mandorla*, a symbol of unity, is a prototype of conflict resolution that has long been secreted in the gathering dust of medieval Christianity.

A mandorla is two overlapping circles with an almond-shaped area in the middle, where the contents of each circle integrate. When thus put together, their areas of overlap and integration—their common root—can be found, and perceived opposites can be balanced. And all opposites have a common root because they are, after all, merely different perceptions of the same reality. For example, a glass of water is half full or half empty, depending on one's point of view, but the level of water is the same in either case.

Once the overlap is identified, acknowledged, and accepted, people can begin working collectively, extending the area of overlap and integration. Although the overlap is tiny at first, like the sliver of a new moon, it is a beginning, the first healing of the split between opposites. With diligent work and the passage of time, the sliver becomes as a quarter moon, then a half moon, and a three-quarter moon, until that point is reached where the two circles become as one—a full moon, unity, total healing.

The mandorla as a symbol, a process, and a metaphor fits every social-environmental problem imaginable. The mandorla thus seems a logical metaphor of social-environmental sustainability, which is the necessary next stage of social evolution—the ultimate expression of a working democracy—if society, as we know it, is to survive. If, however, we are to map the country of the mandorla to our best advantage, we must treat one another with compassion and justice while we explore the hidden potential of the almond-shaped land of overlap and integration.

A Curriculum of Compassion and Justice

For mediation to be successful, the process must be as gentle and dignified as possible, which means that it must be a continual lesson in compassion and justice taught through the mediator's example. All parties must emerge with their dignity intact if anything is to be resolved. It is therefore important to remember that *now* is always the time for compassion and justice because, as Mahatma Gandhi points out, "An eye for an eye only makes the whole world blind."[4] In this sense, mediation, as a democratic process, is perhaps at its best when the people involved must continue dealing with one another after the dispute is resolved.

Compassion is the deep feeling of sharing another's suffering, of giving aid and support to another person in the person's time of need, which is the act of forgiving another's perceived trespass—of extending mercy. The essence of compassion is best acknowledged in a French proverb: "To know all is to forgive all." This is but saying that as I do the level best I can in all I do, so does everyone else, so where, therefore, is the judgment? Thus, when we forgive all, when we fix no judgment and place no blame, we have compassion.

When someone is unkind to me (Chris), I do my best to accept that it is not a personal act but rather one that reflects the other person's inner distress, and I know that neither of us will gain anything if I shame or shun that person. I do not always succeed in my endeavors, however, and I cannot count the times I have fallen short of my ideal of unconditional compassion, which to me is the understanding through which the act of forgiveness may flow.

Forgiveness, in turn, is to see the fear and the pain out of which another person acts and to extend love as an alternative. To have compassion, therefore, demands far greater courage than does retaliation in any form at any time because compassion demands that one is responsible for one's own behavior and thereby abnegates the role of victim.

Although I (Chris) cannot experience how the other person is feeling, I can ask. If that person can relax long enough to answer, I may be able to imagine myself for a moment in their situation and see if I would act any differently under the particular circumstances. I have inevitably found that I would do the same were I the other person. It is therefore up to me to forgive rather than up to the other person to change, which means that I must do unto others as I would have them do unto me in any given circumstance.

I (Carol) remember my first day on a new job, when I learned that I had one employee working in a different office—not for the obvious reasons (operational need, lack of space, etc.), but because he had made a serious mistake ten years prior that had resulted in injury to a visitor. Nelson had never been forgiven for this error in judgment and had been isolated from the remaining employees of the division by placing his desk in an empty building (a shed, really). I was shocked not only by the situation but also by the fact that this incident had happened more than ten years ago. Nelson had more than thirty years of field experience, yet he had been pushed aside and prevented from interacting with the work group and thus sharing his wealth of knowledge.

I asked him to move over to the main building, telling him that I really needed him there to help me learn all of the operation I was responsible for and to be part of my team. A year later, my chief ranger asked me, "What did you do to [Nelson]? He seems so happy now, he's like a different person!" All I had done was forgive him because, like Chris, I do my best to treat people the way I want to be treated. I try to put myself in others' shoes and ask myself, "How would I want to be treated?" and then respond accordingly.

We have often heard it said that "all's fair in love and war" and that "nothing's fair in life." If this is the way people really feel, perhaps we must shift our attention from fairness to justice, or that which is just. If I (in the generic) am just, I am honorable, consistent with the highest morality, and equitable in my dealings and actions. If I do unto others as I would have others do unto me, then I can be a just person.

One can also choose to be just in a practical sense. Being just and equitable with others encourages them to treat you justly, which is another lesson you can teach by example. It is wise to cultivate such kindly behavior for yourself by extending it first to others. And if, for some reason, the person with whom you were just is unjust with you, they give you an opportunity to practice compassion. Being compassionate requires nothing from anyone else—only your courage and the wisdom to love enough to forgive. Such compassion is one of the gifts passed forward through an ideal mediation process.

Mediation As a Gift Is Free but As a Trade Has a Cost

What do a gift and a trade have in common with mediation? They have much to do with it because mediation must be an unconditional gift. To define an unconditional gift, consider what you, as a mediator, might expect out of the process. Do you want something specific to happen, a certain outcome, for example, or is any outcome okay?

A gift is free of expectations, but a trade has a specific outcome attached to it. Both a gift and a trade are circumstances to which the recipient must respond, and the choice of response is one of either trust or distrust.

A gift is a feeling made visible through an object, but the object is not the real gift. The feeling is the real gift because it is the cause for giving the object.

A gift, which most people think of as an object, is free of conditions. If I (in the generic) give you a gift, I have, by definition, also given you title and ownership free of encumbrances. You may do with it as you wish because I have no vested interest in what you do with what you own, which means no strings are attached. Further, your unconditional acceptance of my gift is your unconditional gift to me because I cannot give you my gift if you refuse to accept it. This thought is in keeping with an Aboriginal American proverb: "You must humble yourself to receive before you can truly give."

If, for example, I give you a chocolate cake, but you are on a diet, so you graciously accept the cake and give it to someone else, then you have accepted my gift and given me one through your acceptance. In addition, you have given a gift of your own by passing on the cake. If the second person accepts the cake but does not like chocolate and gives the cake to a third person, then the second person has accepted your gift and given one of their own. In each case, the apparent or perceived gift was the cake, but the true gift was the unconditional love embodied in the thought of giving by one person and in the thought of receiving by the other. At no time was the real gift the cake itself.

A trade, on the other hand, is an exchange of one thing for another, beginning with the thought or expectation of a specific outcome. By definition, therefore, a trade cannot be a gift because a gift, truly given and received, is something bestowed without thought of compensation. A trade, however, is a way of realizing a known expectation, a way to control the outcome.

Let us go back to the chocolate cake. If I give you a chocolate cake on the condition that you eat it, I have given you a condition—a prison cell—instead of a gift. I have traded a chocolate cake to you for your compliance with my expectations of your behavior—to eat the cake in spite of your diet. I have used the cake to control you. I have covertly said: "If you really love me, you will eat the cake for me in spite of your diet." The inference is that if you choose to honor your diet and not eat the cake, then you do not really love me. I have laid guilt on you to control your behavior and give me the outcome I want.

Unless all parties agree to the rules of the trade beforehand, the "trade" is really coercion. Such was the case with the meeting on the livestock grazing fee program discussed previously. The facilitators wanted something from the participants. They wanted compliance with their wishes, which, if forthcoming, would please the Secretary of the Interior and might bring in more business. Although the participants were not privy to what they wanted, it became clear during the mediation process that they had a hidden agenda.

People trade because an unexpected outcome will force them out of their comfort zone and make them deal with the unknown, and that is not what they want. It is the unknown—that which they think is unknowable, that which demands the risk of uncontrollable change—that is frightening.

One of the many places fear of the unknown can be seen in people is in airports. Passengers have their tickets, and their schedules are confirmed, but not beyond change. A flight is suddenly cancelled or baggage is lost, and carefully controlled plans are nowhere to be found. This is distressing because the known expectation suddenly evaporates, and the worst-case scenario of the unknown becomes reality. The dreaded unknown—your not knowing what to expect—has happened. You see no immediate, clear choice. You have suddenly lost control.

This is when frightened people get angry and yell at ticket agents. In so doing, they are trying to trade their anger for compliance with their wishes or more comfortable boundaries within which they can operate "normally." The more frightened they are, the nastier their behavior becomes.

But unknown expectations are also gifts of adventure, which always hold lessons about our lives if we will but look for them. One of my (Chris's) college professors, for example, had such an unexpected experience. He had purchased an expensive microscope in Switzerland, only to have it stolen in Naples, Italy, on his way home. He went to the police station to report the theft. While he stood there waiting, the police chief talked to an American sailor whose wristwatch had been stolen:

"Which pier is your ship docked at?" asked the chief.
"Pier 10," said the sailor.
"I think I know who has your watch. You two come with me," said the chief
motioning to both the sailor and the professor.

When they reached the pier, the chief went up to a young boy and said, "Give this man his wristwatch." The boy reluctantly complied.

This, however, did nothing for the professor's microscope. In fact, the chief told him that his problem was much more difficult to solve, probably impossible, and since the microscope was not insured against theft, the professor was probably out of luck.

The professor returned home, angry that he had been ripped off. It had, retroactively, spoiled his whole trip; it was all he could think about. He stewed about the microscope and the money for six months. With time, he finally accepted what was; he let go of what he could not control— the circumstance—and took responsibility for what he could control—his attitude, his response to the circumstance.

Several months later, the professor got a telephone call from customs at the Seattle-Tacoma Airport in Washington advising him that a package had arrived for him. Lo and behold, his microscope had arrived in perfect condition. All of his stewing and internal discord had been a total waste of time and energy.

Thus, you must be detached from the outcome of your mediation and must become dispensable to all parties as soon as possible by helping them, should they so choose, to establish the processes necessary to resolve their own conflicts and create a vision for their own future. The gift you have to give is helping parties get ready for the next step—bringing the conflict to resolution through a shared vision on which to act.

References

1. Anna F. Lemkow. Our common journey toward freedom. *The Quest,* 7 (1994):55–63.
2. Ibid.
3. Myles Horton and Paulo Freire. *We Make the Road by Walking.* Brenda Bell, John Gaventa, and John Peters (eds.). Temple University Press, Philadelphia, 1990.
4. Louis Fischer. *The Essential Gandhi: An Anthology of His Writings on His Life, Work, and Ideas.* Random House, New York (1962).

10

Resolution: Destructive Conflict Brought to a Shared Vision

Introduction

An ancient custom of the Aboriginal Americans was to call a council fire when decisions affecting the whole tribe or nation needed to be made. To sit in council as a representative of the people was an honor that had to be earned through many years of truthfulness, bravery, compassion, sharing, listening, justice, being a discreet counselor, and so on. These qualities were necessary because a council fire, by its very nature, was a time to examine every point of view and explore every possibility of a situation that would in some way affect the whole of the people's destiny.

When someone called a council, that person had to have the courage to accept the council's decision with grace because, when the good of the whole is placed before the good of the few, all are assured a measure of abundance. The timeless teaching of the council fire is that until all of the people are doing well, none of the people are doing well.

The council fire worked well for the Aboriginal Americans because they knew who they were culturally, and they had a sense of place within their environment. Today, however, the global society is in transition, which robs many people of their original sense of place and substitutes some vague idea of location.

This transition is largely the result of massive shifts in human populations over the last three centuries. These shifts have altered the composition of peoples and their cultural structures throughout the world. All of this activity results in growing interconnectedness, interactivity, interdependence, and cultural uncertainty as some political lines change physically and others blur culturally. Cultural uncertainty is particularly true for those people caught between two cultures, such as the warring religious factions around the world: Millions of refugees have not only their sense of culture disrupted but also their sense of place transformed into an alien location, where their lives hang in limbo. These changes pose necessary questions for some people (such as "Who are we as a culture?"), which must be answered before a statement of vision and goals can be fruitfully considered.

Who Are We As a Culture?

Who are we now, today? This is a difficult but necessary question for people to deal with if they want to create a vision for the future. They must decide, based on how they define their cultural identity, what kind of vision to create. The self-held concept of who a people are is critical to their cultural future because their cultural self-image will determine what their community will become socially, which in turn will determine what their children will become socially.

Thus, how well a people's core values are encompassed in a vision depends first on how well the people understand themselves as a culture and second on how well that understanding is reflected on paper. Let us consider three examples: the Japanese, Aboriginal Canadians, and Aboriginal Americans.

In Japan, a religious system of belief, today known as Shinto, has been observed since the founding of the country. Shinto gained systematic form spontaneously from within the social life of communities. As a result, it has no specific founder or clearly defined body of scripture. Since ancient times, the Japanese have transmitted the legends and myths of the deities or *kami* as a genealogy of their way of life.

Shinto, in its broadest sense, refers to the entirety of indigenous culture, as opposed to Buddhism and other religious systems imported from outside Japan. Shinto is established against a background of hydraulic rice agriculture, which is uniquely suited to Japan's warm and humid climate.

When used in the narrow sense, Shinto refers to the rites offered to deities—primarily those deities of heaven and Earth listed in classical Japanese works of the ancient period. The physical facility used for the performance of this worship is called *jinju* or "shrine."

That Nature and natural phenomena are revered as deities is a result of the Japanese view of Nature as a kind of parent who nurtures life and provides limitless blessings. Shinto shrines all over Japan are surrounded by luxuriant groves of trees. Backed by the Shinto view that untouched Nature is itself sacred, the groves surrounding the shrines are themselves an important composite element of each shrine.

About 1,300 years ago, Emperor Tenmu ordained the practice of removing the old shrine, such as the Grand Shrine of Ise in Ise City, every twenty years and rebuilding a new, exact replica next to it. Why Emperor Tenmu stipulated that the rebuilding of the shrine should take place every twenty years is not clearly known, but it is most likely that twenty years was considered to be the optimum period for allowing the exact replication of the Grand Shrine, considering that it has a thatched roof and unpainted or otherwise preserved structures and is erected on posts sunk into the ground with only the benefit of foundation stones.

Twenty years is perhaps also the most logical interval in terms of passing from one generation to the next the technological expertise needed for the exacting task of duplicating a shrine. The Shinto shrine can be thought of as sacred architecture created from within the prayer and technical skills of the Japanese people themselves. Passing technical skills and the prayer embodied in the sacred architecture from generation to generation is the context within which lies the real significance of the regular rebuilding. The cultural knowledge has thus far been passed on for 1,300 years without change.

Herein lies the challenge for Japan. Although the sacred Shinto architecture can be passed from generation to generation through the perpetuation of the shrines, the belief system is being eroded by the introduction of Western philosophy. This psychic split seems to occur largely because Shinto is based in the belief of the primacy of Nature through cycles and processes, whereas Western philosophy is based in the primacy of linear technology and consumer products. The Japanese are therefore caught between two worlds—their ancient, ritualized, spiritual world and the new Western materialistic free-market one.

The Aboriginal Canadians have a somewhat similar dilemma. They have departed from their old culture because they have—against their will—been forced to adopt European-Canadian ways, which means they have given up or lost ancestral ones. Yet they have not—by choice—totally adopted white culture and want to retain some degree of their ancestral culture. Thus, the question they must ask and answer is: Which of our ancestral ways still have sufficient cultural value for us to keep them? Which of the white ways do we want to adopt? How do we put the chosen elements of both cultures together in such a way that we can today define who we are culturally?

Although Aboriginal Americans have the same task as the Aboriginal Canadians, they have even fewer options because the European Americans did a much more thorough job of destroying their culture and forcing them to adopt foreign ways. Nevertheless, the question of who we are today is still valid for any vision the people of an Indian reservation in the United States might want to create for their own lands. Here, I (Chris) suggest that we all face the question of who we are today as a culture, especially at the community level. This is an important question because how it is answered will determine the legacy inherited by our children.

For example, in 1993 I was asked to review an ecological brief for a First Nation of Aboriginal Canadians whose reservation was located between the sea and land that a timber company wanted to cut immediately upslope from the reservation. The problem lay in the fact that the timber company could only reach the timber it wanted to cut by obtaining an easement through the reservation, which gave the First Nation some control over the timber company. The First Nation, on the other hand, wanted some control over how the timber company would log the upper-slope forest because the outcome would for many years affect the reservation, which is just below the area to be cut.

Before meeting with the timber company, the chief of the First Nation asked me for some counsel. My reply was as follows:

Before I discuss the ecological brief I've been asked to review, there are three points that must be taken into account if what I say is to have any value to the First Nation. What I'm about to say may be difficult to hear, but I say it with the utmost respect.

Point 1: Who are you, the First Nation, in a cultural sense? You are not your old culture because you have—against your will—been forced to adopt some white ways, which means you have given up or lost ancestral ways. You are not—by choice—white, so you may wish to retain some of your ancestral ways. The questions you must ask and answer are: What of our ancestral ways still have sufficient value that we want to keep them? What of the white ways do we want to or are we willing to adopt? How do we put the chosen elements of both cultures together in such a way that we can today define who we are as a culture?

Point 2: What do you want your children to have as a legacy from your decisions and your negotiations with the timber company? Whatever you decide is what you are committing your children, their children, and their children's children to pay for the effects of your decisions unto the seventh generation and beyond. This, of course, is solely your choice, and that is as it should be. I make no judgments. But whatever you choose will partly answer point 3.

Point 3: What do you want your reservation to look like and act like during and after logging by the timber company? How you define yourselves culturally, what choices you make for your children, and the conscious decisions you make about the condition of your land will determine what you end up with. In all of these things, the choice is yours. The consequences belong to both you and your children.

After they answered these questions for themselves, they had to determine what they wanted to leave for their children.

What Legacy Do We Want to Leave Our Children?

Once a group of people, whether a community such as an Indian tribe or perhaps your own hometown, has defined itself culturally, it can then decide what legacy it wants to leave its children. This must be done consciously because whatever decisions the group makes under its new cultural identity, the consequences of those decisions are what the group is committing its children, their children, and their children's children to pay.

Having defined who they are culturally and having determined what legacy they want to leave their children, the people of a community are now ready to craft a vision of what they want because only now do they really know.

The rest of my reply to the First Nation applies here:

Now to my comments: This is a difficult task at best. As with every definition, it is a human invention and has no meaning to Nature. Therefore, you must tell the timber company, clearly and concisely, what the terms in this ecological brief mean to you and how you interpret them with respect to the company's actions that will affect your reservation.

1. Every ecosystem functions fully within the limits imposed on it by Nature and/or humans. Therefore, it is the type, scale, and duration of the alterations to the system—the imposed limits—that you need to be concerned with. If your reservation looks the way you want it to and functions the way you want it to, then the question becomes: How must we and the timber company behave to keep it looking and functioning the way it is? If, on the other hand, your reservation does *not* look the way you want it to and does *not* function the way you want it to, then the question becomes: How must we and the timber company behave to make it look and function the way we want it to? But regardless of your decisions or the company's actions, your reservation will always function to its greatest capacity under the circumstance Nature, you, and the company impose on it. The point is that your decisions and the company's actions, excluding what Nature may do, will determine how your reservation both looks and functions. This reflects the importance of the preceding point 3 and what you decide.

2. If you want the landscape of your reservation to look and function in a certain way, then how must the timber company's landscape look and function to help make your reservation

be what you want it to be? Keep in mind that the landscape of your reservation *and* the company's are *both* made up of the collective performance of individual stands of trees or "habitat patches." Therefore, how the stands look and function will determine how the collective landscape looks and functions.

3. Remember that any undesirable ecological effects are also undesirable economic effects over time. Your interest in your reservation will be there for many, many years, generations perhaps, but the company's interest in the forest may well disappear just as soon as the trees are cut. So the company's short-term economic decision may be good for them but may at the same time be a bad long-term ecological and a bad long-term economic decision for you.

4. To maintain ecological functions means that you must maintain the characteristics of the ecosystem in such a way that its processes are sustainable. The characteristics you must be concerned about are (1) composition, (2) structure, (3) function, and (4) Nature's disturbance regimes.

    The composition or kinds of plants and their age classes within a plant community creates a certain structure that is characteristic of the plant community. It is the structure of the plant community that in turn creates and maintains certain functions. In addition, it is the composition, structure, and function of a plant community that determine which animals can live there and how many. If you change the composition, you change the structure, you change the function, and you affect the animals. People and Nature are continually changing a community's structure by altering its composition, which in turn affects how it functions.

    For example, the timber company wants to change the forest's structure by cutting the trees, which in turn will change the plant community's composition, which in turn will change how the community functions, which in turn will change the kinds and numbers of animals that can live there. These are the key elements with which you must be concerned because an effect on one area can—and usually does—affect the entire landscape.

    Composition, structure, and function go together to create and maintain ecological processes both in time and across space, and it is the health of the processes that in the end creates the forest. Your forest is a living organism, not just a collection of trees—as the timber industry usually thinks of it.

5. Scale is an often-forgotten component of healthy forests and landscapes. The treatment of every stand of timber is critically important to the health of the whole landscape, which is a collection of the interrelated stands.

   Thus, when you deal only with a stand, what is ignored is the relationship of that particular stand to other stands, to the rest of the drainage, and to the landscape. It's like a jigsaw puzzle, where each piece is a stand. The relationship of certain pieces (stands) constitutes a picture of the drainage. The relationship of the pictures (drainages) makes a whole puzzle (landscape). Thus, relationships of all the stands within a particular area make a drainage, and the relationships of all the drainages within a particular area make the landscape.

   If one piece is left out of the puzzle, it is not complete. If one critical piece is missing, it may be very difficult to figure out what the picture is. So each piece (stand) is critically important in its relationship to the completion of the whole puzzle (landscape). Therefore, the way each stand is defined and treated by the timber company is critically important to how the landscape, encompassing both the company's land and your reservation, looks and functions over time.

6. Degrading an ecosystem is a human concept based on human values and has nothing to do with Nature. Nature places no value on anything. Everything just is, and in being it is perfect. Therefore, if something in Nature changes—it simply changes—but no value is either added or subtracted. Therefore, whether or not your reservation becomes degraded depends on what you want it to be like, what value or values you have placed on its being in a certain condition, to produce certain things for you. If your desired condition *is* negatively affected by the company's actions, then your reservation *becomes* degraded. If your desired condition is *not* negatively affected by the company's actions, then your reservation is *not* degraded. Remember, your own actions can also degrade your reservation.

7. It is important that you know—as clearly as possible—what the definitions in this brief really mean to you and your choices for your children and your reservation. Only when you fully understand what these definitions mean to you can you negotiate successfully with the timber company.

To negotiate with the timber company, however, the First Nation must have a vision, goals, and objectives for their reservation.

Vision, Goals, and Objectives

Although the word *vision* is variously construed, it is used here as a shared view of the future—a view based on the coalescence of myriad little, personal decisions, which in concert evolve into a big, collectively shared decision, *the vision*. Defining a vision and committing it to paper goes against our training, however, because it must also be stated as a positive in the positive, which is something we are not used to doing. Stating a positive *in the positive* means stating what we mean directly. For example, a town has an urban growth boundary that it wants to keep within certain limits, which can be stated one of two ways: (1) We do not want our urban growth boundary to look like that of our neighbor (a negative stated as a positive), or (2) we want our urban growth boundary to remain within a half mile from where it is now situated (a positive stated as a positive).

Further, to save our planet and human society, as we know it, we must be willing to risk changing our thinking to have a wider perception of the world and its possibilities, to validate one another's points of view or frames of reference. The world can be perceived with greater clarity when it is observed simultaneously from many points of view. Such conception requires open-mindedness in a collaborative process of intellectual and emotional exploration of that which is and that which might be, the results of a shared vision.

The movie *Spartacus* depicted the story of a Roman slave forced to become a gladiator, who led an army of slaves in an uprising in 71 BCE. They twice defeated the Roman legions but were finally conquered by General Marcus Licinius Crassus after a long siege and battle in which they were surrounded by and had to fight three Roman legions simultaneously.

The battle over, Crassus faced the thousand survivors seated on the ground as an officer shouted: "I bring a message from your master, Marcus Licinius Crassus, Commander of Italy. By command of his most merciful Excellency, your lives are to be spared. Slaves you were, and slaves you remain. But the terrible penalty of crucifixion has been set aside on the single condition that you identify the body or the living person of the slave called Spartacus."

After a long pause, Spartacus stands up to identify himself. Before he can speak, however, Antoninus leaps to his feet and yells, "I am Spartacus!" Immediately thereafter another man stands and yells, "No, I'm Spartacus!" Then another leaps to his feet and yells, "I'm Spartacus!" Within minutes, the whole slave army is on its feet, each man yelling, "I'm Spartacus!"

Each man, by standing, was potentially committing himself to death by crucifixion. Yet their loyalty to Spartacus, their leader, was superseded only by their loyalty to the vision of themselves as free men, the vision that Spartacus had inspired. The vision was so compelling that, having once tasted freedom, they willingly chose death over submitting to slavery. By withholding their obedience from Crassus, they remained free because slavery requires the oppressed to submit their obedience to the oppressor.

In more recent times, a vision of freedom and equality inspired thirteen colonies to formally declare their independence from England on July 4, 1776. The vision of human freedom and equality was so strong that a whole nation, the United States of America, was founded on it. In 1836, the fall of the Alamo, the Franciscan mission in San Antonio, Texas, and the slaughter of the men defending it inspired Texans in their vision of freedom from Mexican rule. In both cases, the strength of the vision carried a people to victory against overwhelming odds.

Although a vision may begin as an intellectual idea, at some point it becomes enshrined in one's heart as a palpable force that defies explanation. It then becomes impossible to turn back, to accept that which was before, because to do so would be to die inside. Few, if any, forces in human affairs are as powerful as a shared vision of the heart.[1]

In its simplest, intellectual form, a shared vision asks: What do we want to create? Beyond that, it becomes the focus and energy to actively create that which is desired. Few people, however, know what a vision, goal, or objective is; how to create them; how to state them; or how to use them as guidelines for development.

A statement of vision is a general declaration that describes what a particular person, group of people, agency, or nation is striving to achieve. A vision is like a "vanishing point," the spot on the horizon where the straight, flat road on which you are driving disappears from view over a gentle rise in the distance. As long as you keep that vanishing point in focus as the place you want to go, you are free to take a few side trips down other roads and always know where you are in relation to where you want to go, your vision. It is therefore necessary to have at hand a dictionary and a thesaurus when crafting a vision statement because it must be as precise as possible; through it, you must say what you mean and mean what you say.

Gifford Pinchot, the first chief of the U.S. Forest Service, had a vision of protected forests that would produce commodities for people in perpetuity. In them, he saw the "greatest good for the greatest number in the long run."[2] Through his leadership, he inspired this vision as a core value around which everyone in the new agency could, and did, rally for almost a century.

I (Chris) spoke in 1989 to a First Nation of Aboriginal Canadians who owned a sawmill in central British Columbia. I had been asked to discuss how a coniferous forest functions, both above and below ground, so that the First Nation could better understand the notion of productive sustainability, something that greatly concerned them. After I spoke, a contingent from the British Columbia provincial government told the

Aboriginal Canadians what they could and could not do in the eyes of the government. The government officials were insensitive at best. The Aboriginal Canadians tried in vain to tell the officials how they *felt* about their land and how they were personally being treated. Both explanations fell on deaf ears.

After the meeting was over and the government people left, I explained to the Aboriginal Canadians what a vision is, why it is important, and how to create one. In this case, they already knew in their hearts what they wanted; they had a shared vision, but they could not articulate it in a way that the government people could understand because their dealings with the First Nation were strictly intellectual.

They committed their feelings to paper as a vision statement for their sawmill in relation to the sustainable capacity of their land and their traditional ways. They were thus able to state their vision in a way that the government officials could understand, and it became their central point in future negotiations.

In another instance, I helped a president and vice president frame a vision, goals, and objectives for their new company. Although the president became frustrated during the two-day process, he told me a couple of years later that it had been the most important exercise that he had ever been through for his company, and he uses it constantly as the company grows.

In contrast to a vision, a *goal* is a general statement of intent that remains until it is achieved, the need for it disappears, or the direction changes. Although a goal is a statement of direction, which serves to further clarify the vision statement, it may be vague, and its accomplishment is not necessarily expected. A goal might be stated as, "My goal is to see Timbuktu."

There is, however, a saying in Nova Scotia for a person without a goal: "If you don't know where you're going, any path will take you there." Thus, without a goal, we take "potluck" in terms of where we will end up, which was Alice's dilemma when she met the Cheshire cat in Lewis Carroll's story of *Alice's Adventures in Wonderland*.

Alice asked the Cheshire cat:

"Would you tell me, please, which way I ought to go from here?"
"That depends a good deal on where you want to get to," said the Cat.
"I don't much care where … " said Alice.
"Then it doesn't matter which way you go," said the Cat.
" … so long as I get somewhere," Alice added as an explanation.
"Oh, you're sure to do that," said the Cat, "if you only walk long enough."[3]

An *objective*, on the other hand, is a specific statement of intended accomplishment. It is attainable, has a reference to time, is observable and measurable, and has an associated cost. The following are additional attributes of an objective: (1) It starts with an action verb; (2) it specifies a single outcome or result to be accomplished; (3) it specifies a date by which the accomplishment is to be completed; (4) it is framed in positive terms; (5) it is as specific and quantitative as possible and thus lends itself to evaluation; (6) it specifies only the "what, where," and "when" and avoids mentioning the "why" and the "how"; and (7) it is product oriented.

Let us consider the previous goal: My goal is to see Timbuktu. Now let us make it into an objective: I *will* see Timbuktu on *my twenty-first birthday*. My stated objective is action oriented: I will see. It has a single outcome: seeing Timbuktu. It specifies a date, the day of my twenty-first birthday, and is framed in positive terms: I will. It lends itself to evaluation of whether or not I achieved my stated intent, and it clearly states what, where, and when—but says nothing of the why or how. Finally, it is product or outcome oriented: to see a specific place.

As you strive to achieve your objective, you must accept and remember that your objective is fixed, as though in concrete, but the plan to achieve your objective must remain flexible and changeable. A common human tendency, however, is to change the objective—devalue it—if it cannot be reached in the chosen way or by the chosen time. It is much easier, it seems, to devalue an objective than it is to change an elaborate plan that has shown it will not achieve the objective as originally conceived.

Recently, I (Carol) have been involved in implementing the practice of *adaptive management* within the U.S. Fish and Wildlife Service. The term is defined by the Department of Interior as "a decision process that promotes flexible decision making that can be adjusted in the face of uncertainties as outcomes from management actions and other events become better understood."[4] This decision process includes crafting a vision and developing goals and objectives to achieve a desired result. The difference is that the process is used when there is a great deal of uncertainty—a situation we often face in making environmental decisions.

As mentioned, an objective is fixed, but the plan to achieve it must remain flexible and changeable. The steps of the adaptive management process are to (1) assess the problem, (2) design an action to address it, (3) implement, (4) monitor, (5) evaluate results, and (6) adjust/adapt the action. This is a tool that can be used to help formalize flexibility and, when used during the mediation process, can allow a group to make decisions that achieve a defined objective yet maintain the necessary flexibility to "adapt" the plan or course of action in the future. As stated by the Department of Interior, "Adaptive management focuses on learning and adapting, through partnerships of managers, scientists, and other stakeholders who learn together how to create and maintain sustainable ecosystems."[5]

It is important to understand what is meant by vision, goal, and objective because they collectively tell us where we are going, the value of getting there, and the probability of success. Too often, however, we "sleeve shop." Sleeve shopping is going into a store to buy a jacket and deciding which jacket we like by the price tag on the sleeve.

The alternative to sleeve shopping is first to determine what you want by the perceived value and purpose of the outcome. Second, you must make the commitment to pay the price, whatever it is. Third, you must determine the price of achieving the outcome. Fourth, you must figure out how to fulfill your commitment—how to pay the price—and make a commitment to keep your commitment. Fifth, you must act on it.

Alexander the Great, the ancient Greek conqueror, provides an excellent example of knowing what one wants and how to achieve it. When he and his troops landed by ship on a foreign shore that he wanted to take, they found themselves badly outnumbered. As the story goes, he sent some men to burn the ships and then ordered his troops to watch the ships burn, after which he told them: "Now we win or die!"

Once you have completed your statement of vision, goals, and objectives, you will be able to answer the following questions concisely: (1) What do I want? (2) Why do I want it? (3) Where do I want it? (4) When do I want it? (5) From whom do I want it? (6) How much (or many) do I want? (7) For how long do I want it (or them)? If a component is missing, you may achieve your desire by default but not by design.

Only when you can concisely answer all of these questions are you ready for planning. Only then do you know where you want to go, the value of going there, and can calculate the probability of arrival. Next, you must determine the cost, make the commitment to bear it, and then commit yourself to keeping your commitment.

Although it is we who define our vision, goals, and objectives, it is the land that limits our options, and we must keep these limitations firmly in mind. At the same time, we must recognize that they can be viewed either as obstacles in our preferred path or as solid ground on which to build new paths. Remember, Nature deals in trends over various scales of time. Habitat (food, cover, space, and water) is a common denominator among species; we can use this knowledge to our benefit. Long-term social-environmental sustainability requires that short-term economic goals and objectives be considered within the primacy of environmental postulates and sound long-term ecological goals and objectives.

How might such a process work? As an example, I (Chris) was asked to help the staff of a national forest in New Mexico come to grips with a vision, goals, and objectives for moving their forestry practices toward biological sustainability and hence economic sustainability. In so doing, I had to be careful of my boundaries, which was sticky because I was, of necessity, wearing three hats.

I helped plan, participated in, and facilitated the outcome of a week-long conference on the management of old-growth trees within a biologically sustainable forest. This conference was requested because of a long-standing and growing conflict, which was becoming increasingly destructive, both environmentally and culturally, among conservationists, three groups of Pueblo Indians, Latinos, Anglos, the timber industry, and the U.S. Forest Service. The conflict was over old-growth forests, logging practices, traditional forest uses by both the Aboriginal Americans and the Latinos, and changes necessary for sustainable forestry.

The first three days were spent viewing slides accompanying scientific presentations on how a forest and its streams function above and below ground (soils, water, trees, microbiology, mycology, animals, and people). Simultaneously with the ecological data, my task was to walk the audience through systems thinking, understanding the consequences of decisions, and how to link social-environmental sustainability ecologically and culturally.

The scientific presentations were followed by presentations of core values and points of view from each participating ethnic group. Throughout this period, there was free and open discussion among the collective group (over fifty people). During this time, people were asked to look at numbered color photographs on a wall and rank them from the most old-growth-like forest to the least. The participants were also asked to write a short description of what old growth was to them, including poetry if they wished.

The fourth day was spent in an open discussion in several age classes of forest in which the participants expressed verbally which ones felt the most "old-growthy" to them and why. The point was for people to be able to express themselves in whatever way they were most comfortable and in the process convert the abstractions of the conference room into concrete social-environmental experiences.

The last day was again spent in the field, using a flip chart to come to grips with the notion of a collective vision and goals. Not only did a collective vision and goals gel, but also the group agreed to rewrite the forest plan together. This was accomplished within a few months, as opposed to the year within which the forest supervisor had originally hoped to be able to revise the plan.

During this whole process, there were two detractors, both from the timber industry. Both of these gentlemen thought systems thinking (social-environmental sustainability) was "just philosophy" and beyond the purview of both science and such "emotional things" as visions. The rest of the group, however, outvoted them in the democratic process.

There was another gentleman, however, who purchased timber for one of the companies. After tentative beginnings as the representative of the timber industry on the planning committee, he became so caught up in the vision of biologically sustainable forestry that he departed from the hard-line stance of the industry. The power of the vision was so great for him that when the company he worked for fired him because he changed his mind and heart, he said that while it was tough and frightening, he felt better about himself. His willingness to give up his job to accommodate his expanding consciousness is the kind of courage that continually strengthens my faith in humanity and in the power of transformative mediation.

What About the Children?

As we the people build our shared visions of a sustainable future in which each person's core values and expertise are acknowledged, we must exercise the good sense and humility to ask our children, beginning at least with second and third graders, what they think and how they feel about their future.

I (Chris) say this because I remember that as a child whenever I expressed my opinion about what I thought the world needed to be like or how I wanted it to be, I was inevitably invalidated as "just a child who knew nothing" and was therefore summarily dismissed. But consider for a moment that the children must inherit the world and its environment as we adults leave it for them. Our choices, our generosity or greed, our morality or licentiousness will determine the circumstances that will become their reality.

Why, then, do adults assume that we know what is best for the children, their children, and their children's children when we are blatantly destroying their world with our blind greed and competitiveness? Why are children never asked what they expect of us as the caretakers and the trustees of the world they must inherit? Why are they never asked what they want us to leave them in terms of environmental quality? Why are they never asked what kinds of choices they would like to be able to make when they grow up? (For that matter, why do we not ask our elders where we have come from, how we are repeating the mistakes of history, and what we have lost, such as fundamental human values discussed in Chapter 4, along the way?)

Where do we, the adults of the world, get the audacity to assume that we know what is good for our children when all over the world they are being abused at home by parents who are out of control of themselves, are being slaughtered in the streets in the egotistical squabbles of adults over everything imaginable, and are being starved to death by adults using the allocation of food for political gain? We do not even know what is good for us. How can we possibly speak for them?

This lack of responsible care was keenly felt at the June 1992 worldwide Conference on the Environment, held in Rio de Janeiro. A twelve-year-old girl delivered to the entire delegation a most poignant speech about a child's perspective of the adult's environmental trusteeship. I (Chris) saw a video of the speech in which a child was pleading for a more gentle hand on the environment so that there would be some things of value left for the children of the future. I saw an adult audience moved to tears—but not to action.

In the society of the future, it is going to be increasingly important to listen to what the children say because they represent that which is to come. Children have beginner's minds. To them, all things are possible until adults with narrow minds, who have forgotten how to dream, put fences around their imaginations.

We adults, on the other hand, too often think we know what the answers should be and can no longer see what they might be. To us, whose imaginations were stifled by parents and schools, things have rigid limits of impossibility. We would do well, therefore, to consider carefully not only what the children say is possible in the future but also what they want. The future, after all, is theirs.

Each generation must be the conscious keeper of the generation to come—not its judge. It is therefore incumbent on us, the adults, to prepare the way for those who must follow. This will entail, among other things, wise and prudent planning—beginning with the idea of social-environmental sustainability.

References

1. Robert D. Garrett. Mediation in Native America. *Dispute Resolution Journal*, March (1994):38–45.
2. Gifford Pinchot. *Breaking New Ground*. Harcourt, Brace, New York (1947).
3. Lewis Carroll. *Alice's Adventures in Wonderland*. Doubleday, Doran, New York (1933).
4. B.K. Williams, R.C. Szaro, and C.D. Shapiro. *Adaptive Management: The U.S. Department of the Interior Technical Guide*. Adaptive Management Working Group, U.S. Department of the Interior, Washington, DC (2009).
5. Ibid.

11

Modifying Our Belief Systems Regarding Change

In 1969, Elisabeth Kübler-Ross published a book titled *On Death and Dying*,[1] which simultaneously is a book "on life and living." Elisabeth described five stages that a terminally ill person goes through when told of their impending death: denial and isolation, anger, bargaining, depression, and acceptance. Before relating these stages to our thought processes and how we change, let us examine each stage:

1. Denial, refusing to admit reality or trying to invalidate logic, is the first stage a terminally ill person goes through. Denial leads to a feeling of isolation, of being helpless and alone in the universe. At some level, however, the person knows the truth but is not yet ready or able to accept it emotionally.

2. Anger, which is a violent outward projection of fear, can be called *emotional panic*. The person is emotionally out of control because he no longer can control circumstances.

3. Bargaining is when a person attempts to bargain with God to change the circumstances, to find a way out of having to deal with what is.

4. Depression is a somewhat different type of issue because it comes in two stages. In the first stage, a person is in the immediate process of losing control of circumstances, such as a job and her identity with that job. The second stage is one in which a person is no longer concerned with past losses, such as a job, but is taking impending losses into account, such as leaving loved ones behind.

5. Acceptance, the final stage, is creative and positive. With acceptance returns trust, a faith in the goodness and the justice of the outcome. Acceptance allows us to acknowledge our problem, which allows us to define it, which in turn allows us to transcend it.[2] But first we must *accept what is*, which is *freedom* from fear.

Now let us see how understanding these stages of dying helps the living to understand the dying and the living. Although we are alive, we die daily to our ideas and belief systems, and in so doing, we go through the five stages of dying, which really are five stages of grieving. These stages are necessary as a process that prepares the way for change, a dying of the old thoughts and their attendant values and relationships within our lives to make way for the birth of the new:

1. Denial of or resistance to change is the first stage of a dying belief system in which we isolate ourselves because we see change as a condition to be avoided at almost any cost. We become defensive, fearful, and increasingly rigid in our thinking; we harden our attitudes and close our minds. If one becomes defensive about anything, starts to form a rebuttal before someone is finished speaking, filters what is said to hear only what one wants to hear, one is in denial.

2. Anger is the violent projection of uncontrollable fear. One is so afraid of change, of the dying of an old belief system, that one becomes temporarily insane: "I won't accept this!" One's anger, however, is not aimed at the person on whom it is projected; it is aimed at one's own inability to control the circumstances that seem so threatening.

3. Bargaining is looking for a way to alter the circumstances based on more "acceptable" conditions, which is the purpose of such things as labor unions.

4. Depression occurs when one becomes resigned to an inability to control or change the "system," whatever that is, to suit personal desires. One feels helpless and deliberately gives up trying to alter circumstances. One becomes a "victim" of "outside forces," and one's defense is to become cynical—distrustful of human nature and motives. A cynic is a critic who stresses faults and raises objections but assumes no responsibility. A cynic sees the situation as hopeless and is therefore a prophet of doom who espouses self-fulfilling prophecies of failure regardless of the effort invested in success.

5. Acceptance of what is allows one to transcend the purely emotional state of mind and reach an integrated point of logic. In doing so, one can define the problem and in turn transcend it. Acceptance of the problem, however, must come before a resolution is possible.

Why do we (in the generic) fear unwanted, uncontrollable change so much? We resist such change because we are committed to protecting our existing belief system. Even if it is no longer valid, it represents the safety of past knowledge in which there are no unwelcome surprises. We try to take our safe past and project it into an unknown future by skipping the present, which represents change and holds both uncertainty and accountability.

When confronted with change, we try to control the thoughts of others by accepting what to us are "approved" thoughts and rejecting "unapproved" thoughts. We see such control as a defense against unwanted change. But, as author George Bernard Shaw said, "My own education operated by a succession of eye-openers each involving the repudiation of some previously held belief."[3]

Change is the death of an accepted, "tried-and-true" belief system through which we have coped with life and which has become synonymous with our identity and therefore our security. When we get too "comfortable" with our belief systems, we might think of the turtle, for which only two choices in life exist: pull its head into its shell, where in safety it starves to death, or stick its neck out and risk finding something to eat and live.

Dysfunctional communities and their organizations with vested interests tend to hide within their self-serving ways by systematically distorting information. Such distortions do not depend on deliberate falsifications by individuals. Instead, people who are competent, hard working, and honest can sustain systematic distortions by merely carrying out their organizational roles in an uncritical—and therefore personally safe—manner. Unchecked by outside influences or the undeniable realities of catastrophic failures, organizational systems can sustain self-serving distortions, even though the potential for catastrophic consequences is significant.

A technological culture, such as ours, faces two choices: It can wait until catastrophic failures expose systemic deficiencies, distortions, and self-deceptions (the turtle with its head sucked into its shell), or it can provide social checks and balances to correct for systemic distortions prior to catastrophic failures (the turtle with its head outside its shell, risking a view of the world). The second, more desirable alternative, however, requires the active involvement of independent people who must ask "uncomfortable" questions and pursue "unfavorable" inquiries. Without such initiatives, checks and balances are undermined, and catastrophic possibilities are likely to increase as the scope and power of organizational technology expand.[4]

As we move forward in social-environmental sustainability, remember that success or failure is a crisis of the will and the imagination, not the possibilities. Remember also that to protect the best of what we have in the present for the present and the future, we must all continually change our thinking and our behavior to some extent. The saving grace of society is that we have a choice. Therefore, whatever needs to be done can be—when enough people want it to be done and decide to do it.

References

1. Elisabeth Kübler-Ross. *On Death and Dying*. Macmillan, New York (1969).
2. Ibid.
3. Leonard Roy Frank. *Quotationary*. Random House Reference, New York (2001).
4. Chris Maser. *Global Imperative: Harmonizing Culture and Nature*. Stillpoint, Walpole, NH (1992).

Index

80 percent agreement, xiii

A

Aboriginal Americans, 202, 203
 council fires, 201–202
Aboriginal Canadians, 146, 147–149,
 202
 ecological brief, 203–204
 sawmill owners, 209–210
Abstractions, 129
 concretizing by field work, 134–136
Abuse, 110
Acceptance, 104
 choice originating from, 115–116
 and stages of change, 218
 in terminal illness, 217
 unconditional, 115
Access
 loss of, in England, 80
 vs. equality, 21
Accountability, 14
 appraisers' fear of, 101
 for outcomes of resource use, 37–38
Acquisitiveness, 81
Action items, 14
Adaptability
 dependence on biodiversity, 71
 simplicity and, 84
Adaptive management, 211
Affluence
 in hunter-gatherer societies, 76
 as measure of success/value, 24
Aggression, as coping mechanism,
 99–101
Agreement
 80/20 rule, xiii
 areas of, 10
 voluntary, 139
Agriculture
 antibiodiversity mindset of, 80
 and birth of civilization, 80

combining with hunting and
 gathering, 79
historical origins of, 79
and origin of wilderness concept,
 78
Air
 as breath of life, 70
 cleaning, 74
 as global commons, 67, 69
Air pollution, xvi, 70, 73
Air quality, and biodiversity, 38
Airports, fear of unknowns in, 199
Alexander the Great, 212
Alice's Adventures in Wonderland, 210
Allen, James, 118–119
Aloneness, paradox of, 68–69
Alternatives, 15
 identifying and evaluating, 15
Amberization, 44
Analogies, 161–162
 brass buckle, 142
 broadening experiential transfer
  through, 136–138
 cattle driving, 153
 chocolate cake trades, 198–199
 city services, 137
 complex systems, 136
 jigsaw puzzle and forests, 207
 mandorla, 195–196
 toothpicks game, 172–173
 turtle, 219
Anger
 as avoidance, 100
 as coping mechanism, 99–101
 as fear projected outward, 168
 as hallmark of fear, xiii
 internalizing, 169
 non-response to, 169
 and stages of change, 218
 taking personally, 169
 in terminal illness, 217
 venting safely, 168

.